OCCUPATIONAL STRESS AND ORGANIZATIONAL EFFECTIVENESS

OCCUPATIONAL STRESS AND ORGANIZATIONAL EFFECTIVENESS

Edited by
ANNE W. RILEY and STEPHEN J. ZACCARO

New York
Westport, Connecticut
London

Library of Congress Cataloging-in-Publication Data

Occupational stress and organizational
  effectiveness.

  Papers presented at the 7th Annual Applied
Behavioral Science Symposium, sponsored by the Dept.
of Psychology at Virginia Polytechnic Institute and
State University, held in 1984.
  Bibliography: p.
  Includes index.
  1. Job stress—Congresses. 2. Employee assistance
programs—Congresses. 3. Personnel management—
Congresses. 4. Organizational effectiveness—
Congresses. I. Riley, Anne W. II. Zaccaro,
Stephen J. III. Virginia Tech Symposium on Applied
Behavioral Science (7th : 1984) IV. Virginia
Polytechnic Institute and State University.
Psychology Dept.
HF5548.85.O24   1987   158.7   86-25250
ISBN 0-275-92281-2 (alk. paper)

Library of Congress Catalog Card Number: 86-25250
ISBN: 0-275-92281-2

First published in 1987

Praeger Publishers, One Madison Avenue, New York, NY 10010
A division of Greenwood Press, Inc.

Printed in the United States of America

∞″

The paper used in this book complies with the Permanent
Paper Standard issued by the National Information Standards
Organization (Z39.48-1984).

10 9 8 7 6 5 4 3 2 1

The editors gratefully acknowledge the encouragement and direction provided by Joseph A. Sgro, head of the Department of Psychology, Virginia Tech. We are also most appreciative of the editorial assistance of Dorothy Grapsas and Ruth Cargo, and the word-processing contributions made by Barbara Moore, Phyllis Morena, and Laura Charping.

We gratefully acknowledge the assistance of Robert H. Rosen, Ph.D., Washington Business Group on Health.

CONTENTS

Preface   ix

1. Stress, Coping, and Organizational Effectiveness
   Stephen J. Zaccaro and Anne W. Riley   1

2. Stress Measurement and Management in Organizations:
   Development and Current Status
   Lawrence R. Murphy and Joseph J. Hurrell   29

3. The Experience and Management of Stress: Job and
   Organizational Determinants
   Cary L. Cooper   53

4. The Themes of Social-Psychological Stress in Work
   Organizations: From Roles to Goals
   Terry A. Beehr   71

5. Person-Environment Fit in Organizations: Theories,
   Facts, and Values
   Robert D. Caplan   103

6. Managing Stress in Turbulent Times
   *Susan E. Jackson, Randall S. Schuler, and
   Donald J. Vredenburgh*   141

7. A Systems Assessment of Occupational Stress: Evaluating
   a Hotel during Contract Negotiations
      Michael S. Neale, Jefferson A. Singer, and
      Gary E. Schwartz   167

8. Employee Assistance Programs: Managing
   Organizational Stress and Strain
      Steven C. Nahrwold   205

9. Innovations in Employee Assistance Programs: A Case
   Study at the Associaton of Flight Attendants
      Barbara Feuer   217

10. Utility Analysis: A Primer and Application to
    Organizational Stress Interventions
       Philip Bobko   229

11. Occupational Mental Health: A Continuum of Care
       Robert H. Rosen and Frederick C. Lee   245

Bibliography   269

About the Contributors   273

Index   279

PREFACE

This book developed from the recognition of a need. It is an urgent need, one that is reflected in the health statistics and the productivity problems experienced by virtually all industrialized nations today. It is the need to develop work environments that are both healthy and highly productive. The impact of work stress and strain on health and productivity is significant, but not well defined. Much has been accomplished in the study and management of work stress, providing an understanding that, though incomplete, is mature enough to be tested. However, the issues of work stress have too long been addressed by groups of researchers on one hand and by managers on the other. In order to solve problems of stress-related illness and impaired performance, the knowledge and understanding garnered by each group must be meaningfully communicated. This has not typically occurred, not because there is a lack of interest, but because there has been a lack of appreciation of the other's perspective and potential contribution.

It was in an attempt to provide a forum for sharing these perspectives that the Department of Psychology at Virginia Polytechnic Institute and State University organized the Seventh Annual Applied Behavioral Science Symposium on organizational stress. The intent was to provide an integration of the views on stress and productivity to ensure an appreciation of the methods used for addressing stress problems, by both practitioners and researchers, and to facilitate the development of realistic research directions and useful applications in the workplace. This book is the product of that effort. Its aim is to further contribute to the continuing development of stress theory and to encourage the application of theory and research findings to real organizational problems, providing an integration that is currently lacking.

The authors represent a range of professionals interested in stress in the workplace. Many have devoted their careers to its study, others are charged with the responsibility of developing effective policies and interventions for the management of stress in their organizations. Consequently, these chapters present varying and sometimes dissimilar perspectives on work stress. They share a common idea, however: any organizational problem, if it is to be understood and managed effectively, must be seen in the context of the overall system. In order to develop accurate concepts about stress at work, to provide realistic approaches to optimizing levels of stress, and to prevent stress-related problems, stress and strain must be considered in context. This is the perspective of a systems approach and is a recurring theme throughout this volume.

The first chapter, written by the editors, Steve Zaccaro and Anne Riley, provides an overview of stress at work and lays the foundation for understanding what is current and important in this field. Particular emphasis is given to the issues of organizational effectiveness and to the effects that stress-management programs have demonstrated.

Larry Murphy and Joseph Hurrell of the National Institute for Occupational Safety and Health review the development of the field and summarize the critical research findings. They provide a perceptive discussion of the current status of stress knowledge, putting what is known and not known about stress into context by considering the influence of the questions that have been posed and the methods chosen for studying stress. This analysis provides insights into what the directions for applying the findings from stress research should be and for formulating future investigations.

Cary Cooper, another leading researcher, initiates the discussion of work stress in terms of the impact of involuntarily not working. His conclusion that being out of work is probably more stressful than working does not discount the fact that work is stressful, but underscores the reality that stress is an integral aspect of life. Cooper reviews the stressors found to have the most impact at work and the potential of social support to moderate the impact of work stress.

The predominant theoretical perspectives in workplace stress are presented in the chapters written by several organizational researchers. The contributions of Terry Beehr, Robert Caplan, Susan Jackson, Randall Schuler, and Donald Vredenburgh provide a comprehensive review of the current theories driving research and understanding in this field.

Terry Beehr, an early contributor to the stress literature, provides a review of the scope of work stress and its history, with particular reference to the evolution of role stress concepts. He provides a recently developed, integrative model of job stress that has as its foundation the accomplishment of organizational and personal goals.

Bob Caplan, an originator of the well-established theory of person-environment fit, outlines the basics of the concept and relates it specifically to social support, one of the key mediators of the stress-strain relationship. He provides an articulate description of how social support may intervene to reduce the impact of stress and strain.

Susan Jackson and her colleagues propose a unifying theory of organizational functioning and performance. Employing the construct of uncertainty as a framework, they have integrated an enormous volume of information about organizations. This chapter provides a comprehensive framework for understanding the influences and behaviors of organizations with particular reference to the effects of uncertainty.

An integration of a systems-theory approach and practical issues of work stress is provided in the chapter by Michael Neale, Jefferson Singer, and Gary Schwartz at Yale. Their contribution recounts a workplace stress assessment performed in a labor union in the midst of a strike. Their systems evaluaton of the problems and opportunities for managing stress will undoubtedly become the model approach to intervening in organizational problems.

Extending this focus on practical responses to organizational stress are the chapters by Steve Nahrwold of Continental Illinois National Bank and Barbara Feuer of the Flight Attendants Association. Nahrwold provides a management perspective, while Feuer describes the approach of a labor union to the development and functioning of employee assistance programs. The programs they describe address similar organizational issues in contrasting ways, making it clear that the nature and functioning of a good program must be defined in terms of specific organizational needs.

Philip Bobko addresses another practical question of pivotal importance, that of determining the utility of interventions designed to reduce stress and enhance health. It is widely acknowledged that in order for stress-reduction methods to be worthwhile, they must have a demonstrable impact. Dr. Bobko lucidly discusses several methods for measuring the impact of programs in terms of organizational and individual costs and benefits.

A unifying perspective on the entire question of mental health in the workplace concludes the book. This contribution by Robert Rosen and Frederick Lee, both of the Washington Business Group on Health, presents a range of options for the manager or practitioner addressing the issues of stress and health in the workplace. Familiar with the difficulties of changing organizational cultures, they discuss each of the methods for enhancing health and productivity in terms of the constraints and potential involved. The commitment Bob Rosen has made to healthy workplaces is reflected not only by this thoughtful work, but also by his significant interest in and contribution to the development of this book.

We, along with all the authors, are hopeful that these discussions will provide insightful encouragement for both investigating and managing stress at work. As it becomes increasingly feasible to maintain optimal levels of stress in the workplace, the potential for healthy and highly productive organizations also increases.

AWR
Baltimore, Maryland

SJZ
Blacksburg, Virginia

OCCUPATIONAL STRESS AND ORGANIZATIONAL EFFECTIVENESS

1

STRESS, COPING, AND ORGANIZATIONAL EFFECTIVENESS

STEPHEN J. ZACCARO
and ANNE W. RILEY

The question of stress at work is at once pervasive and confusing. The controversy over whether job-related stress is good or bad is a reflection of just how basic this confusion is. Whatever one's views on the issue, they are likely to be strongly held and may conflict with those of colleagues, superiors, and subordinates.

There is some agreement among researchers and managers that excessive stress can diminish the health and quality of work life for employees. Less agreement exists regarding the effects of stress on organizational effectiveness. Some researchers note that different stressors can, at times and under certain circumstances, result in higher performance (McGrath 1976; Sales 1970) and lower absenteeism (Arsenault and Dolan 1983). Others maintain that stress lowers performance, job satisfaction, and organizational commitment and increases absenteeism, turnover, and other forms of organizational withdrawal (Beehr and Newman 1978; Cohen 1980; Jamal 1984; Parasuraman and Alutto 1984; Van Sell, Brief, and Schuler 1981).

The practical reality is that stress is neither good nor bad. There are optimal levels of stress at work as there are in life. The issue is not one of presence or absence, but rather of the nature, intensity, and duration of stress and the resources available to respond to it. Our purpose in this chapter is to provide an overview of stress, coping, and organizational effectiveness. A framework based on systems theory is presented as a tool for understanding stress at work. Following this, the next section highlights the multiple effects that stress may have on individual, group, and organizational performance. After the discussion of stress and organizational performance, the chapter focuses on the issues of coping with stress in organizations and includes a review of organizational stress management interventions. There are two important concepts underlying these discussions: (1) a distinction exists between the terms *stressors*, *stress*, and *strain*; and (2) organizations are complex systems comprising different parts operating at various levels, each of which uniquely influences, and is influenced by, stress and its outcomes. These concepts are based on a broad, systems view of the issues and have important implications both for stress management and organizational effectiveness.

STRESS: RESEARCH VERSUS MANAGERIAL PERSPECTIVES

In the stress literature, there has been an unfortunate divergence between the perspectives of researchers and managers. The value of each perspective has not been apparent to those maintaining the other. For example, managers have shown relatively little interest in the stress process itself, which is described as the "fight or flight" response. Selye (1956) originally described the stress response (which he termed the "general adaptation syndrome") as a three-stage process involving an initial alarm reaction, a stage of resistance, and, if resistance fails, a final stage of exhaustion.

The alarm stage is the experience most people associate with stress. A threat or challenge is experienced, and there is an increase in various bodily activities such as breathing rate, heart rate, and perspiration. Associated with these noticeable reactions of increased sympathetic nervous system activity are the remaining aspects of the response: increased blood pressure, increased release of sugar and cholesterol into the blood, dilated pupils, increased flow of blood to the extremities, and decreased blood flow to the stomach.

The next stage in Selye's model, resistance (response to stressors), is an important concern in the workplace. That is, how do individuals, groups, and organizations cope with stressors? Similarly, the exhaustion stage, or outcome of an unsuccessful response to stress, is of keen interest to organizations because it entails both the negative health effects and performance decrements typically related to too much stress at work.

One aspect of the stress response that was not reflected in Selye's early work is the outcome associated with successful coping. The early research involved extreme physical stressors with animals. Consequently, this research reflected only the negative effects of stress. It is little wonder that our understanding of the consequences of stress has been focused on negative health outcomes with little attention, until very recently, to the impact of successful coping.

There are many other issues that contribute to the difficulties of understanding stress at work, from inadequate definitions and poor measures to interdisciplinary rivalry for the dominant perspective. Most managers and stress practitioners find such debates irrelevant. Managers' definitions of stress are practical; they tend to be derived from the apparent effects stress has on individual and group effectiveness. When the link between an obvious stressor and a change in functioning is clear, managers learn about the effects of stress. Generally, managers have more experience in seeing the relationship between increases in demand (stress) and increases in performance.

The negative effects of stress are not as easily seen for several reasons. Negative effects of stress usually take longer to develop and are moderated by many factors. Thus, the links between stress and poor health, organizational withdrawal, and poor performance are less directly apparent. This reality has reduced management's awareness that too much stress can be bad for the employee and the organization and has impeded the ability of managers and practitioners to approach work stress as they would other organizational problems. This difficulty is compounded by the small contribution researchers have made to the practical issues of organizational stress management. The differences in perspective have kept these various professionals from communicating their experiences and valuing one another's approaches. This problem is a common one, even within individual organizations. However, a systems theory approach has emerged as a useful tool in bridging the gap between the various perspectives.

SYSTEMS THEORY AND OCCUPATIONAL STRESS

The following model of stress employs a systems theory approach to organize what is known about occupational stress and its consequences. Our proposal is not a definitive but a generic model that will introduce the reader to the important general issues. Our model is based on four principles that have received a general consensus in the literature.

First, the stress experience is a process that occurs when a person (or group or organization) is confronted by a demand that is perceived to exceed the resources available to effectively respond to it (Caplan, Chapter 5, this volume). The demand creates stress because, if not dealt with effectively, it interferes with progress toward important goals (cf. Beehr, Chapter 4, this volume; Beehr and Bhagat 1985). These goals range from personal (maintenance of self-esteem) to professional (success at selling a product).

Second, distinctions must be made in the definitions of stressors, stress, and strain.

- *Stressors* are the events, people, or thoughts that lead an individual to perceive that some potentially threatening demand is being made on him or her. Change is widely recognized as a stressor, even when it is "good" change.

- *Stress* is the actual process—the fight-or-flight response. It is associated with the awareness of a potential threat and is defined on a physiologic level as the sympathetic response of the autonomic nervous system.

- *Strain* is one outcome of stress. It includes any negative effects of unsuccessful coping, which can include negative self-evaluations, frustration, muscle tension, elevated blood pressure, absenteeism, lower performance, and, in the long term, serious illness and psychological problems, including job burnout.

Third, psychosocial stress at work occurs as a result of either a potential or actual conflict between an employee and some aspect of the organization. This principle incorporates the concepts of person-environment fit (Caplan, Chapter 5), uncertainty (Jackson, Schuler, and Vredenburgh, Chapter 6) and role stress (Beehr, Chapter 4).

Fourth, an individual's process of coping involves two cognitive elements (cf. Lazarus and Folkman 1984): (1) an appraisal that a stressor exists that threatens ongoing goal-related behavior, and (2) a choice of a coping strategy and tactics for coping.

Most models of stress acknowledge these four basic tenets, although they may differ in the emphasis or weight they give each one. The emerging model of stress in the workplace integrates these principles into a framework based on systems theory. As interpreted by Katz and Kahn (1978), systems theory views an organization as an interrelated set of "embedding" systems that can be analyzed at several different levels. The three levels of major importance (and the focus of later discussion) are the individual, group, and organizational levels. At the simplest level of analysis there are the individual members of an organization. All members of the organization, from the production line worker to the chief executive officer, are included in the individual perspective. Individuals work within an immediate social structure (for example, work group, production department, top management) that is guided by a specific organizational purpose. Each of these social systems is embedded within a larger system. For example, work groups are integrated into departments that are further embedded in the organizational structure. Within the organization, each social system interacts with other subsystems to yield products linked to the organization's purposes and goals. In a well-managed organization, each subsystem is guided by a purpose that contributes to the accomplishment of the organization's overall purpose. For example, the general production department is responsible for creating out of raw materials the products to be completed in the finishing unit. The personnel department is responsible for procuring the employees needed to maintain the production system. The presence of subsystems that are interrelated and embedded within one another is a defining characteristic of organizations.

Katz and Kahn (1978) note that the organization itself is embedded in social, cultural, political, and economic systems. It is constantly influencing, and is influenced by, its environment. A system receives inputs from a supportive environment and transforms them into products that are then converted into resources. These resources are subsequently converted into inputs to the system. In this way, the organization maintains itself.

Thus, an important aspect of systems theory is the interaction that occurs between an embedded subsystem and the "larger" system. A critical reality of organizations is that the component systems and people who comprise the organization constantly interact with one another. Rarely do these exchanges between employees and organizational systems proceed without conflict. The needs, expectations, and resources of the individual do not always match the resources, requirements, and constraints of the organizational unit. For example, an employee may be assigned a particular task but not be given the information and resources necessary to complete the assignment. Conversely, the individual may be lacking the skills necessary to complete the task. In both cases, the demands of the organization conflict with the resources of the employee.

A model of occupational stress, using conflicts in employee-environment exchanges as a starting point, is shown in Figure 1.1. Conflict arising from employee-environment exchanges results in a stress reaction when the individual makes the appraisal that a situation threatens progress toward personal goals (cf. Beehr, Chapter 4, this volume; Schuler 1980). This stress reaction is composed of both physiological and psychological characteristics. In addition to the well-known sympathetic nervous system responses (increased heart rate, pupil dilation, inhibited digestive activity, higher blood pressure, increased heart and breathing rates, etc.) stressed individuals experience heightened arousal. The psychological aspects of increased arousal include a greater perceptual orientation to the task, increased alertness and interest, and higher task anxiety and motivation (Hebb 1955, 1972). Furthermore, stressed workers may react to exchange conflicts with at least two different perceptions, one of threat and the other of challenge (Schuler 1980). Indeed, both may exist at once, as when a person feels threatened by the potential loss of important goals and challenged by the opportunity for growth and achievement if the conflict and stress can be successfully mastered. Thus, stress can, and frequently does, produce both anxiety and exhilaration.

The assessment that progress toward a goal may be blocked by a stressor is based on the belief that one's own resources may not be adequate to resolve problems. Beliefs are not facts; they are not always accurate assessments. A person's disposition and personality (including characteristics such as self-esteem and locus of control) may influence how the person both perceives and responds to stressors (Schuler 1980). Furthermore, some personality traits may "manufacture" stressors by changing environmental conditions so that potential stressors become more salient. Examples of such traits include type-A personality and achievement motivation. The type-A or coronary-prone individual tends to react aggressively to even minimal threats to control, which has the potential of generating conflict

Figure 1.1 A model of occupational stress

Exchanges between the employee and the workplace may result in stress which may, in turn, be effectively or ineffectively coped with. The outcome of the coping episode has an effect on the later experience of stress and strain.

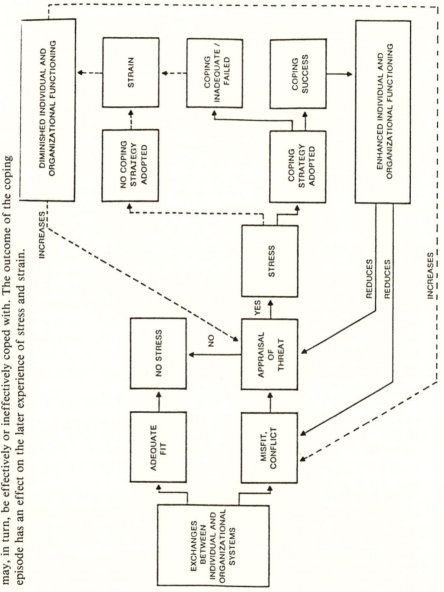

and competition with co-workers (Glass et al. 1980; MacDougall et al. 1985). The effect of these self-generated challenges is the frequent activation of the stress response. The negative health impact of this lifestyle has been nicely documented by continuous monitoring of blood pressure. These minute-to-minute measures show the association between constant struggles and repeated increases in blood pressure (Chesney 1983).

Once a potential stressor is appraised as threatening goal progress, stress is experienced. According to Lazarus and Folkman (1984), a stressed individual will select from among the possible coping responses one that is believed to have the highest probability of reducing or eliminating the stressor. If the chosen coping strategy is indeed successful, the individual experiences a relaxation of arousal and, at a cognitive level, increased confidence in his or her own ability to resolve the occurrence of future similar and, to a lesser extent, dissimilar stressors (Bandura 1982). If, on the other hand, coping behavior (such as working harder or minimizing the problem) does not result in a reduction of the threat or conflict, stress continues.

If new strategies are not tried or are tried but are unsuccessful, this prolonged experience of stress typically results in strain. The strain may appear as fatigue, irritability, heart palpitations, inability to concentrate, lower self-esteem, and other "minor" signs of extended stress. Or it may develop into more severe situations such as high blood pressure, ulcers, insomnia, depression, anxiety, or chronic absenteeism. At high levels of prolonged stress, ineffective coping through the use of alcohol, drugs, or risk-taking becomes a strain in itself. The existence of strain and its symptoms can result in diminished individual and organizational capacities, which in turn increase the likelihood that future events may be experienced as stressful.

STRESS, STRAIN, AND ORGANIZATIONAL EFFECTIVENESS

The distinction between stress and strain, noted in Figure 1.1, permits us to understand how stress can be either beneficial or detrimental to organizational effectiveness. Successful coping with stress can provide opportunities for new solutions, for growth, and so on. However, strain, the outcome of unsuccessful coping, is likely to have detrimental effects. Despite the laboratory demonstration of these effects, there is, as yet, little research establishing the relationships between organizational stress and actual indexes of organizational performance (Beehr and Newman 1978; Schuler 1980). We suspect that this omission is due to the complexity of the relationships among stressors, stress, various moderators (for example, personality traits), and organizational performance. What is known then, about the effects of stress and strain on organizational effectiveness?

According to open systems theory, an organization maintains itself by transforming inputs into sustaining outputs. Generally, organizational effectiveness refers to the success with which components of the organization complete the tasks of transformation. Key measures of effectiveness include costs, timeliness, and quality. Other measures of organizational effectiveness traditionally include productivity (quantity and quality), work attendance, and turnover. Effectiveness is influenced by how well individual inputs and resources are coordinated between subsystems, how well tasks and goals are coordinated within subsystems, and whether the organization maintains adequate amounts of inputted resources. Each of these measures is differently affected by stress and varies in the accuracy with which we are currently able to measure it. The one of keenest interest, productivity, is one of the hardest to quantify, particularly in the service industries.

The Inverted-U Hypothesis

One popular hypothesis regarding stress and performance is that the relationship is represented by an inverted U—performance is lowest at both extremely low and extremely high levels of stress. This hypothesis is based on the Yerkes-Dodson law (Yerkes and Dodson 1908), which states that a curvilinear relationship exists between arousal (one component of stress) and performance. Moderate stress is considered optimum for positive effects on performance. However, the optimum is not fixed; optimal levels vary across individuals and tasks (Selye 1976). Furthermore, optimal arousal levels vary as a function of task difficulty. As task difficulty increases, the level of arousal considered optimal for performance decreases.

There has been considerable discussion and debate regarding the reasons for the inverted-U-shaped function between stress and performance. Hebb (1955, 1972) suggests that the amount of information an individual processes is highest under moderate levels of arousal. That is, as arousal increases, events become more and more effective as guides for behavior. Past a certain point, however, arousal becomes too high, the individual is overwhelmed, and functioning decreases. This model suggests that, at optimal levels, stress can have a beneficial effect on individual effectiveness. Unfortunately, in their research, job stress theorists have paid little more than minimal attention to this performance-enhancing aspect of stress.

Although activation theory (Scott 1966) has been generally acknowledged to explain the effects of low to moderate levels of stress on performance, there has been considerably more confusion and disagreement about the reduction in performance that typically results when stress increases from moderate to high levels (McGrath 1976). Activation theorists contend that extremely high levels of arousal produce psychological disorientation resulting from overstimulation (Hebb 1955, 1972). Hebb (1972) suggests that this condition "approxmates paralysis, either of thought or of bodily movement" (p. 199). These descriptions pertain to situations of extreme stress such as fires and combat. Our concern, however, is with the effects of prolonged levels of moderate to high stress at work.

High or moderately high levels of prolonged stress require continued vigilance and coping responses that eventually produce psychological fatigue in a person (or a group or organization). The resulting strain negatively influences future attempts at coping, and the likelihood of success is further diminished. With an increase in strain, the individual is forced to put more effort into coping with the effects of strain and less into resolution of the stressful situation (Anderson 1976; Vroom 1964). Behaviors that are dysfunctional for the organization (such as downturns in performance, work delays, errors, tardiness, and absenteeism) become more likely. Thus, the right side of the inverted-U relationship reflects impaired performance, due at least in part to increases in frustration and decreases in attention. Over time, ineffective coping with high levels of stressors has negative effects on the person's (group's, organization's) ability to respond to additional stress, and performance drops further.

Making the distinction between stress and strain aids in understanding when and how stress enhances and diminishes performance. Those who fail to make this distinction often fail to note the beneficial effects of stress. To this group, stress is seen as a resource-diminishing rather than a potentially resource-enhancing phenomenon. It is described as a negative influence that always reduces organizational effectiveness. This view, however, is too narrow and disputes managers' experience. By focusing only on the negative consequences of stress, researchers and health providers appear to have alienated managers who understand how stress can motivate employees and improve performance.

Unfortunately, managers often oversubscribe to this resource-enhancement view of stress. The view that stress is a necessary component to effective performance in an organization must be balanced by the understanding that stress enhances performance best when employees cope successfully with stressful circumstances. Thus, facilitating successful coping is in the interest of good management. Managers must also understand that when coping fails repeatedly, strain occurs, resulting in burdens on both the individual and organization. By explicitly separating stress and strain, several bedeviling theoretical and practical issues related to stress and its consequences may be more easily resolved.

The Impact of Stress on Determinants
of Organizational Performance

Organizational effectiveness depends on the performance of individuals and groups within the organization. Those performances are dependent on the abilities, skills, motivation, and constraints that exist within individuals and groups (Campbell and Pritchard 1976; Porter and Lawler 1968). *Ability* refers to the employee's capability in fulfilling task requirements and involves a measure of the employee's skill and resources and the difficulty or complexity of the task. *Motivation* refers to the direction, intensity, and persistence of an individual's work-related responses (Campbell and Pritchard 1976). *External constraints* refer to factors outside the individual's apparent control that may inhibit performance efforts (Peters and O'Connor 1980). One such constraint widely studied in the stress literature is ambiguity about one's purpose or role (Porter and Lawler 1968). Such ambiguity can reduce performance despite high ability and motivation.

The abilities and resources of work groups are dependent on the abilities and task-relevant resources of individual members and the quality of the intra-group process (Steiner 1972). Group level motivation refers to group cohesiveness and to the level of effort or energy willingly expended by members to reach group goals (that is, group synergy; Cattell 1948). Examples of external constraints on group performance include availability of production resources and clarity of group standards and goals (Zander 1971).

At the organizational level, goals and purposes as well as leadership skills shape the effectiveness of the remainder of the organization (Simon 1964). Indeed, the actions and processes at any one level clearly influence behavior at other levels. For example, if organizational goals are unclear or in conflict, then the purposes of work groups and individual role expectations will probably also be unclear (Riley and Frederiksen 1984). Stress and strain can produce distinctive effects that spread to different levels of the organization. Jackson, Schuler, and Vredenburgh (Chapter 6, this volume) note a similar phenomenon in their "cascading flow characteristic" of uncertainty. Uncertainty at the organizational level is manifested at the lower levels of group and individual functioning. The effects of organizational stressors (such as changing market demands) or organizational strain (such as constantly changing marketing strategies) can "cascade" to affect group and individual performance.

At the group level, stress plays a complex role, producing various effects on performance. Deleterious effects on several components of group performance occur when groups are confronted by a significant external threat. The most common effect is to discourage or minimize intra-group communication. This sometimes reduces the group's ability to resolve the threat (Janis 1982). For example, Janis (1982) describes how Richard Nixon and his advisors reacted as a group to the stressful circumstances engendered by the Watergate affair. Many of their actions suggest that stress impaired the group's capacity for effective process. Nixon's advisors suppressed dissension and disagreements (which can minimize the input of fresh or perhaps better ideas), failed to explore a wider variety of options for responding to the crisis, and tended to engage in collective rationalization and misguided conclusions (Janis 1982: 198-241). This type of "group think" is a reaction to stress that diminishes the group's resources and reduces its effectiveness.

Note, however, that stressful circumstances can, at times, enhance group motivation and bring group standards and goals into sharper focus. Just as is the case with the individual, certain characteristics of the group, such as cohesion and external support, can moderate the impact of stressors. The impact of stress, then, is determined by the degree to which there are decrements in healthy group processes such as information storing, idea generation, constructive debate, and group member support. When groups are cohesive and loyal to the goals of the organization, group members may act to overcome the stressors, thereby strengthening subsequent group performance. Stress, then, can have a beneficial effect on group performance.

Impact of Different Stressors and Strains

The intensity and duration of stress are known to influence its impact. Furthermore, the source or specific type of stressor appears to exert unique influence. Indeed, Beehr and Newman (1978) note that "the relationship [between stress and measures of organizational effectiveness] may vary by type of stressor and/or by the type of performance measured and it may be moderated by various personal and situational factors" (p. 690).

Different stressors may have different consequences for individual, group, and organizational performance. For example, one stressor, role uncertainty, typically decreases individual performance, but in some circumstances it can have a healthy effect on the performance of groups. Highly cohesive groups, which generally have strong group process and effective intra-group communication (Cartwright 1968; Steiner 1972), may substitute their own role prescriptions for those being (or not being) delivered by others who are outside the group. When such groups are loyal to organizational goals, the results can be better overall performance and, subsequently, more efficient group process (Zander 1977; 1982). As another example, time pressures (deadlines) tend to increase individual performance, but they can reduce the initial development of healthy group processes, thereby interfering with the group's ability to perform.

In contrast to the effects of stressors, the effects of job-related strain are likely to be more universally deleterious. Strain is characterized by reactions that are psychological (job dissatisfaction, depression, burnout, anxiety), physiological (high blood pressure, exhaustion, headaches), and behavioral (smoking, drug use, alcohol abuse). Strains diminish the individual's capabilities and motivation. As physical well-being deteriorates, the individual is less capable of responding to task demands. Also, severe job strain reduces task motivation as recipients focus more on alleviating the personal consequences of strain and less on task performance (Anderson 1976). Organizational escape behaviors, such as tardiness and absenteeism, increase in frequency. An individual may lower his or her performance expectations when trying to cope with the negative emotions and sense of threat. Lowered expectations may, in turn, improve the chances for future perceived success (Baumgardner and Arkin 1985). If, however, altered expectations and perceptions clash with organizational reality, the worker will continue to experience job failure and increases in job strain.

Similar effects are probable at group and organizational levels of performance. Groups under strain experience diminished cohesion and more inefficient process. Members of such groups often spend an inordinate amount of time focusing on process and socio-emotional issues. The result is diminished goal achievement. Similarly, organizations under strain devote greater amounts of energy to symptoms and consequences of strain than to production demands. These responses diminish the probability of success and increase the amount of felt strain.

Because excessive or prolonged job stress and strain often negatively influence job performance, organizational effectiveness, and individual health, there is a clear need for effective coping strategies. What is the nature of coping with stress at work? How can managers enhance coping to ensure that an optimal level of stress exists for individuals and groups in the organization?

MANAGEMENT OF COPING

Individuals, groups, and organizations have two purposes in coping with stress: (1) to effectively overcome the threat or meet the challenge; and (2) to prevent strain. Coping is something employees and managers do constantly. There are fundamental similarities between coping with stress and managing a work unit. Managing and coping can be reactive endeavors, characterized by waiting for problems to occur, or they can be proactive endeavors in which general and specific planning takes place to organize resources to prepare for both predictable and unpredictable demands. Good management requires frequent monitoring of the environment, skillful assessment, practical decisions, and a range of potential responses in one's repertoire. The same is true of coping. The skills of generating resources, enlisting support, communicating needs, and responding creatively are valued assets in both effective management and successful coping.

In coping with or managing a stressor, some appraisal of threat must initially occur. Lazarus and Folkman (1984) maintain that two processes are involved in this evaluation stage. An individual must determine the possible meaning of a situation to determine whether it is likely to be stressful, irrelevant, or positive. If the appraisal suggests that the situation involves a loss, threat, or challenge, then the individual must appraise the options for coping and determine what to do.

Coping has been defined by Lazarus and Folkman (1984) as a process involving "constantly changing cognitive and behavioral efforts to manage specific external and/or internal demands that are appraised as taxing or exceeding the resources of the person" (p. 141). An important aspect of coping, then, is that it is a response. Coping is initiated when a person realizes that there is a specific challenge, threat, or loss that must be dealt with. Coping has primarily been studied at the level of the individual. However, the concepts appear to be generic and provide a framework for a discussion of the process of coping at group and organizational levels.

Coping Strategies and Tactics

The process of coping can be understood in terms of the general strategies used and the specific tactics employed to accomplish each. Pearlin and Schooler (1978) suggest that there are basically three ways or strategies of coping: (1) changing the potentially stressful situation before it occurs; (2) controlling the meaning of stressful experiences once they occur; and (3) managing the effects of the stress response. These strategies characterize the process of coping at all levels—individual, group, and organizational.

The first coping strategy, if successful, prevents the occurrence of stress by eliminating the threatening or challenging event. This approach is basic prevention of problems and requires prior knowledge of likely stressors and plans to circumvent them—proactive management. Even the good manager, however, cannot forestall all demanding or challenging situations. Nor would that be desirable. Many demands on the organization and the individual constitute challenges or opportunities for growth and development. Good stress management in an organization means optimizing the levels of stress. Too little stress (for example, boredom, routinization) can be as detrimental to performance and satisfaction as too much. Demands and threats that have little or no potential benefit are targets for prevention. Such stresses as uncertainty regarding purpose, conflict over job performance requirements, boredom, underutilization, and lack of opportunity for development have little to recommend them from the standpoint of improving individual or organizational performance. Each of these has been repeatedly identified as a powerful source of stress at work and is discussed fully in the chapters that follow.

The second coping strategy, managing the meaning of the stressful experiences, offers a way of reframing the nature of those problems that cannot be avoided. Warren Bennis, in a discussion of the competencies of 60 leaders of Fortune 500 companies, maintains that the management of meaning is one of the key behaviors of successful managers (Bennis 1984). Translating the demanding aspects of a work situation from threats, annoyances, and "the same old problems" into opportunities to make change, to develop one's position, and to fix the problem once and for all provides everyone with renewed vigor and motivation for problem-solving. Those favorites of management, individuals who seem to thrive on stress, are often able to cope using this strategy to foster their long-range goals. They recast demands as opportunities to learn, expand, develop, and achieve. (Note, however that some stress-loving employees are type-A individuals who are generating challenge and demand in many situations and who too frequently work themselves into strains such as heart disease.) Managing meaning by focusing on the positive aspects of situations not only feels better; there is a developing body of empirical research that suggests that a situation interpreted as a challenge produces a diffrent and less harmful stress reaction than the same situation appraised as a threat (Frankenhauser 1980).

Other tactics useful in managing the meaning of stressful situations include shifting priorities, minimizing the importance of outcomes, and ignoring certain types of problems. For example, the employee who has earned a promotion but misses out because of a reorganization of the company is likely to adapt by minimizing the importance of the promotion and shifting his/her priorities from the promotion to the opportunity for new learning, or if very disgruntled, to the opportunity of finding a better job. In short, if he/she adapts successfully, part of the adaptation will involve finding the silver lining in this dark cloud.

The third coping strategy, managing the effects of stress once they occur, involves an even broader array of tactics. Because this approach involves reducing the impact of stress, it can be either a reactive response to a significant stress or a planned strategy. Individuals and organizations will continuously experience stress and can plan for this reality. By providing an environment that fosters opportunities to release tension, obtain support, clarify the meaning of events, and evaluate progress toward goal attainment, the effects of inevitable stress can be managed on an ongoing basis. The lifestyles of people and the cultures of organizations reflect the existence (or lack) of strategies designed to manage the stress that will certainly occur. An organizational culture that is characterized by ignorance of the needs that individuals and groups have for understanding, input, and feedback, except on an annual or semiannual basis, provides little opportunity for employees to manage the effects of routine stress.

The strategies of coping are the general approaches used to deal with stressors. The best choice among the strategies is often defined by the situation. Often, the three strategies can be applied at different times to different aspects of the problem.

The tactics of coping, on the other hand, are those more specific behaviors chosen to accomplish the strategic objectives of preventing the occurrence of a stressor, managing its meaning, or reducing its impact. The tactics of coping fall into two general categories, emotion-focused and problem-focused coping responses (Pearlin and Schooler 1978). Emotion-focused coping involves attempts at lessening emotional distress, including avoidance, minimization, distancing, selective attention, positive comparisons, and wresting positive value from negative events (Lazarus and Folkman 1984).

The tactics of problem-focused coping are similar to those used for problem-solving. Such efforts are often directed at defining the problem, generating alternative solutions, weighing the alternatives in terms of their costs and benefits, choosing among them, and acting. A frequent focus of problem-focused coping is environmental change. However, problem-solving tactics are also basic to the management of a healthy and satisfying lifestyle, and to the management of a successful career.

Which coping tactics an individual chooses depends on how he/she appraises problems and his/her repertoire of available tactics (Lazarus and Folkman 1984; Pearlin and Schooler 1978). If, for example, an employee confronts a problem situation that he or she believes can be changed (whether or not that belief is true), then the coping efforts chosen are likely to be attempts to solve the problem head-on. If, on the other hand, it is clearly a situation that cannot be changed by the employee, then the coping strategies will likely involve emotion-focused coping that reduces involvement, such as avoiding, minimizing, and distancing oneself from the situation. If such persistent stressors continue over a long period, effects of coping can eventually result in emotional withdrawal, a primary aspect of burnout (Maslach and Jackson 1984).

A too common example is that of the employee whose career motivation and training have encouraged the view that dedication and hard work can solve important social or organizational problems. This view is not uncommon for employees in human service areas, urban planning, and administrative sciences (Maslach and Jackson 1984). The individual devotes several years of intense effort to solving the critical problems. Not only do the problems turn out to be intransigent, but the lack of concern and support from persons who appear to have more ability to effect real solutions leaves the employee frustrated and overwhelmed. The life history of such experiences often involves a shift from predominantly problem-solving to coping that is emotion-focused, in an attempt to reduce the arousal and strain caused by such important failures. When the coping tactics are primarily avoidance and withdrawal, the opportunities for satisfaction and achievement are significantly reduced. A negative spiral is set up, potentially leading to a state of withdrawal and emotional exhaustion termed "burnout." This is organizational strain in its most destructive form. Burnout involves a mechanized approach to people, routinization of work efforts, and cynicism. It is "contagious," negatively influencing co-workers and decreasing the job performance of all persons involved (Cherniss 1980; Jackson and Schuler 1983).

High-performing, committed persons can and too frequently do lose their ability to cope effectively in jobs that involve high levels of people contact.

This situation is not inevitable; several approaches are being taken in work organizations throughout the industrialized world to sustain and direct effective coping. Approaches to solving the problem of organizational stress and strains fall into three categories, paralleling the three basic coping strategies for individuals: (1) attempts to directly change the situations (prevention); (2) attempts to manage the meaning of the stress (management); and (3) attempts to cope with the effects of stress (damage control). All are the prerogative of the manager, each strategy potentially facilitating the other.

A FRAMEWORK FOR COPING WITH ORGANIZATIONAL STRESS

We have seen that an understanding of stress and strain must be based on the recognition that the interdependent levels of a system (individual, group, and organizational) influence the experience and production of stress and the development of strain at all other levels. Similarly, management efforts to optimize work stress must be based on this framework. Any intervention directed at one level will influence other parts of the organization. These "side effects" have the potential to be positive or negative, depending to a great extent on the information employees have about how the intervention will influence them.

A key to this issue of intra-organization influence is the way individuals approach problems. Each employee's unique perspective results from personal characteristics and her or his position in the system. Recall the parable of the blind men describing the elephant. The parts each one took hold of—the trunk, the tail, or the ears—dictated very different views of the animal and what it might be good for. A person's position in an organization strongly influences the problems that are seen. More importantly, the way problems are defined determines the strategies and tactics considered.

A particularly good example of how definitions inherently limit solutions is the recent history of organizational stress interventions in the workplace. The stress-related problems of the individual—poor health, dissatisfaction, and burnout—prompted the interventions. The individual was seen as the source and focus of the problems. Naturally, the individual was also seen as the appropriate target of the solution. The primary solution chosen in organizations throughout the country was "innoculation" of employees against stress. There are two assumptions involved in this solution. First, it assumes that the individual is the primary party responsible for the development of strain. Second, it assumes that the individual level is the best or only place to make the changes.

These assumptions notwithstanding, employees often do have the motivation and some ability to manage their personal experience of stress. Each person has the basic coping strategies for preventing the occurrence of stressors by managing his or her lifestyle, home life, and work environment; managing the personal perception or meaning of demanding situations; and managing the effects of unavoidable stress to reduce the development of significant strains. Table 1.1 outlines a range of tactics involved in these strategies of personal stress management in terms of primary, secondary, and tertiary prevention of stress (Quick and Quick 1984).

Many people continue to be uninformed about the fundamental relationships between lifestyle, stress, and health. Didactic and skill development programs for employees can therefore be a useful adjunct in developing an optimal work environment. In addition to providing information and skills, such programs can help employees define their role in managing stress in both their personal and work lives. As the following sections on individual and organizational stress interventions will demonstrate, programs must be supported by appropriate organizational policies and practices.

Table 1.1 Individual-Level Preventive Management Techniques

Primary prevention: Stressor-directed	
Managing personal perceptions of stress	*Lifestyle management*
• Constructive self-talk	• Prioritizing one's goals
• Psychological withdrawal	• Maintaining a balance
• Recognizing the inevitable	• Leisure time use
• Disputing cognitive distortion	• Sabbaticals
• Changing the type-A behavior pattern	• Balanced diet
	• Regular exercise
Managing the personal work environment	• Moderate use of caffeine and alcohol
	• Minimal use of psychoactive drugs
• Planning	
• Time management	
• Overload avoidance	
• Other methods (social support, task variation, leave job)	

Secondary prevention: Response-directed	
Relaxation training	*Emotional outlets*
• Progressive relaxation	• Talking with others
• The relaxation response	• Writing it out
• Meditation	• Acting it out
• Medical hypnosis & autogenic training	
• Biofeedback training	
• Momentary relaxation	
• Traditional methods	

Table 1.1 (continued)

Physical outlets

- Aerobic exercise
- Recreational sports
- Flexibility and muscular
  relaxation activities
- Muscle strength and endurance
  building

Tertiary prevention: Symptom-directed

Counseling and psychotherapy	*Medical care*
• Symptom-specific programs	• Medications
• Individual psychotherapy	• Surgery
• Behavior therapy	• Physical therapy
• Group therapy	
• Career counseling	

Source: Adapted with permission from *Organizational Stress and Preventative Management*, by J. C. Quick and J. D. Quick (New York: McGraw-Hill, © 1984).

Individually Focused Stress Management Interventions

The most widely acclaimed approach to stress management in organizations is the multicomponent, individually focused, stress-management course based on the notion of inoculating employees against stressors. The previous discussion suggests that, given their exclusive individual focus, stress-management courses should not have a powerful impact. Murphy (1984a) and Newman and Beehr (1979), in their comprehensive reviews of such programs, conclude that, indeed, there is little evidence to suggest that these courses have an appreciable impact. It is instructive to note that although the reported outcome of the stress-management programs reviewed by Murphy (1984a) and Newman and Beehr (1979) were frequently positive, over two-thirds did not involve a control group. People reported that they felt better. But without making a comparison with another untreated group, the noted improvement tells us little about the reduction of stress. The few programs that employed adequate controls to evaluate program effects typically report two primary outcome measures: (1) in-session response on physiological measures; and (2) post-program self-report of improvement. A few of these studies suggest some beneficial effects. Benson and his colleagues have demonstrated that daily relaxation breaks can have a positive effect on blood pressure and self-reports of well-being (Peters, Benson, and Peters 1977). Carrington et al. (1980) demonstrated that home relaxation practice of New York Telephone employees resulted in reductions of symptoms ratings on the SCL-90. However, the control group also reported sizable reductions.

Two studies supported by the National Institute for Occupational Safety and Health have employed two-week programs in muscle relaxation and biofeedback to reduce stress among hospital nurses (Murphy 1983) and highway maintenance workers (Murphy 1984b). The active treatment groups reported some beneficial effects such as increases in their ability and efforts to cope with stress, their level of work energy, and self-assessments of coping effectiveness. However, both trained and untrained control groups reported improvements in measures of emotions and symptoms.

To date, only one empirical evaluation of a work-site stress-management program has reported significant health-related effects that were sustained over time. Ganster et al. (1982) evaluated an eight-session, cognitive-behavioral, stress-management program delivered to highly stressed employees of a public agency ($N = 79$). Using a control group design with one replication, they assessed anxiety, depression, symptoms, and urinary catecholamines (epinephrine and norepinephrine) at three-month intervals. A statistically significant reduction in urinary catecholamines and irritation was produced in the first treatment group. In the replication, epinephrine increased following the program, but irritation and norepinephrine were reduced. The findings at follow-up indicate that the reliability of epinephrine measurements may have been influenced by extraneous factors such as seasonal variation. This possible non-program effect suggests the need for caution in interpreting the primary finding of urinary catacholamine reduction. Additionally, if one accepts this study as documentation of a positive effect of such interventions, it is important to note that it was not delivered to a general sample of employees but to those who were initially highly stressed.

A study of an organization in the midst of planned and unplanned transition suggests that stress-management interventions may not be without their negative side effects. In a design similar to that of Ganster et al. (1982) but involving employees in the normal stress range, Riley, Frederiksen, and Winett (1984) employed a two-group, waiting-list control format. During a time of major change, including layoffs of approximately 15 percent of the employees, roughly half of the volunteer employees received a six-session, stress-management program. Three months later, the remaining interested employees went through the stress-management program. Measures of information, program satisfaction, stress, symptoms, job satisfaction, absenteeism, productivity, and health-care claims were taken four times, before and after each administration of the program. There were significant increases in knowledge, high levels of consumer satisfaction, and moderate improvement in the daily measure of stress as a result of the program. Unlike the results found when the same program was delivered to a sample of chronically stressed individuals, there was not a statistically significant change in symptom ratings or characteristic stress level (Riley, Frederiksen, and Winett 1984). Most notably, job satisfaction decreased significantly in each group after completion of the program. The loss of a number of participants who were laid off compromised the balanced design of the study. However, it is unlikely that those remaining in the program would have been less satisfied with their jobs than those who did not remain.

An indirect indication of the power of these organizational events was the finding of a significant decrease in absenteeism for both groups throughout the study period, apparently in response to the threat of job loss. The increase in job dissatisfaction is more difficult to explain. There were no direct means of interpreting this finding. There is, however, a probable explanation. It appeared that these low-level (non-exempt, hourly) employees were sensitized by the program to their lack of control and inability to manage the major stressors at work, thereby increasing their dissatisfaction.

At this time it appears that this study is the only one to employ comprehensive, organizationally relevant measures. However, it is only one study and it was influenced in unexplainable ways by the loss of employees. Still, it argues for caution in the implementation of individual stress-management programs in isolation from other supportive changes in organizational policy and practices.

In sum, there is little scientific evidence that individually oriented, stress-management education has a beneficial effect on organizationally relevant outcomes. Indeed, such interventions, when delivered without support at other levels of the organization, may have an untoward, boomerang effect. The widely acclaimed value that such add-on programs can improve morale, attendance, and performance, and reduce absences (Shea 1981), can only be attributed to individual satisfaction with such programs (which is consistently high, as with virtually all training programs) and the success of the marketing efforts of stress-management training organizations.

Group and Organizational Approaches to Managing Work Stress

The research of Pearlin and Schooler (1978) on the process of coping suggests a fundamental reason that individual coping efforts, when used in isolation, are inadequate. In a large-scale, prospective survey, they found problem-focused coping to be most successful in preventing strain in marital and family relationships. In contrast, emotion-focused coping, designed not to change the situation but to reduce one's involvement, was the most effective response to work-related stress. The work environment is commonly unresponsive to individual attempts at effecting change; group-level efforts are typically more rewarding. As the necessary resources are rarely in one's complete control, even for those at the upper levels of an organization, an individual is rarely in the best position to manage sources of organizational stress.

A look at the common stressors at work (ambiguity, work overload, conflict of purpose, lack of feedback, inadequate opportunity for advancement, and relationships with co-workers) supports the concept that the opportunity for significantly affecting organizational stress exists primarily at the levels of the group and organization. These stressors are issues of the work group, the supervisor-employee relationship, and the shop floor. Organizational-level methods of preventing stress include those that address the task and physical demands of the workplace and those that target relationships between employees at all levels. There is, of course, the possibility that the same methods can have positive effects at the group level as well. For example, participative management is typically implemented at both the organizational and group levels and has effects on both task requirements and the support experienced from co-workers. Group-level interventions are typically directed toward the management of role and interpersonal demands. Those interventions at the organizational level are primarily concerned with modifying the formal organization in order to alter the demands it places on individuals. They may include task redesign, participative management, flexible work schedules, career development, and design of physical settings (Quick and Quick 1984). A comprehensive discussion of these methods is beyond the scope of this chapter. However, Table 1.2 lists interventions that can be implemented at the group and organizational levels to manage work stress, and a few comments are relevant.

The concept that an optimal "fit" between workplace demands and a worker's needs results in optimal levels of stress, performance, and satisfaction is basic to the approach of job redesign (Hackman and Oldham 1980). The basis of efforts to redesign the nature or flow of work to fit the employee's abilities and needs is the theory of person-environment fit (French and Caplan 1973; French, Caplan, and Harrison 1984). The premise of this theory is that the employee's experience of stress approaches an optimum level as the fit between the employee's needs and resources, on one hand, and organizational requirements and supplies, on the other, improves.

One type of organizational-level intervention that offers the potential to improve the fit between the employee and the organization is participative management. The research supporting participative management as a strategy that minimizes organizational strains while maximizing performance comes from a number of sources. In the early investigations of Kurt Lewin (Lewin, Lippitt, and White 1939), Coch and French (1948), Likert (1961), and Tannenbaum and Massarik (1950), employees were found to have more freedom and less turnover, absenteeism, conflict, and grievances in participatively managed situations. Although similar outcomes have been experienced in many of the organizations currently employing variations of participative management (Nightingale 1982), this management approach is

Table 1.2   Group- and Organizational-Level Methods for Preventing
Work Stress

Role and Interpersonal Demands	
Clarify role expectations	*Social support*

• Define job requirements clearly
• Make resources accessible
• Make rewards contingent on
  performance
• Eliminate conflicting expectations
• Provide frequent feedback on
  performance
	• Encourage constructive
	  relationships
	• Provide group or unit goals
	  and rewards
	• Encourage accessibility of
	  supervisors
	• Provide accessible counseling

Goal setting	*Team building*

• Establish reasonable performance
  goals
• Define area of responsibility
• Provide frequent feedback on
  goal-related performance
	• Provide opportunity to address
	  and resolve conflicts
	• Provide methods for integrating
	  new employees

Task and Physical Demands	
Task redesign	*Flexible work schedules*

• Assessment of task demands
• Restructures to provide more
  satisfying, less stressful work
	• Employee manages time to fit needs
	• Enhances fit between work and
	  home responsibilities

Participative management	*Career development*

• Reduces authoritarianism
• Increases employee control and
  responsibility
• Increases co-worker support
	• Involves self- and organizational
	  assessment
	• Requires clarification of career paths

Design of physical settings	
• Involves assessment and reduction of stressful environments • Facilitates task accomplishment	

Source: Compiled by the authors.

not without risks. It has the potential for increasing stress in the form of
ambiguity, demands, responsibility, and so on. Kanter (1983) discusses participative management in terms of those situations that are most enhanced
by the participative approach and those that are not. High levels of expert

decision-making and the need for immediate decision-making are examples of work situations that typically are not best suited to participatively managed organizations. The actual process of implementation is often a key factor in determining the success of such interventions both from the standpoint of enhancing productivity and optimizing levels of stress. As with most reorganizations, the implementation period is often one of lowered productivity and increased stress.

Cohesive work groups have, in themselves, the potential for managing the effects of stress. Such groups provide the opportunity for peer support, for a "sounding board," and for getting things done. Recently, Revicki and May (1985) documented that occupational stress experienced by family physicians directly influences the level of depression they experience. This stress-strain relationship was modified by the influence of social support from others, especially family. That is, even in the face of high stress, strain, in the form of depression, was low if there was good support from the family. This study did not assess the effects of co-worker support, presumably because many family physicians do not typically have a network of such relationships at work. There is evidence, however, that support from co-workers has a similar moderating effect on the experience of various types of strain (see Chapter 5 for a further discussion).

In his comprehensive comparison of democratic and hierarchically managed companies in Canada, Nightingale (1982) has contributed much to our understanding of these forms of management. He found that the differences between them were experienced primarily among rank-and-file employees rather than at middle and upper levels of management. Significant differences on measures of internal communication, levels of conflict, mental health, and job satisfaction were found between rank-and-file employees in democratically and hierarchically organized companies. Participatively managed employees rated their experience more positively on each of these measures. Additionally, these employees were significantly lower on measures of alienation and high on measures of organizational commitment. The limitation of these results primarily to the rank and file may, in part, be a function of the fact that participative management is often implemented at the lower levels of organizations where control and responsibility are typically less and jobs are typically more easily defined. It is important to note that when differences were found at the managerial level, they tended to be due to more positive ratings of the participatively managed companies (Nightingale 1982).

Finally, there is research support suggesting that managing for productivity and managing for optimal stress levels may enhance rather than oppose one another. An analysis by Katzell and Guzzo (1983) of 207 U.S. productivity programs reported between 1971 and 1981 demonstrated that those programs typically implemented at the group level (training, feedback, and goal-setting) increased at least one measure of productivity 92 to 95 percent of the time and had "side effects" of improving measures of strain. Specifically, attitudes improved 67 to 78 percent of the time, and withdrawal and disruption decreased 60 to 80 percent of the time. The success of training, feedback, and goal-setting programs in reducing these measures of strain may be due to their ability to improve clarity about one's job requirements, reduce conflict and ambiguity, and provide more potential for advancement.

CONCLUSIONS

In sum, there is substantial theory and evidence to give direction to efforts to optimize levels of stress at work. Individual and organizational distress are not inevitable. In summarizing the research in a paper that received a Distinguished Contributions Award from the American Psychological Association, Rudolf Moos states, "Most generally, [an individual's] personal growth or goal orientation dimensions channel the direction of change, while the relationship and system maintenance dimensions influence [his/her] commitment to the environment as well as the extent of change and the personal costs involved" (Moos 1984: 10). Given opportunities for flexibility, support, adequate resources, and a sense of control, employees at all levels have an enhanced potential of successfully coping with the demands placed on them. Indeed, when such opportunities are available, employees are likely to seek additional demands to keep their level of stress and challenge at optimal levels.

The nature of stress in the workplace has only begun to be appreciated as both resource-enhancing and resource-depleting. This understanding supports the view that an appropriate level of organizational stress is that which challenges employees in the context of an environment that provides adequate clarity, recognition, and resources. When viewed in this manner, managing stress becomes another aspect of managing for overall organizational effectiveness.

Acknowledgments—Comments and suggestions on an earlier draft of this chapter were offered by Lee W. Frederiksen and Christopher Peterson. The authors gratefully acknowledge the editorial assistance of Ruth Cargo and the word-processing expertise and efforts of Laura Charping in the preparation of this chapter.

REFERENCES

Anderson, C. R. 1976. "Coping Behaviors as Intervening Mechanisms in the Inverted-U Stress-Performance Relationship." *Journal of Applied Psychology* 61: 30-34.

Antonovsky, A. 1979. *Stress, Health and Coping: New Perspectives on Mental and Physical Well-Being* (San Francisco, CA: Jossey-Bass).

Arsenault, A. and S. Dolan. 1983. "The Role of Personality, Occupation and Organization in Understanding the Relationship between Job Stress, Performance, and Absenteeism. *Journal of Occupational Psychology* 56: 227-40.

Bandura, A. 1982. "Self-Efficacy Mechanism in Human Agency." *American Psychologist* 37: 122-47.

Baumgardner, A. and R. Arkin. 1985. "Playing It Safe: Social Anxiety and Protective Self-Presentation." Paper presented at the 93rd annual convention of the American Psychological Association, Los Angeles.

Beehr, T. A. and R. S. Bhagat. 1985. *Human Stress and Cognition in Organizations* (New York: Wiley & Sons).

Beehr, T. A. and J. E. Newman. 1978. "Job Stress, Employee Health, and Organizational Effectiveness: A Facet Analysis, Model, and Literature Review." *Personnel Psychology* 31: 665-99.

Bennis, W. 1984. "The Four Competencies of Leadership." *Training and Development Journal* 38 (August): 15-19.

Billings, A. G. and R. H. Moos. 1982. "Work Stress and the Stress Buffering Roles of Work and Family Resources." *Journal of Occupational Behavior* 3: 215-32.

Campbell, J. P. and R. D. Pritchard. 1976. "Motivation Theory in Industrial and Organizational Psychology." In *Handbook of Industrial and Organizational Psychology*, edited by M. Dunnette (Chicago, IL: Rand McNally), pp. 1455-1525.

Carrington, P., G. H. Collings, H. Benson, H. Robinson, L. W. Wood, P. M. Lehrer, R. L. Woolfolk, and J. W. Cole. 1980. "The Use of Meditation-Relaxation Techniques for the Management of Stress in a Working Population." *Journal of Occupational Medicine* 22: 221-31.

Cartwright, D. 1968. "The Nature of Group Cohesiveness." In *Group Dynamics: Research and Theory*, edited by D. Cartwright and A. Zander (New York: Harper & Row).

Cattell, R. B. 1948. "Concepts and Methods in the Measurement of Group Synergy." *Psychological Review* 55: 48-63.

Cherniss, C. 1980. *Staff Burn-Out: Job Stress in the Human Services* (Beverly Hills, CA: Sage Publications).

Chesney, M. 1983. "The Lockheed Hypertension Project." Paper presented at the Fourth Annual Scientific Sessions of the Society for Behavioral Medicine, Baltimore, MD (March).

Coch, L. and J. R. P. French, Jr. 1948. "Overcoming Resistance to Change." In *Group Dynamics: Research and Theory*, edited by D. Cartwright and A. Zander (New York: Harper & Row).

Cohen, S. 1980. "After-Effects of Stress on Human Performance and Social Behavior: A Review of Research and Theory." *Psychological Bulletin* 88: 82-108.

Frankenhauser, M. 1980. "Psychobiological Aspects of Life Stress." In *Coping and Health*, edited by S. Levine and H. Ursin (London: Plenum Press).

Frederiksen, L. W., A. W. Riley, and J. B. Myers. 1984. "Matching Technology and Organizational Structure: A Case Study in White Collar Productivity Improvement." In *Computers, People and Productivity*, edited by L. W. Frederiksen and A. W. Riley (New York: Haworth).

French, J. R. P. and R. D. Caplan. 1973. "Organizational Stress and Individual Strain." In *The Failure of Success*, edited by A. J. Marrow (New York: AMACOM).

French, J. R. P., Jr., R. D. Caplan, and R. V. Harrison. 1984. *Mechanisms of Job Stress and Strain* (New York: Wiley).

Ganster, D. C., B. T. Mayes, W. E. Sime, and G. D. Tharp. 1982. "Managing Organizational Stress: A Field Experiment." *Journal of Applied Psychology* 67: 533-42.

Glass, D. C., L. R. Krakoff, R. Contrada, W. F. Hilton, K. Kehoe, E. G. Mannucci, C. Collins, B. Snow, and E. Elting. 1980. "Effect of Harrassment and Competition upon Cardiovascular and Plasma Catacholamine Responses in Type A and Type B Individuals." *Psychophysiology* 17: 453-63.

Hackman, J. R. and G. R. Oldham. 1976. "Motivation through the Design of Work: Test of a Theory." *Organizational Behavior and Human Performance* 3: 69-106.

_____. 1980. *Work Redesign* (Reading, MA: Addison-Wesley).

Hebb, D. O. 1955. "Drives and the C.N.S. (Conceptual Nervous System)." *Psychological Review* 62: 243-54.

_____. 1972. *Textbook of Psychology* (Philadelphia, PA: W. R. Saunders).

Jackson, S. E. and R. S. Schuler. 1983. "Preventing Employee Burnout." *Personnel* 60 (March-April): 58-68.

Jamal, M. 1984. "Job Stress and Job Performance Controversy: An Empirical Assessment." *Organizational Behavior and Human Performance* 33: 1-21.

Janis, I. L. 1982. *Groupthink* (Boston, MA: Houghton Mifflin).

Kanter, R. M. 1983. "Dilemmas of Managing Participation." In *The Change Masters: Innovation for Productivity in the American Corporation*, edited by R. M. Kanter (New York: Simon and Schuster).

Katz, D. and R. L. Kahn. 1978. *The Social Psychology of Organizations* (New York: Wiley & Sons).

Katzell, R. A. and R. A. Guzzo. 1983. "Psychological Approaches to Productivity Improvement." *American Psychologist* 38: 469-78.

Lazarus, R. S. and S. Folkman. 1984. *Stress, Appraisal and Coping* (New York: Springer).

Lewin, K., R. Lippitt, and R. K. White. 1939. "Patterns of Aggressive Behavior in Experimentally Created 'Social Climates.' " *Journal of Social Psychology* 10: 271-99.

Likert, R. 1961. *New Patterns of Management* (New York: McGraw-Hill).

MacDougall, J. M., T. M. Dembroski, J. E. Dimsdale, and T. P. Hackett. 1985. "Components of Type A, Hostility, and Anger-In: Further Relationships to Angiographic Findings." *Health Psychology* 4: 137-52.

Magnet, M. 1982. "Managing by Mystique at Tandem Computers." *Fortune* 105: 84-91.

Main, J. 1981. "Westinghouse's Culture Revolution." *Fortune* 60: 74-93.

Maslach, C. S. and S. E. Jackson. 1984. "Burnout in Organizational Settings. *Applied Social Psychology Annual* 5: 237-259.

McGrath, J. E. 1976. "Stress and Behavior in Organizations." In *Handbook of Industrial and Organizational Psychology*, edited by M. Dunnette (Chicago, IL: Rand McNally), pp. 1351-95.

Moos, R. H. 1984. "Context and Coping: Toward a Unifying, Conceptual Framework." *Journal of Community Psychology* 12: 5-25.

Murphy, L. R. 1983. "A Comparison of Relaxation Methods for Reducing Stress in Nursing Personnel." *Human Factors* 25: 431-40.

_____. 1984a. "Occupational Stress Management: A Review and Appraisal." *Journal of Occupational Psychology* 57: 1-15.

_____. 1984b. "Stress Management in Highway Maintenance Workers." *Journal of Occupational Medicine* 26: 436-442.

Newman, J. E. and T. Beehr. 1979. "Personal and Organizational Strategies for Handling Job Stress: A Review of Research and Opinion." *Personnel Psychology* 32: 1-42.

Nightingale, D. V. 1982. *"Workplace Democracy. An Inquiry into Employee Participation in Canadian Work Organizations* (Toronto: University of Toronto Press).

Parasuraman, S. and J. A. Alutto. "Sources and Outcomes of Stress in Organizational Settings: Toward the Development of a Structural Model." *Academy of Management Journal* 27: 330-50.

Pearlin, L. I. and C. Schooler. 1978. "The Structure of Coping." *Journal of Health and Social Behavior* 19: 2-21.

Peters, L. H. and E. J. O'Connor. 1980. "Situational Constraints and Work Outcomes: The Influences of Frequently Overlooked Construct." *Academy of Management Review* 5: 391-97.

Peters, R. K., H. Benson, and J. M. Peters . 1977. "Daily Relaxation Response Breaks in a Working Population. II. Effects on Blood Pressure." *American Journal of Public Health* 67: 954-59.

Porter, L. W. and E. E. Lawler. 1968. *Managerial Attitudes and Performance* (Homewood, IL: Richard D. Irvin).

Quick, J. C. and J. D. Quick. 1984. *Organizational Stress and Preventive Management* (New York: McGraw-Hill).

Revicki, D. A. and H. J. May. 1985. "Occupational Stress, Social Support and Depression." *Health Psychology* 4: 61-77.

Riley, A. W. and L. Frederiksen. 1984. "Organizational Behavior Management in Human Service Settings: Problems and Prospects." In *Improving Staff Effectiveness in Human Service Settings,* edited by L. W. Frederiksen and A. W. Riley (New York: Haworth Press).

Riley, A. W., L. W. Frederiksen, and R. A. Winett. 1984. "Stress Management in the Workplace: A Time for Caution in Organizational Health Promotion." Paper submitted to NIOSH under contract no. 84-1320.

Sales, S. M. 1970. "Some Effects of Role Overload and Role Underload." *Organizational Behavior and Human Performance* 5: 592-608.

Schuler, R. S. 1980. "Definition and Conceptualization of Stress in Organizations." *Organizational Behavior and Human Performance* 25: 184-215.

Scott, W. E. 1966. "Activation Theory and Task Design." *Organizational Behavior and Human Performance* 1: 3-30.

Selye, H. 1956. *The Stress of Life* (New York: McGraw-Hill).

_____. 1976. *The Stress of Life,* 2d ed. (New York: McGraw-Hill).

Sharit, J. and G. Salvendy. 1982. "Occupational Stress: Review and Reappraisal." *Human Factors* 24: 129-62.

Shea, G. F. 1981. "Profiting from Wellness Training." *Training and Development Journal* 35 (October): 32-37.

Simon, H. 1964. "On the Concept of Organizational Goal." *Administrative Science Quarterly* 9: 1-22.

Steiner, I. 1972. *Group Process and Productivity* (New York: Academic Press).

Tannenbaum, R. and F. Massarik. 1950. "Participation by Subordinates in the Managerial Decision-Making Process." *Canadian Journal of Economics and Political Science* 16: 408-18.

Thompson, P. C. 1982. "Quality Circles at Martin Marietta Corporation." In *The Innovative Organization: Productivity Programs in Action*, edited by R. Zager and M. P. Rosow (Elmsford, NY: Pergamon Press).

Trist, E. and C. Dwyer. 1982. "The Limits of Laissez-Faire as a Sociotechnical Change Strategy." In *The Innovative Organization: Productivity Programs in Action*, edited by R. Zager and M. P. Rosow (New York: Pergamon, Work in American Institute Series).

Van Sell, M., A. P. Brief, and R. S. Schuler. 1981. "Role Conflict and Role Ambiguity: Integration of the Literature and Directions for Future Research." *Human Relations* 34: 43-71.

Vroom, V. H. 1964. *Work and Motivation* (New York: Wiley).

Walters, R. W. 1982. "The Citibank Project: Improving Productivity through Work Redesign." In *The Innovative Organization: Productivity Programs in Action*, edited by R. Zager and M. P. Rosow (New York: Pergamon, Work in America Institute Series).

Winett, R. A. and M. S. Neale. 1981. "Flexible work schedules and Family Time Allocation: Assessment of a System Change on Individual Behavior Using Self-report Logs." *Journal of Applied Behavior Analysis* 14: 39-46.

Yerkes, R. and J. D. Dodson. 1908. "The Relationship of Stimulus to Rapidity of Habit Formation." *Journal of Comparative Neurological Psychology* 18: 459-82.

Zander, A. 1971. *Motives and Goals in Groups* (New York: Academic Press).

_____. 1977. *Groups at Work* (San Francisco, CA: Jossey-Bass).

_____. 1982. *Making Groups Effective* (San Francisco, CA: Jossey-Bass).

2

STRESS MEASUREMENT AND MANAGEMENT IN ORGANIZATIONS: DEVELOPMENT AND CURRENT STATUS

LAWRENCE R. MURPHY
and JOSEPH J. HURRELL

This chapter provides a developmental review of occupational stress research, focusing on how our current understanding of job stress has evolved from the assessment methodologies selected for use. Early definitional work that shaped how stress was conceptualized is represented first, followed by an examination of the contribution of major research methodologies and their limitations. The chapter ends with a discussion of stress-reduction strategies and health promotion/health protection activities in work settings.

EARLY CONCEPTUAL AND DEFINITIONAL WORK

Occupational stress as a field of scientific inquiry examining job conditions and their consequences crystallized in the early 1970s. Its conceptual roots can be found in Selye's (1936) animal research on stress and Cannon's (1929) work on emotional stressors in humans. Selye (1936) discovered that a wide range of harmful stimuli (stressors) such as exposure to temperature extremes, physical injury, or injection of toxic substances evoked an identical pattern of change in specific bodily organs. In each case, the cortex of the adrenal gland became enlarged, the thymus and lymphatic structures became involuted, and deep bleeding ulcers developed in the stomach and intestines. Selye (1946) later described this somatic response to harmful stimuli as the *general adaptation syndrome* (GAS) and defined stress as the *nonspecific response* of the body to any demand.

Cannon (1914, 1929) had earlier described a "fight or flight" response in humans confronted by potentially dangerous situations. The response was an integrated mobilization of the body's resources which included elevated heart rate and blood pressure, a redistribution of blood flow to the major muscle groups and the brain and away from distal body parts, and a decrease in vegetative functions. One need only read Cannon's review of cases of death by fear or terror in the classic article "Voodoo Death" published in 1942 (reprinted in Monat and Lazarus, 1977) to appreciate the role of perceptual factors in ill health.

Lazarus (1966) described in more specific terms how one's perception of events or situations determines the health valence of objective events. Cognitive appraisal was described as the intrapsychic process that translates objective events into stressful experiences. The importance of this formulation lies in its recognition that subjective factors can play a much larger role than objective factors in the experience of stress. Indeed, any objective event can at once be perceived in a positive way by one person and as stressful by another—"one man's meat is another man's poison."

The focus on health consequences in occupational stress research was given impetus by the establishment of the National Institute for Occupational Safety and Health (NIOSH) by Public Law 91-596 (Occupational Safety and Health Act of 1970), whose stated goal was to ensure, as far as possible, safe working conditions for America's working men and women. NIOSH is the principal federal agency in the United States engaged in research aimed at the recognition and control of job-related hazards. That behavioral and motivational factors had an important bearing on the attainment of this objective was acknowledged in certain research provisions of the OSH Act (1970). For example, Sections 20(a)(1) and 20(a)(4) explicitly directed NIOSH to include psychological, behavioral, and motivational factors in researching problems of worker safety and health, and in developing remedial approaches for offsetting such problems. Job conditions were broadly interpreted to include those of a psychological nature, consisting of undue task demands, work conditions, or work regimens which, apart from or combined with exposures to physical and chemical hazards, may degrade a worker's physical or mental health (Cohen and Margolis 1973).

In view of the historical events outlined above, it is not surprising that measurement techniques in occupational stress have focused on subjective definitions of work characteristics and have used health outcomes (versus performance) to identify job characteristics as stressful. As will be seen later in this chapter, these themes are also to be found in stress reduction studies.

One of the first tasks facing occupational stress researchers in the early 1970s was characterizing the job stress concept. Job stress implied so many events and processes that it was (and to many is still) a nebulous construct difficult to study in a scientific manner. A seminal conference held in 1972 helped to limit this confusion by bringing together representatives of various disciplines to present their points of view on the subject of job stress (McLean 1974). A method of study was adopted at this Occupational Mental Health Conference that would have far-reaching consequences. In this paradigm, job stress was viewed as the condition in which some factor or combination of factors at work interacts with the worker to disrupt psychological or physiological homeostasis (Margolis and Kroes 1974).

The concept in this paradigm of factors that interact with the worker was significant. Indeed, a broad and diverse literature was known to exist that dealt with individual differences in physical and psychological states that can alter human response in a variety of situations. What was not completely clear was how much of this information was relevant to occupational situations. In this regard, a literature review published in 1975 (Sleight and Cook 1975) focused on (a) questions of hypersusceptibility or predisposition of certain workers to job-related illnesses and injuries, (b) selection criteria for placing workers in stressful or hazardous jobs, (c) needs for standards or guidelines to protect worker groups with special physical or psychological characteristics, and (d) relationships among life stress factors and work performance. The results of the review were significant in that they highlighted (1) the paucity of empirical data linking job conditions, individual characteristics, and health consequences, and (2) problems with existing research methodologies. This early work shaped the job stress concept and the kinds of methodologies needed for its study.

OCCUPATIONAL STRESS MEASUREMENT

Distributing self-report questionnaires to a large cross section of workers at one point in time represents the most common data collection strategy used by stress researchers. Such cross-sectional surveys typically solicit worker perceptions of job characteristics, work environment factors, individual psychological and physical health status, and maladaptive behaviors. Data analysis strategies have generally sought to identify associations between work factors on one hand and health complaints on the other. Those work factors associated with health complaints are deemed stressful.

Cross-sectional questionnaire surveys have identified a long list of stressful work factors. Examples include too much or too little workload, too easy or too difficult work, role conflict and ambiguity, lack of worker participation in decision-making, repetitive work, and rotating shiftwork, to name a few. Perhaps the most widely referenced study of this nature is *Job Demands and Worker Health*, sponsored by NIOSH and conducted by Caplan et al. (1975) at the University of Michigan's Institute for Social Research. In this study, a questionnaire designed to tap a wide variety of psychological stressors and health complaints was administered to 2,010 men employed in 23 occupations. The hypothesis that job stressors produce affective strains was strongly supported. Job dissatisfaction, for example, was strongly influenced (correlations greater than 0.30) by underutilization of skills and abilities, simple and repetitive work, low participation in decision-making, job insecurity, and little support from one's supervisor.

Given the reliance of researchers on the cross-sectional survey method, it is appropriate to examine some limitations in the kind of information that such surveys can supply. Two classes of limitations will be discussed: (1) those inherent in the methodology and (2) those imposed by researchers.

One major limitation of cross-sectional surveys involves response bias. Response biases can take numerous forms, reflecting misrepresentation of work factors (intentional and unintentional), poor memory recall, and non-response to the survey (or parts of the survey). This last bias can be particularly troublesome since, on one hand, some workers may be unable to read or understand questionnaire items, while others may be highly motivated to complete and return questionnaires for emotional or political reasons. It is not uncommon in job stress surveys to achieve less than a 50 percent response rate, and the obvious question becomes whether nonrespondents differ from respondents along sociodemographic and/or job stress variables. The extent to which these groups differ determines the representativeness of the respondent sample for the work population of interest and, consequently, the generalizability of obtained results.

Self-administered questionnaires also lack flexibility. With no interviewer present, variation in questions posed to the worker and probing for greater insight are not possible. This can lead to some misleading conclusions. For example, interview studies of police officers (for example, Kroes, Margolis, and Hurrell 1975) have found role conflict and role ambiguity to be major job stressors for police officers, yet questionnaire studies using traditional role stress measures fail to replicate these findings (Caplan et al. 1975). Upon closer examination, it is evident that questionnaire items typically used in job stress surveys (such as those developed by Kahn et al., 1964) tap conflict and ambiguity within the organization. However, for police officers, conflict and ambiguity involve not only organizational but community and societal expectations, the latter of which is missed in most questionnaire studies.

Finally, cross-sectional surveys provide only a "snapshot" view of stress, with no information on dynamic aspects like worker adaptational strategies, which evolve over time with experience. Accordingly, issues of assortive mating and "drift" are not elucidated. Of course, causal attributions regarding the direction of effects (that is, do stressors cause distress or does distress serve as a stressor) are also limited.

A second set of limitations of cross-sectional questionnaire surveys stems from conceptual perspectives of researchers who design the survey instruments. It is obvious that the knowledge gained from survey studies is a function of the questions posed to worker respondents. In this regard, we know a good deal about job demands, task characteristics, work role factors, and work routines, and how they relate to health complaints. At the same time, less attention has been paid to variables that may *moderate* stress-health relationships. Examples of such variables include extra-organizational stressors, lifestyle habits, coping skills, stage in career development, social relationships at work and home, and workplace exposure to physical and chemical agents.

The lack of knowledge regarding contextual variables and interactions of factors that may affect worker health and productivity compromises the ecological validity of many occupational stress studies. It is not sufficient to enumerate work factors that correlate individually to one degree or another with health complaints. For studies to be ecologically valid, a more holistic approach is required in which contextual factors are assessed as the backdrop against which job stressors occur. In this way, a clearer picture may emerge of how the occurrence of stress on the job at particular times will affect workers with particular qualities.

It is noteworthy that many questionnaires have emphasized negative features of work as predictors of health complaints. Kanner, Kafry, and Pines (1978) suggested that distress results from both the presence of negative work features *and* the absence of positive features. In their study of over 200 workers from various occupations, the authors reported that negative and positive features were statistically independent and both were associated with distress. However, work satisfaction/dissatisfaction was exclusively a function of the absence of positive features of work.

Moderator Variables

The ecological validity of occupational stress research has been significantly improved by attempts to assess and determine statistically the impact of moderator variables on stress/health relationships.

One of the earliest moderator variables examined in job stress research was social support. House and Wells (1978) provided evidence that the presence of a stressor or set of stressors at work was not the sole determining factor affecting health. It was shown that social support from one's supervisor, spouse, and co-workers could buffer the health effects of certain job stressors. Workers reporting high levels of job stress along with high levels of social support reported fewer health complaints than comparably stressed workers with little social support. The source of the support was also a significant variable. Social support from one's supervisor or one's wife were more powerful buffers than support from co-workers or from friends or relatives. Also, total social support buffered the effects of stress on some health conditions (for example, neurosis and ulcers) more so than others (such as angina). More recent research has confirmed the protective role of social support on workers' health (Thoits 1982).

Another potent moderating variable is stress coping. There is extensive literature on coping with stress, but little of this knowledge has been included in occupational stress/health formulations until recently. Lazarus and colleagues (Cohen and Lazarus 1979; Folkman and Lazarus 1980) have indicated that coping is not a trait or disposition but is a continuous, transactional process that is modified by experience within and between stressful episodes. Further, a specific coping strategy that can serve to alleviate stress in one situation may be maladaptive in others (Cohen and Lazarus 1979).

Pearlin and Schooler (1978) suggested that the coping responses people use are a function of the social and psychological resources at their disposal. Social supports and psychological resources (for example, mastery and self-esteem) are what people draw upon in developing coping strategies. Research has shown that these resources vary by sex, educational level, and income, such that men appear to have more psychological resources than women and use them to develop more effective coping responses. In the same way, the better educated and the more affluent possess more resources and a wider range of coping alternatives (Pearlin and Schooler 1978).

What is more important, aside from what people actually do to cope with stress, is the relative effectiveness of coping responses. Pearlin and Schooler (1978) considered a coping response effective if it reduced (buffered) the relationship between stressors and strains. The authors concluded that no single coping response was strikingly protective across life and work areas, but that having a larger and more varied coping repertoire was effective in reducing stressor/strain relationships. In this regard, the effectiveness of problem-focused versus emotion-focused coping for buffering ill health seemed to be a function of the controllability of the stressor—coping of any type is relatively ineffective in situations beyond the individual's control (Caplan, Naidu, and Tripathi 1984; Felton, Revenson, and Hinrichsen 1984; Fleishman 1984; Krause and Stryker 1984).

Particularly important in the present context was the finding by Pearlin and Schooler that while various problem-solving coping responses were effective in the areas of marriage, child-rearing, and household finances, this type of active coping was strikingly ineffective when applied to occupational problems. The authors suggested that the resistance of occupational stress to problem-focused coping may be due to the impersonal nature of work and the lack of worker control over stressors.

Evidence from other recent studies suggests that some coping behaviors that workers use actually *increase* distress. Parasuramen and Cleek (1984) identified adaptive and maladaptive coping responses used in work settings. They found that adaptive coping responses (planning, organizing, and prioritizing assignments, enlisting the support of others) had no buffering effects on felt stress or job satisfaction, but were associated with *elevated* trait anxiety. Maladaptive coping (working harder, making unrealistic promises, avoiding supervision) contributed to felt stress. Both types of coping were inversely related to organizational tenure, indicating that experience on the job did not necessarily lead to better stress-coping skills.

It is clear from the foregoing that the coping responses that workers use may increase, decrease, or have no effect on stressor-health relationships. Those that increase or decrease stress reactions need to be factored into job stress assessment instruments to increase ecological validity and "fine tune" descriptions of stressor-health relationships. Coping behaviors that have a buffering effect provide insights into the types of stress reduction strategies that are likely to be successful.

The effect of coping on worker productivity, work accidents, and organizational effectiveness in general has not been researched. Again, although it is logical to assume that workers who cope more efficiently with job stressors and suffer fewer health consequences will perform better and increase organizational effectiveness, an empirical demonstration is needed.

A final moderating factor is extra-organizational stress, which interacts with and provides a context for work stressors. While nearly every model of job stress and health acknowledges the interaction of work and nonwork stressors affecting health outcomes, few studies have incorporated measures of extra-organizational stressors into assessment designs and partialed out respective health effects. Some studies have incorporated a life-events scale (Holmes and Rahe 1967) into job stress surveys and attempted to assess its relative contribution to health status. However, generic life-event scales provide only a rough indication of social, familial, and financial stressors that workers may experience. Finer-grained measures are required that tap interpersonal, marital, financial, and child-rearing stressors. For example, a life-event scale will be sensitive to events like divorce, but is not designed to measure marital dissatisfaction, which may be present in varying degrees and for an extended period of time *before* divorce. Life-event scales record only the occurrence of events, not their perceptual valence. In some cases, divorce may serve to reduce total stress levels and be viewed as a positive event by one or both parties. Whichever the case, it would be useful to additionally assess perceptions of extra-organizational events, and to do so in greater depth (Bhagat et al., 1985).

Interactions among Variables

Bivariate associations between work factors and health complaints limit the apparent complexity of stress-health relationships. Such associations are not sensitive to *interactions* among work factors, which affect perceptions of work events as well as health outcomes.

One type of interaction is exemplified in the work of Karasek (1979), who identified two traditions in occupational stress research, one focusing on job demands and the other on worker issues. Each set of factors had been independently associated with health complaints in the research lierature. Based on his analyses of job characteristics and health complaints from the Quality of Employment Surveys (Quinn and Shepard 1974; Quinn and Staines 1979), Karasek (1979) proposed that the experience of stress is a function of the interaction of job demands and job decision latitude (control) such that health consequences were more frequent in occupations where job demands are high *and* job decision latitude is low. High-strain jobs identified by Karasek included nurse's aide, mason, waiter, laborer, excavator, stack handler, cook, cleaner, freight handler, assembly worker, firefighter, and cashier. Jobs falling in the low-strain quadrant included photographer, therapist, dentist, natural scientist, programmer, tool and die worker, civil engineer, and forester.

Karasek, Schwartz, and Theorell (1982) examined the predictive status of job characteristics for clinically determined coronary heart disease (CHD) from the Health and Nutrition Examination Survey (1971-74). Jobs with high scores on psychological workload and low scores on decision latitude were associated with a higher prevalence of myocardial infarction and elevated blood pressure after controlling for age, race, and sex. The magnitude of the elevated CHD risk in high-strain jobs was roughly equivalent in size to other risk factors, such as cholesterol and blood pressure (Karasek, Schwartz, and Theorell 1982).

House et al. (1979) highlighted another type of interaction whereby distress increases worker susceptibility to the effects of exposure to physical and chemical agents in the workplace. The authors found that stress was never associated with respiratory symptoms in workers with no exposures to dust, fumes, temperature variations, and noise. In contrast, stress was almost always associated with respiratory symptoms in workers exposed to three or more agents. Thus, workplace exposures can mediate associations between psychosocial stressors and health complaints.

Other Methodologies

Approaches other than cross-sectional surveys have contributed to current understanding of occupational stress-health relationships, but are relatively less common in the research literature. Examples here include longitudinal surveys, record studies, ergonomic evaluations, laboratory studies, and natural experiments.

Longitudinal studies involve repeated measurements over time on the same group of workers, and allow one to establish an adequate baseline, assess the reliability of measures, and associate changes in independent and dependent measures over time. As such, they have fewer limitations than the cross-sectional approach and provide a more dynamic view of stress but, at the same time, are much more costly. Moreover, the use of a longitudinal design does not guarantee "better" or more understandable results. For example, Chadwick et al. (1979) examined stress-health relationships in a group of 400 managers at Lockheed Missiles and Space Company. A baseline examination was administered to all 400 subjects, and approximately 220 were followed in repeat examinations administered each 2.5 months over a period of one year. Both the baseline and the repeat examinations included a large number of questionnaire items dealing with workload, job satisfaction, work pressure, personality, working environment, family environment, life events, and psychological distress. Data was also collected at each exam on the status of various known or suspected CHD risk factors, and participants completed weekly workload assessments and subjective appraisals of work pressures and felt stress during the repeat examinations.

There were a fairly large number of low-grade, but seemingly consistent relationships between psychosocial variables defining job stress and physiological measurements believed to relate to CHD risk. For example, the Involvement and Support subscales of the Work Environment Scale (Moos and Insel 1974) correlated negatively with psychological distress and some CHD risk factors. Most measures of work pressure correlated with psychological distress and CHD status. Broad occupational categories tended to be related to CHD either very weakly or not at all. Individual characteristics, the job environment, and interactions between these two elements seem to be implicated about equally in the processes that heightened CHD risk (Chadwick et al. 1979).

The data did not support the concept of job stress and behavior as an *extraordinary* component of CHD risk, that is, as a component much larger than conventional CHD risk factors. The data was consistent with the concept of job stress and behavior, in combination as ordinary components of CHD risk, having effects that are comparable to the classic factors.

In contrast to surveys, record studies start with outcomes of interest (for example, absenteeism) and work backwards to attribute stressful characteristics to jobs. Employer records regarding absenteeism, insurance/time lost claims, clinic/dispensary visits, and accidents and community-based records from population studies, hospitals, mental health centers, or insurance agencies are common sources of archival data. For example, Colligan, Smith, and Hurrell (1977) examined the records of 22 of the 27 mental health centers operated by the state of Tennessee. The records of all first admissions to the 22 participating mental health centers from January 1972, through June 1974 constituted the sampling frame. Data was recorded for a total of 8,450 cases.

The results indicated a disproportionate incidence of mental health disorders among hospital/health-care professions that comprised seven of the top-ranked occupations. The interpretation of results was complicated by the high proportion of females in health-care professions. Women in general and health-care workers in particular are more likely to report mental health disorders relative to the general population due to heightened sensitivity to and acceptance of emotional disturbances. This factor, and not excess job stress, could explain the obtained results (Colligan, Smith, and Hurrell, 1977).

Mental health admissions provide, at best, a crude index of distress, and the causal direction of the relationship between occupation and admission rate is certainly tenuous. It is noteworthy in this case that more recent studies have supported the conclusion of excess mental health problems and stress-related disorders among health-care workers (Gundersson and Colcord 1982; Hoiberg 1982).

Record surveys have distinct advantages in the study of occupational stress, including large enough numbers of workers to permit comparisons among occupational groups; discreet, relatively objective outcome measures across time measures of variables; and relatively low cost. A retrospective approach also offers the security of hindsight, and the investigator can control how far back in time she or he reaches in order to obtain an adequate sample of the behavior under study. Accident and illness rates may be examined over multiple years, depending on the needs of the investigator. Furthermore, one can indirectly control the impact of extraneous factors on the data set by selecting for observation only those time periods that were relatively stable (for example, strike-free) and representative of normal plant operations. Finally, the retrospective approach allows a well-defined historical framework within which to interpret the data.

At the same time, the disadvantages of this approach are quite formidable. First, the researcher is at the mercy of the record-keepers and the data-gathering guidelines of the organization. Employer records vary considerably in terms of thoroughness across companies and industries. Changes in record-keeping, many as a result of the OSHA Act (1970), may limit the comparability of longer-term retrospective studies, as do extraneous events like strikes, layoffs, organizational upheavals, and personnel policy changes. For community-based medical records, diagnoses are not as uniform across practitioners (or states) as one might suppose and, for worker compensation and disability, changes in state statutes and determination criteria (namely, functional capacity) may contaminate the acquired data file.

Of course, record studies do not solicit worker perceptions of distress, job dissatisfaction, work pressure, or psychosocial variables, and thus miss the subjective element of cognitive appraisal, the final common pathway of stress reactions (Lazarus 1966; Mason 1975). Accordingly, while record studies have discovered occupational differentials in morbidity and mortality (Kasl 1978), it is not clear which characteristics of the work experience contribute to observed consequences. On the other hand, record studies do provide a basis for selecting occupations for more in-depth study and for targeting high-risk worker groups for stress reduction efforts.

On-site observations of work conditions providing objective assessments of environmental factors, work-station design features, and work-process characteristics that can interact with job demands to elevate worker stress levels, have become more common in recent years. Ergonomic evaluations seek to compare capacities of the worker (visual, auditory, motor, information processing) with requirements of the task and assess the degree of worker-environment "fit." Poor fit between optimum worker capacities and task requirements is considered stressful. In this regard, a number of studies have found that machine-paced work is associated with negative mood states and somatic complaints (Frankenhauser and Gardell 1976; Murphy and Hurrell 1980). Machine-paced work routines, where operator control is minimal or absent altogether, do not allow for variations in individual work capacities, which determine optimum performance ranges (that is, a degree of fit between worker and environment).

Ergonomic studies, if focused exclusively on objective characteristics of work, also will miss the subjective element of job stress. Moreover, individual variations in capacities (visual, auditory, information processing) and worker anthropometric features are difficult to factor into ergonomic checklists for evaluating worker "fit." For example, optimal work-station design characteristics can be recommended, based on averages from a large number of measurements, but these will not result in a good fit for all workers. Ranges for such characteristics, rather than numerical point values, would be more useful data. Moreover, provisions for adjustability of work-station characteristics (for example, chairs, keyboard height, etc.) would facilitate optimal fit between worker and job/task requirements. These are the essence of ergonomic recommendations.

Company reorganizations, alterations in work processes, the introduction of flexible working hours, and changes in job scope/task requirements offer possibilities for designing experiments around planned organizational events and measuring before/after effects on worker well-being. This type of study is appealing because it embodies many advantages of a laboratory study without some of its attendant disadvantages. Natural experiments are not common in the literature, perhaps owing to the intricate logistics and sufficient "front-end" time required to design the study before the event or change is scheduled to take place. Needless to say, cooperation by the organization is a required first step.

Disadvantages of natural experiments are readily apparent. If the planned organizational change involves a number of factors changing simultaneously, such as alterations in the work process, change in job scope, and introduction of flexible working schedules, it will not be possible to tease out factor-specific effects. In addition, the work group under study may be of insufficient size for detecting statistically significant effects. Small sample size also limits generalizability of obtained results.

Natural experiments have been designed around a change from 5-to-4-day work weeks (Bhagat and Chessie 1980), redesign of work processes

(Wall and Clegg 1981), introduction of a compressed shift schedule (Cunningham 1981), shift from a training program to actual work assignments (Parkes 1982), temporary facility shutdown (Caplan and Jones 1975), change in job scope (Bechtold, Sims, and Szilagyi 1981), and job termination (Cobb and Kasl 1977).

The methodologies up to this point represent field studies of job stress in which the researcher has no opportunity to control or manipulate job/task characteristics or work processes. This kind of experimental control can be achieved in laboratory settings where environmental, work-station, and task factors can be changed systematically and relative impact assessed. Such designs permit attributions of cause to measured outcomes (effects) as opposed to associational (correlational) type statements.

Laboratory studies represent the most powerful methodologies in job stress research but, at the same time, have significant disadvantages. Such studies are quite costly in terms of equipment, technical personnel, and subject payments for participation. Lab studies typically involve only a handful of subjects who may be solicited from local universities or temporary employment agencies. In either case, the small sample size and type of participant call into question the representativeness of the sample and may limit the generalizability of the results. Equally significant, lab studies are far removed from the actual work environment and it is difficult to recreate the work *gestalt*, comprising a web of social, economic, and interpersonal factors. This state of affairs also limits generalizability of results to "real world" situations.

METHODOLOGICAL NEEDS

A fundamental methodological need involves evaluating existing tools for measuring job stress and strain and exploring alternative methods. The dominant methodology has been a cross-sectional questionnaire approach involving worker self-reports of job characteristics and health complaints, the former achieving "stressor" status if correlated with the latter. While this strategy has captured the subjective element of stress (cognitive appraisal), objective characteristics of the work environment have been largely ignored. Moreover, some scales used to measure job stressors have not been conceptually orthogonal to some dependent measures, creating what Kasl (1978) has called the "triviality trap." The absence of a generic questionnaire instrument (or at least a core set of questions) retards the development of normative data against which to compare stress levels in specific occupational groups. The use of assessment scales with unknown validity or reliability and the continuous modification of published scales also hinders the formation of normative data bases (Jenkins, DeFrank, and Speers 1984).

Over 50 percent of the U.S. work force is engaged in work activities that are primarily information processing in nature. This work is rapidly being automated via new computer-based technology, with major changes occurring in job design and task structure which impose more cognitive and less physical demands on the worker. There is an acute need for researchers to develop methods and measures for assessing cognitive task demands and to validate them on work groups subject to varying levels of cognitive effort.

A surveillance system for monitoring job stress and strain across occupational categories would be useful. Most existing health data bases were not designed for occupational health surveillance and permit only limited conclusions about the etiological role of the work experience regarding health. For example, the National Health Interview Survey (NHIS) is an annual household survey of approximately 120,000 individuals, of which about 40,000 are in the labor force. However, for nearly one-half of these workers, health information is obtained by proxy from another household member. Another data base, maintained by the Social Security Administration, contains diagnoses from medical examinations of workers who were judged severely disabled and were allowed income protection benefits. While this data base is quite large (about 500,000 annual allowances for severe disability in recent years) and contains sufficient numbers of disabilities due to stress-related conditions, it is not a true health incidence file, since factors other than medical criteria are considered in a percentage of disability determinations. Moreover, analysis of these data files has lagged several years so that such a system would not be sensitive to new technological changes in the workplace.

It is possible that some existing longitudinal data bases (such as Framingham, Evans County, Tecumseh, and Alameda County) could be linked to provide a surveillance system required for work stress. Employer-owned data files, many of which are computerized operations, may likewise offer meaningful surveillance data, but these will need to be merged to provide adequate sample sizes to detect occupational differentials in health conditions. Such a surveillance system would permit comparisons among occupations or job families, and the results could then be related to questionnaire assessments of stress and strain in specific work groups.

A final need involves expanding outcome measures in occupational stress research beyond health indices. For example, although the effects of stress on the performance of simple tasks were documented in early laboratory studies (Beier 1951; Deese and Lazarus 1952), there is little evidence that occupational stressors lead to decrements in worker performance or that health complaints attendant to job stressors reduce productivity. Indeed, Bhagat and Brush (1986) recently reported that the role stressors that predicted affective complaints were not good predictors of performance outcomes. Likewise, the state of knowledge concerning the role of occupational stress in workplace accidents has not changed substantially since Hirschfield and Behan (1963) reviewed 300 accident records, and found indications of heightened anxiety, depression, and low self-esteem in workers just prior to accident occurrences.

STRESS REDUCTION APPROACHES

The foregoing sections describe a growing knowledge base on occupational stress and health, although the area is complex and much additional research is required. Job stress studies have told us a great deal about how role stressors, workload levels, and subjective perceptions of job factors relate to worker reports of health complaints. Very little is known, though, about how job stressors affect worker productivity or organizational effectiveness. Likewise, the contribution to worker health and productivity of individual factors like stage in career development, levels of nonwork stress, and lifestyle behaviors and their interactions with work stressors, is largely unknown.

Despite the complexities in job stress research, the merits for stress reduction of both individual-oriented and, to a lesser extent, work environment-oriented approaches have been explored. Given the conceptual framework emphasizing the subjective element of stress presented earlier, it is not surprising to find that most stress reduction studies in the literature have focused on the individual, rather than the organization, and have used individual-oriented outcome measures to assess program success.

Individual-Oriented Techniques

A rationale for the conceptual viability of individual coping strategies emerges from the pioneering work of Lazarus (1966), who suggested that one's appraisal of an event or situation determines the response. Individual differences are also evident regarding the psychological, behavioral, and somatic reactions (strains) to perceived stressors. The importance of individual differences in both the perception of and reaction to stress suggests the potential efficacy of individual coping strategies. Individual-oriented techniques involve minimal description of work routines and can be easily tailored to individual workers. A number of studies in the literature have supported the efficacy of stress management training (SMT) in work settings for reducing psychophysiological and self-report signs of stress (Murphy 1984a).

A growing number of studies have evaluated prescriptive, relaxation-based strategies for helping workers to recognize stress and reduce arousal levels. Techniques have included biofeedback, muscle relaxation, meditation, and cognition-focused methods, many of which were borrowed from clinical practice, where they have been used successfully to treat psychosomatic dysfunctions (Pomerleau and Brady 1979). As applied in work settings, these techniques have a distinctive preventive flavor with an emphasis on imparting training skills to symptom-free workers. Accordingly, SMT is considered a health promotion activity rather than a strategy to relieve stress problems in troubled workers.

In addition to focusing on individual-oriented training techniques, SMT studies have used individual-oriented measures to evaluate benefits. Research has shown the efficacy of SMT for reducing worker self-reports of anxiety, depression, tension, somatic complaints, sleep disturbances, and psychophysiological arousal levels (Murphy 1984a).

The effects of work-site stress management training on organization-relevant variables such as absenteeism, tardiness, performance ratings, and symptom interference with work need to be evaluated to (1) document any transfer of intra-individual effects on psychophysiological levels of anxiety to employee behaviors and (2) compute cost-benefit ratios. Although such programs are not designed to influence such variables, indirect effects on these behaviors via reductions in arousal level might be evident. In this regard, Kohn (1981) has shown that workers trained in progressive muscle relaxation made fewer performance errors under conditions of high noise stress than did controls. Thus, beyond health-related benefits, relaxation training may directly improve work performance under conditions of elevated stress.

Two recent studies have examined employee behaviors before and after SMT. Riley, Frederiksen, and Winett (1984) used multimodal SMT with hourly employees of a health insurance company and found a significant *decrease* in job satisfaction in trained but not control groups. Both trained and control groups evidenced lower absenteeism and improved productivity after training, but these effects probably reflected known organizational events (for example, moving to a new location, loss of major contract, and consequent transfer and termination of some employees) that occurred during the course of the study.

A second study examined organization records for absenteeism, work performance ratings, equipment accidents, and work injuries among highway maintenance employees who had participated in a previous stress management study (Murphy 1984b). Preliminary analyses indicate significant pre- versus post-training increases in attendance ratings and decreases in Monday or Friday absences in workers taught muscle relaxation compared to nonvolunteer controls. No significant post-training changes were found for biofeedback-trained workers relative to controls.

The SMT techniques described above all contain a relaxation exercise and seek to reduce worker arousal levels. Thus, an important question is, does a relaxation break at work result in restored vigor and lower fatigue *or* does such a break create feelings of drowsiness and inattention, which could reduce worker performance, or worse, predispose toward unsafe behaviors?

Although individual-oriented strategies do not attempt to reduce or eliminate the job stressors themselves (a clear limitation), such techniques may warrant a place in job stress reduction efforts by virtue of their potential for reducing arousal levels, anxiety, somatic complaints, and sleep disturbances, within a health promotion/disease prevention framework. Stress management methods address the issue of individual differences in the perception of events as stressful and can be useful in reducing reactions to work and nonwork stressors that interact with individual characteristics to produce health consequences.

Organization-Centered Approaches

Approaches to job redesign and organizational change focus on reducing or eliminating the sources of stress at work and, hence, are preferred solutions. An example of an organization-centered approach designed to improve satisfaction, morale, and productivity is job enrichment.

Job enrichment strategies were popular in the 1960s and early 1970s. The guiding principle of job enrichment was to make the work activity more challenging and interesting in order to motivate employees to do high-quality work. Variations within this approach included adding more diversity to the work activity (job enlargement), encouraging greater worker participation in decision-making (job involvement), and rotating employees between different jobs (job rotation).

Although organizational change through job enrichment seems a most straightforward approach to reducing job stress (by altering the stressors themselves), equivocal results are found in the scientific literature. As Alderfer (1976) notes, one can find results ranging from completely successful through moderately successful to completely unsuccessful. Apparently, instituting changes at one level in the organization (such as the individual) often resulted in unpredictable and undesirable changes at other levels (such as the group). Indeed, in summarizing the results of 34 job enrichment studies, Caplan et al. (1975) state, "In no case has there been any good evidence that they [job enrichment programs] reduce illness or improve the physical health of the employees" (p. 208).

It should be noted that job stress was not the focus of these early "enrichment" studies. Efforts to scientifically evaluate organizational change or job redesign solutions for reducing work stressors are few. One reason for this state of affairs undoubtedly is the logistical and economic problems inherent in and attendant to such interventions. Some of these issues include (1) the reticence of organizations to undertake substantial reorganization of work outlines or organizational processes, (2) the lengthy time periods necessary to implement proposed changes in the workplace and evaluate benefits, (3) the fact that not all stressors can be eliminated from work (for example, shift work), and (4) the realization that global organizational changes may reduce stress for some employees but increase stress for others, as a function of individual differences in the perception of the work modification.

Organizational strategies that have potential for preventing or reducing stress include quality circles (which bring bench-level workers into the decision-making process); worker representation on health and safety committees; more extensive training programs for workers, especially in emerging technology occupations; alteration of communication channels within an organization; and creation of more psychologically humane evaluation systems to replace those that are either archaic or ones that monitor employee performance in a "Big Brother" fashion, for example, computer monitoring of keystrokes. These interventions have not been subjected to rigorous scientific evaluation, perhaps owing to some of the problems mentioned earlier. Evaluation schemes for such interventions should include an element of cost/benefit in addition to assessments of worker satisfaction, job stressors, performance, absenteeism, and health status. Bobko (Chapter 10, this volume) provides a description of quantifying techniques as well as some application examples for such studies.

While studies of individual-centered stress management approaches have steadily increased over the past 10 years, efforts to reduce or eliminate the sources of stress in work settings remain relatively sparse in the published literature. Reasons for this discrepancy seem straightforward: individual-oriented strategies are easy to implement, can be evaluated in the short term, do not require disruptions in production schedules or organizational structure, and fit nicely with management's view of stress as an individual worker problem (Neale et al. 1982). Individual strategies also ride the coat-tails of the expanding interest among employers in health promotion-disease prevention programs which seem to focus exclusively on individual lifestyle-behavioral change to improve health (Parkinson et al. 1982).

At the same time, approaches to organizational change require an accurrate and valid assessment of work factors that generate undue stress, and an extensive knowledge of the dynamics of change processes in social organizations (Alderfer 1976), so that potentially undesirable outcomes can be minimized. At the same time, organizational change strategies can be expensive and disruptive interventions, making them less palatable to management.

In this regard, developmental and experimental work on the Job Characteristics Model of Work Motivation (Hackman and Oldham 1976) indicates its usability for job redesign interventions. The model includes specific principles for redesigning and enriching jobs, such as forming more natural work groups, combining tasks into meaningful work modules, vertically loading jobs by adding responsibility and control to benchwork tasks, and improving performance feedback systems. These are testable interventions that have a theoretical base; work-site evaluations of their efficacy are warranted.

Recent work in the area of ergonomics suggests a set of concrete, work-centered measures that can reduce stress by improving the fit between the physical, psychological, and information-processing capacities of the worker and task requirements. A case in point involves video display terminal (VDT) work, where the technology has emerged more quickly than our knowledge of "software" or worker adaptational functions. Computerization in the workplace led to the introduction of equipment and routines that did not fit worker capacities, and to an array of worker complaints regarding workload, rest breaks, work content, social interaction, performance appraisal, and health. Computer monitoring of keystrokes, poorly designed office furniture, and inadequacies in terms of VDT equipment (screen size, lighting, character resolution, glare, postural requirements) also may contribute to the apparent dissatisfaction among VDT operators performing routine, clerical duties. Other organizaional-level interventions geared toward reducing worker stress include participative management (quality circles), flexible work schedules, career development programs, autonomous work groups, role analysis, and team building. Careful work-site evaluations are needed to establish the efficacy of such interventions, along with "bottom line" estimates of cost effectiveness.

HEALTH PROMOTION/PROTECTION ISSUES IN WORK SETTINGS

Stress management training is one example of a set of work-site programs designed to promote worker health and prevent disease. Other programs accent weight control, improved nutrition, smoking cessation, hypertension screening, and physical fitness. One reason for the increased interest in work-site health promotion is the belief that lifestyle factors contribute to the etiology of many chronic diseases and play a significant role in seven of the ten leading causes of death (DHHS 1979).

A significant trend toward greater company involvement in health promotion programs has been apparent in recent years, as reflected by the steady growth of employee health programs. Some programs address solitary problem areas such as alcoholism or hypertension, while others offer more comprehensive services, including counseling for workers and their families. Corporate expectations regarding health promotion include enhanced productivity, lower medical and disability costs, reduced absenteeism and turnover, and improved satisfaction and morale among workers.

The workplace represents an ideal site for the implementation of health promotion and disease prevention programs. Work-based programs have access to large numbers of people with social support networks in place, and facilitate participation among individuals with significant familial or community commitments that compete for available schedule time (Parkinson 1982).

Health promotion programs in work settings focus exclusively on the worker and the actions he or she can take to reduce risk and improve health (see *Health Education Quarterly*, Fall 1982, special issue). Job exposure as a risk factor is rarely addressed, and this has led to a conceptual dichotomy between management and labor groups. A NIOSH-sponsored survey of stress management programs in blue-collar settings (Neale et al. 1982) described the conflicting perspectives of union and management groups regarding the nature of stress, its sources, and how best to reduce it. From management's perspective, stress was defined in personal, biological, and physical terms with few, if any, acknowledgments that the work experience contributes to total stress levels (Neale et al., 1982). Emphasis was placed on individual responsibility and coping via lifestyle change. Accordingly, SMT, geared toward reducing the experience of stress by modifying the worker, was management's preferred stress reduction strategy.

The survey found that labor groups, in contrast, viewed stress as arising from the work experience and mentioned physical conditions of work, lack of individual control over work content and processes, unrealistic task demands, and lack of understanding by management as prevalent stress factors affecting worker health. From this perspective, the preferred strategy was to alter working conditions and processes to create a less stressful environment. To accomplish this, labor groups advocated strong contractual control and legislative restraints on management.

Neale et al. (1982) highlighted the selective attention of both management and union groups to certain aspects of stress enumerated in the literature. In reality, the experience of stress appears to be a function of (1) characteristics of the individual, (2) extra-organizational stressors, *and* (3) aspects of the work experience. The relationship of stressors to health and performance outcomes is equally complex and reflects a synergy of stressors from all life areas. To selectively attend to some stressors and deny the importance (impact) of others is not a constructive strategy for improving worker health and well-being.

Acknowledging the obvious interaction of individual lifestyle factors with work conditions affecting worker health status, NIOSH has formulated ideas for fusing health *promotion* with health *protection* concerns. These are contained in a NIOSH position paper (Cohen 1984) that recognizes that health promotion programs could augment the level of worker protection against certain job hazards and, perhaps, have a positive influence in motivating worker adherence to safe work practices. Among some research objectives set forth were: (1) elaborate the interactions of lifestyle factors and health and safety risks posed by the job (for example, smoking as a co-factor in occupational respiratory disease, excessive drinking as a factor in workplace accidents), (2) demonstrate and test strategies for effecting behavioral and lifestyle changes for reducing risks both on and off the job, and (3) identify worker groups in need of work-site health promotion-risk reduction programs owing to combination lifestyle-work-site environmental threats and means for delivering such programs.

REFERENCES

Alderfer, C. P. 1976. "Change Processes in Organizations." In *Handbook of Industrial and Organizational Psychology*, edited by M. D. Dunnette (Chicago, IL: Rand McNally College Publishing).

Bechtold, S. E., H. P. Sims, and A. D. Szilagyi. 1981. "Job Scope Relationships: A Three-Wave Longitudinal Analysis." *Journal of Occupational Behavior* 2: 189-200.

Beier, E. G. 1951. "The Effects of Induced-Anxiety on the Flexibility of Intellectual Function." *Psychological Monographs* 65 no. 365: 1-26.

Bhagat, R. and D. H. Brush. 1986. "Employee Reactions to Stressful Jobs and Life Events: A Longitudinal Analysis." *Organizational Behavior and Human Performance* (under review).

Bhagat, R., S. J. McQuaid, H. Lindholm, and J. Segovis. 1985. "Total Life Stress: A Multimethod Validation of the Construct and Its Effects on Organizationally Valued Outcomes and Withdrawal Behaviors." *Journal of Applied Psychology* 70: 202-14.

Cannon, W. B. 1914. "The Interrelations of Emotions as Suggested by Recent Physiological Researches." *American Journal of Psychology* 25: 256-82.

_____. 1929. *Bodily Changes in Pain, Hunger, Fear, and Rage* (Boston, MA: C. T. Branford).

Caplan, R. D., S. Cobb, J. R. P. French, Jr., R. Van Harrison, and S. R. Pinneau. 1975. *Job Demands and Worker Health*, DHEW (NIOSH) publication no. 75-160 (Washington, D.C.: U.S. Government Printing Office).

Caplan, R. D. and K. W. Jones. 1975. "Effects of Work Load, Role Ambiguity, and Type A Personality on Anxiety, Depression, and Heart Rate." *Journal of Applied Psychology* 60: 713-19.

Caplan, R. D., L. K. Naidu, and R. C. Tripathi. 1984. "Coping and Defense: Constellations and Components." *Journal of Health and Social Behavior* 25: 303-20.

Chadwick, J. H., M. A. Chesney, G. W. Black, R. H. Rosenman, and G. G. Sevelius. 1979. *Psychological Job Stress and Coronary Heart Disease*, final report on contract no. CDC-99-74-42 (Washington, D.C.: U.S. Government Printing Office).

Cobb, S. and S. V. Kasl. 1977. *Termination: The Consequences of Job Loss*, DHHS (NIOSH) publication no. 77-224 (Washington, D.C.: U.S. Government Printing Office).

Cohen, A. 1984. "Health Promotion/Protection at the Workplace: A Position and Planning Guide." Proceedings of the Society of Prospective Medicine, Atlanta, Georgia.

Cohen, A. and B. Margolis. 1973. "Initial Psychological Research Related to the Occupational Safety and Health Act of 1970." *American Psychologist* 28: 600-606.

Cohen, F. and R. S. Lazarus. 1979. "Coping with the Stresses of Illness." In *Health Psychology—A Handbook*, edited by G. C. Stone, F. Cohen, and N. E. Adler (San Francisco, CA: Jossey-Bass), pp. 217-54.

Colligan, M. J., M. J. Smith and J. J. Hurrell, Jr. 1977. "Occupational Incidence Rates of Mental Health Disorders." *Journal of Human Stress* 3: 34-39.

Cunningham, J. B. 1981. "Exploring the Impact of a Ten-Hour Compressed Shift Schedule." *Journal of Occupational Behavior* 2: 217-22.

Deese, J. and R. Lazarus. 1952. "Effects of Psychological Stress on Perceptual-Motor Performance." *Research Bulletin* 52-19 (Human Resources Research Center, Lackland Air Force Base).

Department of Health and Human Services. 1979. *Healthy People: The Surgeon General's Report on Health Promotion and Disease Prevention*. (Washington, D.C.: U.S. Government Printing Office).

Felton, B. J., T. A. Revenson, and G. A. Hinrichsen. 1984. "Stress and Coping in the Explanation of Psychological Adjustment among Chronically Ill Adults. *Social Science and Medicine* 18: 889-98.

Fleishman, J. A. 1984. "Personality Characteristics and Coping Patterns." *Journal of Health and Social Behavior* 25: 229-44.

Folkman, S. and R. S. Lazarus. 1980. "An Analysis of Coping in a Middle-Aged Community Sample." *Journal of Health and Social Behavior* 21: 219-39.

Frankenhauser, M. and B. Gardell. 1976. Underload and Overload in Working Life: Outline of a Multidisciplinary Approach." *Journal of Human Stress* 2: 35-46.

Grandjean, E. and E. Vigliani. 1981. *Ergonomic Aspects of Visual Display Terminals*. (London: Taylor and Francis).

Gundersson, E. K. E. and C. Colcord. 1982. *Health Risks in Naval Operations: An Overview*, Naval Health Research Center Report no. 82-1 (San Diego, CA).

Hackman, J. R. and G. R. Oldham. 1976. "Motivation through the Design of Work: Test of a Theory." *Organizational Behavior and Human Performance* 16: 250-79.

Hirschfeld, A. and R. Behan. 1963. "The Accident Process: Etiological Considerations of Industrial Injuries." *Journal of the American Medical Association* 186: 285-307.

Hoiberg, A. 1982. "Occupational Stress and Disease Incidence." *Journal of Occupational Medicine* 24: 445-51.

Holmes, T. H. and R. H. Rahe. 1967. "The Social Readjustment Rating Scale." *Journal of Psychosomatic Research* 11: 312-18.

House, J. and J. A. Wells. 1978. "Occupational Stress, Social Support, and Health." In *Reducing Occupational Stress*, DHHS (NIOSH) publicaton no. 78-140, edited by A. McLean, G. Black, and M. Colligan (Washington, D.C.: U.S. Government Printing Office).

House, J. S., J. A. Wells, L. R. Landerman, A. J. McMichael, and B. H. Kaplan. 1979. "Occupational Stress and Health among Factory Workers." *Journal of Health and Social Behavior* 20: 139-60.

Hurrell, J. J., Jr. 1985. "Machine-Paced Work and the Type A Behavior Pattern." *Journal of Occupational Psychology* 58: 15-26.

Hurrell, J. J., Jr., A. Pate, and R. Kliesmet. 1984. *Stress among Police Officers*,

DHHS (NIOSH) publication no. 84-108 (Washington, D.C.: U.S. Government Printing Office).

Jenkins, C. D., R. S. DeFrank and M. A. Speers. 1984. *Evaluation of Psychometric Methodologies Used to Assess Occupational Stress and Strain*, final report on P.O. no. 84-2756 (Cincinnati, OH: NIOSH).

Kahn, R. L., D. M. Wolfe, R. P. Quinn, J. D. Snoek, and R. A. Rosenthal. 1964. *Organizational Stress: Studies in Role Conflict and Ambiguity* (New York: Wiley).

Kanner, A. D., D. Kafry, and A. Pines. 1978. "Conspicuous in Its Absence: The Lack of Positive Conditions as a Source of Stress." *Journal of Human Stress* 4: 33-39.

Karasek, R. A. 1979. "Job Demands, Decision Latitude, and Mental Strain: Implications for Job Redesign." *Administrative Science Quarterly* 24: 285-307.

Karasek, R. A., J. Schwartz, and T. Theorell. 1982. *Job Characteristics, Occupation, and Coronary Heart Disease*, final report on contract no. R-01-OH00906 (Cincinnati, OH: NIOSH).

Kasl, S. V. 1978. "Epidemiological Contributions to the Study of Work Stress." In *Stress at Work*, edited by C. L. Cooper and R. Payne (New York: John Wiley & Sons).

Katz, D. and R. L. Kahn. 1978. *The Social Psychology of Organizations* (New York: John Wiley & Sons).

Kohn, J. P. 1981. "Stress Modification Using Progressive Muscle Relaxation." *Professional Safety* 26: 15-19.

Kroes, W. H., B. Margolis, and J. J. Hurrell, Jr. 1975. "Job Stress in Policemen." *Journal of Police Science and Administration* 2: 145-55.

Krause, N. and S. Stryker. 1984. "Stress and Well-Being: The Buffering Role of Locus of Control Beliefs. *Social Science and Medicine* 18: 783-90.

Lazarus, R. 1966. *Psychological Stress and the Coping Process* (New York: McGraw-Hill).

Mason, J. W. 1975. "A Historical View of the Stress Field." *Journal of Human Stress* 1: 6-12.

McLean, A. 1974. *Occupational Stress* (Springfield, IL: Charles C. Thomas).

McNair, D. M., M. Lorr, and L. F. Droppleman. 1971. *Profile of Mood States*. (San Diego, CA: Educational and Industrial Testing Service).

Margolis, B. L. and W. H. Kroes. 1974. "Occupational Stress and Strain." *Occupational Mental Health* 2: 4-6.

Margolis, B., W. H. Kroes, and R. P. Quinn. 1974. "Job Stress: An Unlisted Occupational Hazard." *Journal of Occupational Medicine* 16: 659-61.

Monat, J. W. and R. L. Lazarus. 1977. *Stress and Coping: An Anthology* (New York: Columbia University Press).

Moos, R. and P. Insel. 1974. *Family, Work, and Group Environment Scale Manual* (Palo Alto, CA: Consulting Psychologists Press).

Murphy, L. R. 1984a. "Stress Management in Highway Maintenance Workers." *Journal of Occupational Medicine* 26: 436-42.

_____. 1984b. "Occupational Stress Management: A Review and Appraisal." *Journal of Occupational Psychology* 57: 1-15.

Murphy, L. R. and J. J. Hurrell, Jr. 1980. "Machine Pacing and Occupational Stress." In *New Developments in Occupational Stress*, DHHS (NIOSH) publication no. 81-102, edited by R. Schwartz (Washington, D.C.: U.S. Government Printing Office).

Neale, M. S., J. A. Singer, G. A. Schwartz, and J. Schwartz. 1982. "Conflicting Perspectives on Stress Reduction in Occupational Settings: A Systems Approach to Their Resolution," report to NIOSH on P.O. no. 82-1058 (Cincinnati, OH 45226).

O'Toole, J. 1974. "Work in America and the Great Job Satisfaction Controversy." *Journal of Occupational Medicine* 16: 710-15.

Parkes, K. 1982. "Occupational Stress among Student Nurses: A Natural Experiment." *Journal of Applied Psychology* 67: 784-96.

Parkinson, R. 1982. *Managing Health Promotion in the Workplace: Guidelines for Implementations and Evaluation* (Palo Alto, CA: Mayfield).

Parasuraman, S. and M. A. Cleek. 1984. "Coping Behaviors and Managers' Affective Reactions to Role Stressors." *Journal of Vocational Behavior* 24: 179-83.

Pearlin, L. I. and C. Schooler. 1978. "The Structure of Coping." *Journal of Health and Social Behavior* 19: 2-21.

Pomerleau, D. F. and J. P. Brady. 1979. *Behavioral Medicine: Theory and Practice* (Baltimore, MD: Williams & Wilkins).

Quinn, R. P. and L. J. Shepard. 1974. *The 1972-73 Quality of Employment Survey* (Ann Arbor, MI: University of Michigan, Institute for Social Research).

Quinn, R. P. and G. L. Staines. 1979. *The 1977 Quality of Employment Survey* (Ann Arbor, MI: University of Michigan, Institute for Social Research).

Riley, A. W., L. W. Frederiksen, and R. A. Winett. 1984. *Stress Management in the Workplace: A Time for Caution in Organizational Health Promotion*, final report to NIOSH on P.O. no. 84-1320 (Cincinnati, OH 45226).

Selye, H. 1936. *"A Syndrome Produced by Diverse Noxious Agents." Nature* 138: 32.

———. 1946. "The General Adaptation Syndrome and Diseases of Adaptation." *Journal of Clinical Endocrinology* 6: 217-30.

———. 1976. *Stress in Health and Disease* (London: Butterworth).

Sleight, R. B. and K. G. Cook. 1975. *Problems in Occupational Safety and Health: A Critical Review of Select Worker Physical and Psychological Factors*, DHHS (NIOSH) publication no. 75-124 (Washington, D.C.: U.S. Government Printing Office).

Tasto, D. L., M. J. Colligan, E. W. Skjei, and S. J. Polly. 1978. *Health Consequences of Shiftwork*, DHHS (NIOSH) publication no. 78-154 (Washington, D.C.: U.S. Government Printing Office).

Thoits, P. A. 1982. "Conceptual, Methodological, and Theoretical Problems in Studying Social Support as a Buffer against Life Stress. *Journal of Health and Social Behavior* 23: 145-59.

U.S. Congress. Occupational Safety and Health Act. 1970. Public Law 91-596, 91st Congress, S. 2193.

Wall, T. D. and C. W. Clegg. 1981. "A Longitudinal Field Study of Group Work Redesign." *Journal of Occupational Behavior* 2: 31-49.

3

THE EXPERIENCE AND MANAGEMENT OF STRESS: JOB AND ORGANIZATIONAL DETERMINANTS

CARY L. COOPER

The purposes of this article are twofold: (1) to highlight the sources of stress that people experience in relation to work and (2) to provide examples of what can be done by management and stress practitioners to enhance the well-being of individuals in the workplace.

It will be useful to begin this exploration by examining the complex experience of those who are involuntarily out of work—the unemployed. This growing phenomenon in Western society has long-term implications for the health and attitudes of individuals toward work and toward their society. Following a review of the potent effects of unemployment, the key sources of stress at work and the importance of social support in managing work stress will be discussed.

BEING UNEMPLOYED

Historically, long-term unemployment (over 12 months) has represented, in most developing countries, a small proportion of the total number of unemployed people. Recent statistics from the Organization for Economic Cooperation and Development (OECD) indicate that this may be changing, however, particularly in Europe. Recent figures show that from the early 1970s to 1982, Belgium, France, the Netherlands, Britain, and Germany

Some of the material used in this chapter was drawn from the author's articles in *Small Group Behavior* and the Manchester *Guardian*.

experienced a large increase in the number of long-term unemployed, whereas in North America this figure is still fairly low. For example, the average duration of unemployment in Belgium is 16.1 months; France, 10.9 months; the Netherlands, 9.1 months; and Britain, 8.9 months. In contrast, the figure for the United States is 3.2 months; for Canada, 3.5 months; and for Sweden and Norway, 3.8 months.

In a forthcoming OECD report entitled, "Employment Review and Outlook," the figures for Britain are extremely disheartening. Nearly a third of all those unemployed in Britain have been in this situation for 12 months or more. Nearly 50 percent have been unemployed for over six months. By comparison, in the United States the proportion of those who have been out of a job for six months or more is less than 15 percent, and it is less than 10 percent for those unemployed for over 12 months. The November 1982 Manpower Services Commission quarterly report showed that by late 1982, "450,000 of the 1.1 million long-term unemployed had been registered for 2 years or more and 185,000 of these had not had a job for over 3 years. Numbers in these very long-term categories are increasing at an even faster rate than the over one year category" (Manpower Services Commission 1982: 35).

An even more disturbing view of these findings is that the major increase in the long-term unemployed (12 months or over) in Britain is in young people under 25 years old. In 1973, just over 6 percent of the long-term unemployed were under 25, but by 1981 nearly 25 percent were "out of work" in this age group. The proportions of the long-term unemployed have also shifted. In 1973, 91 percent of the long-term unemployed were men. That figure had declined to just over 78 percent in 1981. For women, however, there was an increase from 9 percent in 1973 to 22 percent in 1981 (as a percentage share of the total of those unemployed 12 months or longer). These trends are also prevalent in several other European countries, such as Belgium and the Netherlands.

Since more and more people are taking early retirement in Britain, the number of older workers unemployed for over 12 months dropped from 70 percent in 1973 to just over 40 percent in 1981. The increase for those "prime age" adults (25-44) was from just over 24 percent to nearly 35 percent during this same period. At these two times, 1973 and 1981, the proportion of young people who were unemployed for over six months also changed dramatically. In 1973 only 10 percent were under 25, whereas in 1981 30 percent of them had been on welfare for over six months.

Another concern expressed by the OECD report is the impact on individual and community health of this increase in long-term unemployment. Preliminary research in Britain indicates that people who endure long periods of unemployment face potential problems in maintaining their self-respect, retaining a high level of job expectation, and sustaining the self-confidence and energy necessary to find another job. In a U.S. government report entitled, "Estimating the Social Costs of National Economic Policy: Implications for Mental and Physical Ill Health and Criminal Aggression," research was reported that related the symptoms of a number of physical and mental illnesses to length of unemployment.

A number of research studies suggest that job loss can have significant consequences on the health and well-being of the unemployed and his or her family. Kahn (1956) looked at redundancy in the car industry in Birmingham, England, where 6,000 men were suddenly left without jobs. Ten percent of the men, mainly unskilled and semiskilled workers, were interviewed two years later. A great deal of data was collected concerning attitudes toward their unemployment, age, length of time out of work, methods of job seeking, and the individual's subjective impression of the new job compared with the old. The interview data revealed that even after two years, some individuals were not only still recovering financially, but were still suffering from the loss of self-esteem and other partially debilitating psychological difficulties.

In addition, Daniel (1972) investigated the effects of several plant closings in a particular area of Britain over a four-year period. He used structured interviews to look at a wide range of factors, including demographics, type of job, and skill level, and related these to variables such as length of time unemployed. He also compared the new job with the old. He found that older workers and men whose skills were important in a particular job or firm (such as supervisors and semiskilled workers), had the greatest difficulties in finding new work and expressed the least satisfaction with their new employment. Daniel also compared methods of job search and found distinct differences between occupational groups, which may reflect the different ways in which jobs come on the market for blue-collar and white-collar workers.

A study by Warr and Lovatt (1975) examined the job status of those left unemployed by the complete closure of Irlam Steel Works and related this to psychological well-being and pre-closure training. They found that psychological well-being was lower for people who were still unemployed at the time of the interview than for those who had found alternative employment, and that this influenced a person's outlook beyond that toward her or his work. For example, the unemployed tended to have more anxieties about their own health and even about the world political situation. Pre-closure training had no impact on well-being. The study also looked at a person's job-seeking behavior in terms of his or her "orientation to work," using a simple measure of motivation for employment. For those individuals who scored high on this work orientation measure, having a job was associated with psychological well-being, but there was no relation for those with low motivation for employment. It is clear that for most people, work is very important both psychologically and financially. Involuntary unemployment can be extremely stressful, producing significant strains for the individual, the family, and society. While being unemployed can be damaging to the individual, employment also poses problems and can be a major source of stress. Work stress need not be damaging, however. In increasing numbers of organizations, psychologists and managers are actively attempting to optimize stress at work, to create environments that are demanding enough to motivate good levels of productivity, while being supportive and responsive enough to ensure that stress levels never become detrimental to the individual or organizational unit. Effectively managing people at work requires understanding the sources of stress and learning how to keep it at healthful levels.

SOURCES OF WORK STRESS

Six major sources of occupational stress have been defined in the literature. These include: (1) factors intrinsic to the job, (2) role in the organization, (3) career development, (4) relationships at work, (5) organizational structure and climate, and (6) home-work interface.

Factors Intrinsic to the Job

Sources of stress that are intrinsic to the job itself across a variety of occupations include: (1) poor working conditions, (2) shift work, (3) work overload, (4) work underload, and (5) physical danger.

Poor working conditions. Poor physical working conditions can enhance stress at work. For example, Otway and Misenta (1980) believe that the design of the control room itself is an important variable in the stress experienced by nuclear power plant operators. They propose that control room designs need to be updated, requiring more sophisticated ergonomic designs. As an example they refer to an important stress factor that was highlighted in the Three Mile Island accident—the distraction caused by excessive emergency alarms. In a study carried out by Kelly and Cooper (1981) on the stressors associated with casting in a steel manufacturing plant, poor working conditions due to heat and danger were found to be major stressors.

Shift work. Numerous occupational studies have found that shift work is a common occupational stressor, affecting neurophysiological rhythms such as temperature, metabolic rate, and blood sugar levels. Mental efficiency and work motivation are both directly and indirectly affected. An occupational study by Cobb and Rose (1973) involving air traffic controllers (a particularly demanding occupation) demonstrated that hypertension was four times more prevalent among the subjects than in a control group of enlisted men in the military. The air traffic controllers also had a higher prevalence of mild diabetes and peptic ulcers than the control group.

Although other job stressors were identified, a major job stressor was reported to be shift work.

Work overload. French and Caplan (1972) classify work overload as either quantitative (having too much to do) or qualitative (too difficult). Others have associated certain behavior malfunctions with work overload. For example, the French and Caplan study indicated a relationship between quantitative overload and cigarette smoking (an important behavior in the development of coronary heart disease). Margolis, Kroes, and Quinn (1974), in their sample of 1,500 employees, found that work overload was associated with such strains as low self-esteem, low work motivation, and escapist drinking. In a study by Cooper, Davidson, and Robinson (1982) investigating stress among British police officers, it was found that work overload was a major stressor among the lower ranks, particularly among sergeants. In particular, sergeants who scored high on the depression scale of the Middlesex Hospital questionnaire tended to be older operational officers who believed they were overloaded and who perceived a number of bureaucratic and outside obstacles to effective police functioning. They complained about the long hours and heavy work load, as well as the increased paperwork, lack of resources, and the failure of the courts to prosecute offenders.

Work underload. Work underload involves repetitive, routine, boring, and understimulating work environments. Machine-paced assembly lines are an example of such a work environment and have been associated with ill health (Cox 1980). Moreover, in certain jobs, such as policing and operating nuclear power plants, periods of boredom must be endured simultaneously with maintenance of sufficient alertness to respond to potential emergency situations (Davidson and Veno 1980). This is difficult to do and is made all the more stressful by awareness of the costs of an ineffective response to an emergency.

Physical danger. There are certain occupations that are known to involve high risk in terms of physical danger—for example, police officers, mineworkers, soldiers, and firefighters (Kasl 1983). However, stress induced by the uncertainty of physically dangerous events is often substantially relieved if the employee feels adequately trained and equipped to cope with emergency situations (Cooper and Smith 1985).

Role in the Organization

The roles one is supposed to fulfill at work can be stressful when they are unclear or ambiguous or when they are in conflict. Responsibility for people has also been demonstrated to be a major organizational stressor (Cooper and Marshall 1976). Authors such as French and Caplan (1972), Beehr, Walsh, and Taber (1976), and Shirom et al. (1973) have related role ambiguity and conflict to such stress-related illnesses as coronary disease. Furthermore, Cooper and Marshall (1976) conclude that those less physically demanding occupations, such as managerial, clerical, and professional positions are more prone to role conflict.

The problems that role conflicts can generate were amply demonstrated by Cooper, Mallinger, and Kahn (1978) in their investigation into the work stress experienced by dentists. It was found that the variables that predicted abnoramlly high diastolic blood pressure among dentists were factors related to the role of the dentist. These included the view that the dentist was "an inflictor of pain" rather than a "healer"; that she had to assume the sometimes conflicting roles of administrator, business person, and clinician; and that her work role was in conflict with her personal life, primarily in terms of time commitments.

Career Development

The next group of stressors in the work environment is related to career development, which, Cooper and Marshall (1976) maintain, refers to "the impact of overpromotion, underpromotion, status incongruence, lack of job security, thwarted ambition. . . ." Career development blockages are most notable among women managers, as a study by Cooper and Davidson (1982) revealed. In this investigation, the authors collected data from over 700 female managers and 250 male managers at all levels of the organizational hierarchy and from several hundred companies. It was found that women suffered significantly more than men on a range of organizational stressors, but the most damaging to their health and job satisfaction were those associated with thwarted career development and allied stressors. These stressors included, for example, sex discrimination in promotion, inadequate training, male colleagues being treated more favorably, and inadequate delegation to women.

Relationships at Work

Both the quality of an individual's work relationships and the social support available from one's colleagues, boss, and subordinates have been related to job stress (Payne 1980). According to French and Caplan (1972), one mechanism for the development of poor relationships with other members of an organization may be role ambiguity. This lack of clarity may produce other psychological strains in the form of low job satisfaction. Moreover, French, Caplan, and van Harrison (1982) found that strong social support from peers relieved job strain and served to mediate the effects of job stress on cortisone, blood pressure, glucose, and the number of cigarettes smoked, and was related to the cessation of cigarette smoking. It is interesting to note that among air traffic controllers, greater help and social support were provided by friends and colleagues than by those in supervisory positions (French and Caplan 1972).

Organizational Structure and Climate

Another potential source of occupational stress is related to organizational structure and climate, which includes such factors as office politics, lack of effective consultation, lack of participation in the decision-making process, and restrictions on behavior. Margolis, Kroes, and Quinn (1974) and French and Caplan (1972) found that greater participation led to high productivity, improved performance, lower staff turnover, and lower levels of physical and mental illness (including such stress-related behaviors as escapist drinking and heavy smoking).

Home-Work Interface

Another cost of the current economic situation is the effect that work pressures (such as fear of job loss, blocked ambition, work overload, and so on) have on the families of employees. When there is a career crisis (or stress from job insecurity as many employees in Europe are now facing), the tensions workers bring with them into the family affect the wife and the home environment in a way that may not meet their ''sanctuary'' expectations. It may be very difficult, for example, for parents to provide the kind of supportive domestic environment children require at a time when they are beginning to feel insecure, and when they are worried about the family's economic, educational, and social future.

Dual career stress. The response of many families to these pressures has been for the wife to become an income earner. Increasingly women are taking on additional roles, often relieving financial pressures, but adding to the demands on every family member. According to the U.S. Department of Labor, the ''typical American family'' with a working husband, a homemaker wife, and two children now makes up only 7 percent of the nation's families. In fact, in 1975, 45 percent of all married women were working, as were 37 percent of women with children under six; in 1960 the comparable figures were 31 percent and 9 percent, respectively. Today about half of all U.S. women with children under six are working outside their homes. It is claimed by many psychologists and sociologists that dual career family development is the primary culprit of the very large increase in the divorce rate over the last 10 years in the United States and Western Europe (Cooper and Davidson 1982).

Not only are these stressors numerous and diverse, but at one time or other, the majority of workers confront them. Furthermore, most people cope with the stress of work fairly effectively most of the time. A condition that has repeatedly been found to aid effective coping is that of available support from others in one's life.

SOCIAL SUPPORT AT WORK

The studies that have produced evidence indicating the importance of the social group as a source of job and life satisfaction are discussed by Cooper and Payne (1978, 1980). The importance of support is recognized in the human relations approach to the workplace, which emphasizes the role of social relationships in achieving satisfying and rewarding work (Cooper and Mumford 1979). There is now substantial evidence that the individual's work group and social group can provide social support that is able to offset the effects of stress and coronary heart disease (Cooper and Marshall 1976). One of the first indications of this appeared in several studies of social stress in Japan, which revealed marked differences in rates of coronary heart disease compared to the United States. In 1962 the ratio of deaths from coronary heart disease to the total death rate was reported to be 33.2 for Caucasians in the United States and 8.7 for the Japanese (Luisada 1962). Matsumoto (1970) reported that two major factors seemed to be implicated in the development of CHD, namely a high-fat diet and emotional stress. The diet hypothesis was strongly supported by the fact that less than 16 percent of the calories in the average Japanese diet comes from fat, whereas 40 percent of the calories in the U.S. diet are from fat. Marmot and his colleagues at the University of California (Marmot et al. 1975) extended this work by looking at the differences between the two cultures in terms of social support and stress, controlling for the fat content in the diet. They studied 11,900 men of Japanese ancestry, aged between 45 and 69 (2,141 living in Japan, 8,006 in Hawaii, and 1,844 in California). It was found that age-adjusted prevalence of CHD increased from Japan to Hawaii, and again from Hawaii to California, where it is approximately double the rate found in Japan. This trend was the same for either of the two criteria of heart disease, electrocardiogram (EKG) and subjective assessments of angina pectoris. The incidence of abnormal EKG per 1,000 of the population (age adjusted) was 5.3 in Japan, 6.2 in Hawaii, and 10.8 in California. The incidence of diagnosed angina pectoris was 11.2 per 1,000 of the population (age adjusted) in Japan, 14.3 in Hawaii, and 25.3 in California. The researchers found that the known risk factors for CHD, hypertension, serum cholesterol levels, and smoking were roughly the same in all three regions, so that these risk factors could not explain the observed increase in the prevalence of coronary heart disease the further one went toward the U.S. mainland. The investigators concluded that the acculturation among the Japanese Americans, that is, the extent to which they have abandoned their traditional way of life and moved toward a mobile, nuclear family, may be responsible for the differences. Marmot and his colleagues suggested further that the more hectic, demanding pace of life in the United States, together with the lack of social support, both at work and home, are likely contributors. Given the value of social support in moderating the effects of stress, it is important to consider how to improve social support in work groups and organizations.

Work Organization Support

Work organizations can provide a wide variety of social support systems to their employees. Payne (1980) suggests a framework for looking at organizational support at work, which explores both the official or formal and the informal support systems (where the individual is both a giver and receiver of support). He also breaks down the areas of "support need" as cognitive, emotional, and behavioral (Table 3.1). Organizations obviously provide material support to accomplish a given task at work. Some organizations care for their employees better than others, that is, design better working environments, use more sophisticated and time-saving machinery, provide more support staff, ensure adequate training, and so on. Furthermore, strategies such as semi-autonomous work groups and greater worker participation in decision-making processes are materially improving the quality of life and the availability of social support networks in industry.

Participation at Work

Volvo, for example, has one of the most talked about worker participation projects in the world. By now, worker participation at Volvo is so complex and far-reaching it is no longer possible to make a simple statement about it. The Kalmar plant is the boldest experiment Volvo has launched. An assembly plant was built to accommodate the principles of worker participation, adding 10 percent to the construction costs. A brief description may provide some understanding of the approach being used.

In the metal-pressing section, workers wear differently colored uniforms, depending on their job. Blue is for worker, yellow for supervisor, and green for quality controller. The workers rotate jobs (and uniforms). The quotas are set by the planning department and the union. No overtime is paid for working overtime. Employees work until the quota is met and then they have free time. If they finish early, employees can take a swim or sauna at the plant.

In the body-finishing section, there are several lines, each with its own characteristics. In one line the workers follow the cars along the conveyor belt doing a different job as the car progresses past various tool stations. On other lines, the workers stand in place and the car passes by. A variety of job rotating schemes are used to involve workers in different aspects of the finishing. In some finishing lines workers are in uniform; in others they are

Table 3.1 Forms of Organizational Support

	Material		Social		
		Cognitive	*Emotional*		*Behavioral*
Formal organization (rules, regulations and specialists) (person is largely a recipient)	Providing Money Tools People Good physical environment Inducements	Advice by experts Doctors Counselors Consultants Superiors	Support provided by experts Counselors Occupational health nurses Welfare officers Supervisors (rarely)		Take person off job or change job Find someone else to solve problem Give early retirement Take responsibility from person
Informal organization (person is both giver and receiver)	Loaning to each other Money Tools People Space	Pooling problem-solving resources by widening information network, which may include "experts" known personally to group members	Support spontaneously marshaled by the group. If given is more likely to be felt as genuine by the recipient		Help person to do the job or do it for him or her while he or she recovers Share responsibility with person

Source: Payne, R. "Organisational Stress and Social Support." In *Current Concerns in Occupational Stress*, edited by C. L. Cooper and R. Payne (London: John Wiley & Sons, 1980).

in their own clothes. Workers make their own decision in this regard.

In the truck frame assembly section, the work is done in small teams of eight or ten who have available all the parts and tools necessary to assemble a complete unit. Workers elect their own supervisors, who are paid marginally higher wages and can be replaced by a vote of confidence at any time. Replacement workers are brought in by consent. The team trains the new workers and brings them up to production standards.

Volvo is an assembly operation located on 21 sites. Six hundred and fifty subcontractors make the components used in assembly. At any one time, there is only about three hours' warehouse supply available. At the corporate level there are special divisions developed to lend support and finance, if necessary, to the subcontractors in order to keep them profitable and up to standard. Flexitime is widely practiced in a variety of forms. Often two employees, including husband-and-wife teams, will cooperate in job sharing, splitting the shift into smaller units or alternate days. There is a commitment to cooperation and fair play at Volvo that seems to be required in worker participation efforts. An example of the cooperation that characterizes Swedish industry is the four goals agreed on by the Swedish Employers Association and the unions in 1972: increased productivity, greater job satisfaction, better working environment, and job security.

Participation at work seems to provide the social support that inoculates people against stress; it provides a kind of substitute family group. As early as the 1940s, Coch and French (1948) explored the impact of greater involvement and participation at work in a study of three degrees of participation in a sewing factory. They found that the greater the participation, the higher the productivity, the greater the job satisfaction, the lower the turnover and the better the relationships between boss and subordinates. These findings were later supported by a field experiment in a footwear factory in southern Norway, where greater participation led to significantly more favorable attitudes by workers toward management and more involvement in the job (French, Israel, and As 1960).

What Organizations Have Failed to Do to Create Support Systems

If we return to Payne's model presented earlier, we can see that work organizations have within their power the opportunity for providing cognitive, emotional, and behavioral support systems to their employees. But what is the reality? In many organizations only advice is offered, usually on issues that are directly related to work (for example, safety). Although they are in the minority, some firms encourage healthy lifestyles more actively by providing full fitness and health facilities for their employees. For example, Pepsico has provided a comprehensive physical fitness program at their world headquarters in Purchase, New York. They have a fully outfitted gymnasium that includes sauna, treadmill, a striking bag, stationary bicycles, whirlpool, baths, showers, and massage facilities. In addition, they have a 1.15-mile running track that circles the headquarters complex. This program is under the supervision of a full-time physical therapist and a physician. Tailor-made exercise programs are planned for any interested employee by the physical therapist and doctor. Although this facility was originally planned for senior executives, it is now used by all interested employees. Specialized programs such as aerobic dancing, weekly yoga sessions, and diet training are also offered to meet the needs of individual employees. The corporate headquarters are located in an attractive park-like setting that encourages a positive quality of life. Increasingly, major corporations are developing premier facilities with similar characteristics. The majority of workplaces, however, do not provide such possibilities for health maintenance.

There is often a failure on the part of work organizations to provide "emotional support." Until recently, very few private- or public-sector institutions actively addressed employees' needs for emotional support systems. When this type of support is available, it is provided by the informal network at work. Although the view is changing, for a long time management maintained that it was outside its scope of responsibility to provide counselors or other sources of human support for their employees, particularly if the problems stemmed from the home environment, even when the problems at home were affecting the work. It has been increasingly recognized that it is difficult to draw a clear line between sources of stress that originate in the home and those that come from the workplace; the distinction is not easily defensible. There are several other factors forcing organizations to take an interest in providing social support systems at work. One is the increasing litigation against companies for the stress that is alleged to exist in the workplace (Cooper 1981a). Another is the increasing incidence of stress-like epidemics in factories and offices in many companies that adversely affect absenteeism (Colligan and Murphy 1979).

The first development is called *cumulative trauma*, which is a type of workers' compensation claim in which an employee contends that a major illness or disability is the cumulative result of job stresses and strains extending back over a period of years of employment. Any employed person, from a shop-floor worker to a corporate executive, if forced to give up work due to any illness (coronary heart disease, mental breakdown, nervous disability, etc.), can claim that the illness was caused in part by work over the years. Since it is relatively easy to show that just about any job contains a certain element of stress and since the law in various states (in particular, California and Michigan) allows a very liberal interpretation of stress-induced illness, the courts and appeal boards are accepting many of these claims. In addition, and more importantly, personnel executives and company medical directors have, in many cases, been unable to provide evidence that they are trying to minimize stresses and strains in the work environment.

In addition to recent court decisions regarding cumulative trauma cases, another aspect of stress at work is worrying employers and health authorities. It is what the National Institute for Occupational Safety and Health terms "mass psychogenic illness." They define it as "the collective occurrence of physical symptoms and related beliefs among two or more persons in the absence of an identifiable pathogen." In other words, it is a situation in which a number of workers at a particular work site develop similar symptoms, although no noxious substance or microorganism can be found. The specific symptoms vary from one industrial situation to another, but they usually consist of subjective somatic complaints, such as headaches, nausea, sleepiness, chills, etc. In all the reported cases of mass psychogenic illness, extensive biochemical and environmental tests (to check for harmful chemicals in the air) have been carried out. No causative agent has been found. What has been found, however, are moderate to severe psychosocial stressors in the absence of discernible social support systems.

Organizational Attempts at Improving Emotional Support

As a result of these developments and a generally more humanistic approach to people at work, there are an increasing number of stress prevention programs oriented toward providing emotional support. The efforts of a large copper corporation provide a good example. Management has focused on the psychological health of its employees, providing extensive counseling facilities for all work- and home-related problems (Marshall and Cooper 1981). Indeed, they have even helped to organize Alcoholics Anonymous groups for employees and their families. In another example, Converse Corporation of Wilmington, Massachusetts, provided a voluntary relaxation program for its employees (Peters and Benson 1979) and had its effectiveness evaluated. Over 140 employees volunteered and were compared to 63 non-volunteers who were selected randomly. The volunteers agreed to keep daily records for 12 weeks and to have their blood pressure measured. In addition, their general health and job performance were assessed during the experimental period. The results indicated that not only were relaxation breaks feasible within a normal workweek, but that they led to general improvements in health, job performance, and well-being, as well as significantly decreasing the blood pressure of employees from the beginning to the end of training.

Another even more adventurous emotional support program was carried out in Britain by a large chemical company. It set up a stress counseling program, what it termed an "employee counseling service" with a full-time counselor (with a psychiatric social work background). The goals of this facility are "to provide a confidential counseling service to all employees and their families," to work with outside helping professions for the welfare of the employee, and to develop other activities that enhance the quality of working life. After four years of operation, the counselor has been consulted by nearly 10 percent of the employees per annum. About half the employees who seek the service come for advice on education, family matters, work-related housing problems, divorce, separation, children, aged parents, and consumer affairs. The other half developed a longer-term case-work or counseling relationship with the counselor on more fundamental individual or interpersonal problems. This is the kind of program that needs to be encouraged in industry and other types of organizations if we are to provide the emotional social support people need in the kind of modern society we all have created. (See the chapters by Nahrwold and by Feuer, this volume, for descriptions of other employee counseling programs.)

Informal Social Support at Work

One of the most important sources of social support is the informal work group. La Rocco and Jones (1978) did a large-scale study of 3,725 U.S. Navy personnel (enlisted men spanning the range of enlisted pay grades) on leader and co-worker support and the stress-strain relationship. They concluded that the effect on coping of support from one's boss and co-workers was both positive and additive. That is, the more support one obtained from one's leader and co-workers, the less likely one was to exhibit signs of strain. This result may explain the desire people have to seek the support of others in situations of danger or stress. Wilson (1975) has suggested that humans are genetically programmed to obtain security from the proximity of others because this supports survival. The complicated nature of relationships at work and their potential for conflict and ambiguity make it necessary for individuals to seek support from their peers. While the organization can have an impact on the support available, there are a number of different approaches that employees can take themselves. Taking responsibility for identifying others who can provide emotional support is an important first step. Acknowledging to others that their support is needed and appreciated and that support will be offered in return helps ensure a strong network.

CONCLUSION

There are those who argue that individuals could survive and, indeed, thrive in Western organizations if only the work environment provided the "social support" it does in Japan. As discussed earlier, coronary heart disease in Japan is much lower than in most Western countries, and there is evidence that the individual's work group and social group provide effective social support, which can offset some of the effects of stress and reduce the development of strains such as coronary heart disease. Although many people in the West ridicule the structure of Japanese corporate life and the "Japanese organizational man," it appears that these very institutions (group affiliations, corporate identity, group counseling, etc.) play an important role in decreasing the frequency of stress-related disease in Japan. As one of the leading researchers in the field has suggested in a special issue of a journal on stress, "the deleterious circumstances of life need not be expressed in malfunctioning of the physiologic or psychologic systems if a meaningful social group is available through which the individual can derive emotional support and understanding" (Cooper 1981b).

REFERENCES

Beehr, T. R., J. T. Walsh, and T. D. Taber. 1976. "Relationship of Stress to Individually and Organisationally Valued States: Higher Order Needs as a Moderator." *Journal of Applied Psychology* 61: 41-47.

Cobb, S. and R. H. Rose. 1973. "Hypertension, Peptic Ulcer and Diabetes in Air Traffic Controllers." *Journal of the Australian Medical Association* 224: 489-92.

Coch, L. and J. R. P. French. 1948. "Overcoming Resistance to Change." *Human Relations* 1: 512-32.

Colligan, M. J. and L. R. Murphy. 1979. "Mass Psychogenic Illness in Organisations." *Journal of Occupational Psychology* 1: 79-90.

Cooper, C. L. 1981a. *The Stress Check* (Englewood Cliffs, NJ: Prentice-Hall).

_____, ed. 1981b. "Stress and Small Groups." *Small Group Behavior*: 251-375.

Cooper, C. L. and M. J. Davidson. 1982. *High Pressure: Working Lives of Women Managers* (London: Fontana).

Cooper, C. L., M. J. Davidson, and P. Robinson. 1982. "Stress in the Police Service." *Journal of Occupational Medicine* 24: 30-36.

Cooper, C. L., M. Mallinger, and R. Kahn. 1978. "Identifying Sources of Occupational Stress among Dentists." *Journal of Occupational Psychology* 51: 227-34.

Cooper, C. L. and J. Marshall. 1976. "Occupational Sources of Stress: A Review of the Literature Relating to Coronary Heart Disease and Mental Ill Health. *Journal of Occupational Psychology* 49: 11-28.

_____. 1978. *Understanding Executive Stress* (London: Macmillan).

Cooper, C. L. and E. Mumford. 1979. *The Quality of Working Life in Western and Eastern Europe* (London: Associated Business Press).

Cooper, C. L. and R. Payne. 1978. *Stress at Work* (London: John Wiley & Sons).

_____. 1980. *Current Concerns in Occupational Stress* (London: John Wiley & Sons).

Cooper, C. L. and M. J. Smith. 1985. *Job Stress and Blue Collar Work* (London: John Wiley & Sons).

Cox, T. 1980. "Repetitive Work." In *Current Concerns in Occupational Stress*, edited by C. L. Cooper and R. Payne (London and New York: John Wiley & Sons).

Daniel, W. W. 1972. "Whatever Happened to the Workers in Woolwich?" *PEP Broadsheets* 38: 537.

Davidson, M. and A. Veno. 1980. "Stress in Police Officers." In *White Collar and Professional Stress*, edited by C. L. Cooper and J. Marshall (New York: John Wiley & Sons).

French, J. and R. Caplan. 1972. "Organizational Stress and Individual Strain." In *The Failure of Success*, edited by A. J. Marrow (New York: Amacon).

French, J. R. P., R. Caplan, and R. van Harrison. 1982. *The Mechanisms of Job Stress and Strains* (New York: Wiley).

French, J. R. P., J. Israel, and D. As. 1960. "An Experiment in Participation in a Norwegian Factory." *Human Relations* 12, no. 1: 3-20.

Kahn, H. 1956. *Repercussions of Redundancy* (London: Allen & Unwin).

Kasl, S. 1983. In *Stress Research: Issues for the Eighties*, edited by C. L. Cooper (New York: John Wiley & Sons).

Kelly, M. and C. L. Cooper. 1981. "Stress among Blue Collar Workers." *Employee Relations* 3: 6-9.

La Rocco, J. M. and A. P. Jones. 1978. "Co-Worker and Leader Support as Moderators of Stress-Strain Relationships in Work Situations." *Journal of Applied Psychology* 63, no. 5: 629-34.

Luisada, A. A. 1962. "Introduction of Symposium on the Epidemiology of Heart Disease." *American Journal of Cardiology* 10: 316.

Manpower Services Commission. 19XX. *Quarterly Economic Report* (London: Manpower Services Commission).

Margolis, B. L., W. H. Kroes, and R. P. Quinn. 1974. "Job Stress: An Unlisted Occupational Hazard." *Journal of Applied Medicine* 16: 654-61.

Marmot, M. G., S. Fyne, A. Kagan, H. Ato, J. Cohen, and J. Belsky. 1975. "Epidemiologic Studies of Coronary Heart Disease and Stroke in Japanese Men Living in Japan, Hawaii, and California: Prevalence of Coronary and Hypertensive Heart Disease and Associated Risk Factors." *American Journal of Epidemiology* 102, no. 6: 514-25.

Marshall, J. and C. L. Cooper. 1981. *Coping with Stress at Work* (Hampshire, England: Gower Press).

Matsumoto, Y. S. 1970. "Social Stress and Coronary Heart Disease in Japan." *Milbank Memorial Fund Quarterly* 48: 14-25.

Otway, H. J. and R. Misenta. 1980. "The Determinants of Operator Preparedness for Emergency Situations in Nuclear Power Plants." Paper presented at Workshop on Procedural and Organizational Measures for Accident Management: Nuclear Reactors. International Institute for Applied Systems Analysis, Laxenberg, Austria, January 28-31.

Payne, R. 1980. "Organizational Stress and Social Support." In *Current Concerns in Occupational Stress*, edited by C. L. Cooper and R. Payne (London: John Wiley & Sons).

Peters, R. K. and H. Benson. 1979. "Time Out from Tension." *Harvard Business Review* (January-February): 120-24.

Selye, H. 1976. *Stress in Health and Disease* (London: Butterworth).

Shirom, A., D. Eden, L. Silberwasser, and J. Kellerman. 1973. "Job Stresses and Risk Factors in Coronary Heart Disease among Occupational Categories in Kibbutzim." *Social Science and Medicine* 7: 875-92.

Warr, P. B. and J. Lovatt. 1975. "Well-Being and Orientation to Work." Unpublished paper.

Wilson, E. O. 1975. *Sociobiology* (Cambridge, MA: Harvard University Press).

4

THE THEMES OF SOCIAL-PSYCHOLOGICAL STRESS IN WORK ORGANIZATIONS: FROM ROLES TO GOALS

TERRY A. BEEHR

It is difficult to find people who will say that their jobs are not stressful. It may be a fact of life that work is stressful, or it may be simply the case that life is stressful; if so, the common assertion that a total lack of stress is found only in death would be on target. Aside from such personal and philosophical observations about the inevitability of stress in life, the extent of stress in the workplace in particular has become one of the exciting, growing areas of research and practice in applied psychology in recent years. A problem common to most topics of such widespread popular interest is the difficulty in getting agreement on definitions. Job stress has had this problem since the beginning of its rapid growth. Chapter 7, by Neale, Singer, and Schwartz (this volume), describes job stress as both "elusive and omnipresent"; Beehr and Newman (1978) and McGrath (1976) have noted the problem of definition, and Ivancevich and Matteson (1980) have gone so far as to compare stress to sin, since both topics are emotionally charged and both are defined differently by different people.

Social psychological stress in the workplace is most often characterized by the relationship between social psychological characteristics of work (this has come to mean almost anything except the physical work environment) and the incidence of poor employee health (health is also very broadly defined). Thus, for example, job stress is often considered the culprit when some work characteristics are found to be related to ill health of employees. Although definitional problems have arisen because of the popularized notions of stress, several problems have arisen from the fragmented nature of psychology itself. Clinical and counseling psychology, borrowing from medicine's "father" of stress, Hans Selye, has usually defined stress as a nonspecific bodily *response* to some environmental demand (Selye 1974, 1976). Clinicians and counselors, of course, are likely to add psychological responses to the bodily responses in Selye's definition. For Selye and many clinical and counseling psychologists, the term *stressor* is reserved for the environmental demands or situations thought to cause the stress. Mason (1975a, 1975b) and Selye (1975) have debated some of the terminology, and Mason has argued that the term *stress* has been used by Selye himself, in his early work, to mean the environmental forces acting on the person (forces that Selye now would term *stressors*). Mason (1975a) has argued, with Selye (1975) disagreeing, that "relatively few workers at present use the term exactly according to Selye's particular definitions and formulations" (p. 10). Selye (1974, 1976) himself has relatively recently labeled one of the causes of stress as "nervous tension," although many would argue that this is a person's response, rather than an environmental demand. All of this is to indicate that even in the medical and psychology communities, the term *stress* is not used entirely consistently.

In contrast to this is the long-standing use of the term *stress* in another area, engineering psychology. In this field, stress has referred to environmental stimuli or demands; and strain is the consequence (usually a cost) to the individual (McCormick 1976). Here, stress is used in a manner opposite from the most common use of the term in the clinical/counseling area, that is, it is an environmental cause rather than a personal consequence. Even in physiology, Mason (1975a) has noted that Cannon developed the terms *stress* and *strain* in 1935 consistently with engineering uses of term. When industrial/organizational (I/O) psychology relatively recently began to study psychosocial elements of the environment in relation to employee health and welfare, many of the writers used the engineering terminology (Beehr 1976; Kahn and Quinn 1970; French and Caplan 1973; Caplan et al. 1975). Currently, however, writers in I/O psychology have become more mixed. Some use "stress" to mean the environmental stimulus, and others use it to mean the resulting individual response. Obviously, it is not clear that research and thinking about job stress has strong links to past (or even current) theories and research on general stress (that is, non-job stress). Nevertheless, there have been attempts to link the two, or perhaps more often, assertions that the two are the same or at least are closely related. A non-exhaustive review of the history of the general stress concept prior to significant amounts of research on job stress reveals some interesting facts. Job stress encompasses performance, health, and environmental aspects of the stress concept.

It is proposed here that the domain of job stress is the relationship between psychosocial stimuli in the working environment and individual health and well-being. It is not assumed that Selye's specific theory is related to social psychological stress in the workplace. Neither is it assumed that the theories from the engineering psychology approach to stress necessarily apply to the psychosocial stressors in the work place. Job performance has been a key variable in engineering psychology studies of stress, but it is nowhere in the description of job stress offered above. Writers have often assumed that psychosocial job stressors would be related in a curvilinear manner to job performance, as engineering psychology has often theorized regarding the relationship between physical stressors and job performance (that is, in the shape of an inverted-U-shaped curve). A recent study by Jamal (1984) failed to uncover a curvilinear relationship, however, and as Landy and Trumbo (1980) indicated, the research supporting the hypothesis over the years has been relatively sparse. It is interesting to note that there is a small amount of support for a curvilinear (inverted-U-shaped) relationship between job stress and employee health and well-being; in particular, it is consistent with parts of the person-environment fit theory of job stress (Caplan et al. 1975; French and Caplan 1973; Harrison 1985).

WORKABLE DEFINITIONS

From this discussion of the confusion of job stress terminology, it is apparent that the word *stress* is itself the problem. The other major terms, *stressor* and *strain*, tend to be used consistently when they are used. Therefore, consistent with some other recent writings (Beehr and Bhagat 1985), Selye's word *stressor* will be used in this chapter to describe environmental stimuli thought to be causal, and the engineering term *strain* will be used to mean the person's aversive physiological, behavioral, or psychological response. These strains are usually mental or physical behaviors or illnesses. The word *stress* will be used here only to describe the general field of study and practice (McLean 1974).

There may also be stress responses that are not, by themselves, aversive. These could include nervous system arousal and secretion of catecholamines into the bloodstream, and are reminiscent of Selye's controversial "first mediators" (Beehr and Newman 1978; Mason 1975a; Selye 1975). Labeling these as stress, however, would imply that (1) these responses necessarily occur when "stress" is present and (2) that these responses are necessary for social psychological stressors to have an effect on employee strains. The first implication seems especially unlikely for some job stressors (such as underutilization of skills), and there is little evidence that such responses are necessary for any strain to occur.

Identification of stressors can be confusing since these definitions of stressor and strain are circular. Stressors are aspects of the work environment that cause strains, and strains are aversive employee responses caused by stressors. Job characteristics that are frequently found related to strains are customarily labeled stressors even though they do not cause strain in every instance. The inconsistency in the relationships between stressors and strains gives hope to those wishing to avoid strains and sends researchers on a quest for moderator variables (characteristics of the employee or the work situation that reduce the strength of the association between stressors and strains).

In summary, then, job stressors are psychosocial characteristics of jobs that cause strains, which are employees' aversive reactions. "Strain" characteristically refers to ill health. However, this does not overlook the fact that other responses to stress can result in decreased productivity and impaired performance. Stress is the area of practice or research focusing on social psychological characteristics of work that are detrimental to employees' health.

THE SCOPE OF WORK-RELATED STRESS

Having defined job stress as the relationship between psychosocial characteristics of work (stressors) and employee ill health or welfare (strains), it is useful to estimate the scope of this problem. This turns out to be a rather difficult task, but there are two common ways of attempting it. The first is to estimate how widespread job stress is in terms of the number of jobs that have it, and the second is to estimate the cost of job stress summed over all jobs. Either of these approaches is fraught with problems that probably cause the estimate to have large but unknown amounts of error. Recognizing this, rough estimates are nevertheless offered.

Using the first method of estimating the scope of job stress, it is instructive that Caplan et al. (1975) have studied 23 jobs in the United States and have found reasonable evidence that there is stress in many of them. Similarly, several studies of job stress within a single organization have examined many different jobs in the organization and have found relationships between potential job stressors and strains (Beehr 1976; Beehr, Walsh, and Taber 1976). This does not prove that the relationship exists in all of the jobs studied, but it is a small piece of evidence that many, perhaps most, of the jobs in the sample may be stressful in some way. After all, if many nonstressful jobs were included in the samples, the statistical evidence for the presence of job stress would be very weak or nonexistent in such studies. A glance through the empirical literature also shows that a number of studies have focused on a single job. Examples include nurses (Jamal 1984), police (Gaines and Jermier 1983), schoolteachers (Payne and Fletcher 1983), accountants (Friedman, Rosenman, and Carroll 1957), managers (Hennigan and Wortham 1975), and coal miners (Axelrod and Gavin 1980).

The accumulation of information about such a large number of jobs, one at time, also indicates that the potential for job stress may be widespread. It is important to remember, however, that most of these studies were conducted with the aim of discovering whether employees in these jobs with large amounts of stressors experienced more strain than employees with small amounts of stressors. As a result, the studies do not show that these jobs always or even on the average have job stress; instead, they show that some of the people in these jobs have job stress, and that the jobs are therefore capable of being stressful.

Along the same lines, the pioneering study by Kahn et al. (1964) included a national (United States) survey of male employees in an examination of the extent of job stress in the work force. They concluded that about one-third of these employees reported experiencing the two stressors in their study (role conflict and role ambiguity) to the extent that they were "bothered" by them. Indeed, if one asks the job incumbents, it seems as if all jobs are stressful some of the time. Overall, then, if the first approach to discovering the scope of job stress is taken, it is possible to conclude that job stress is widespread, because it appears to be present in a fairly wide number of jobs.

The second approach to estimating the scope of work-related stress involves looking more closely at the consequences or strains involved. Here, one can try to estimate the toll of occupational stress in terms of human suffering, organizational productivity losses, or the dollar figures attached to them. Since the techniques of attaching dollar figures to employee behaviors are still evolving, this method may be quite inaccurate (see Bobko, this volume). Some such estimates simply involve the figures showing that the cost of a particular disease (the amount of money spent treating it) is very high. For example, it has been estimated that the cost of two so-called stress-related diseases, peptic ulcers and cardiovascular disease, is about $45 billion per year (Putt 1970; Moser 1977). Similarly, it has been reported by one insurance company that about 15 percent of the disability claims filed by employees and of the benefits paid to them involve back disorders (Warshaw 1979). Greenwood (1978) has estimated conservatively that all sources of executive stress cost between 10 and 20 billion dollars in 1970. Most of these specific figures are virtually meaningless, except to show that there is the belief that the cost of job stress is very large. The problems with such figures are that: (1) it is difficult to attach dollar figures to some of the consequences of work-related stress (note the vast discrepancy between Greenwood's two "conservative" estimates of the cost of executive stress); (2) it is usually unknown in such figures how much psychosocial job stress, physical environment effects on or off the job, genetics, and so on, contribute to the development of the disease in question; and (3) much of the cost may go unrecorded and therefore does not find its way into public figures at all. Using this second method of estimating the scope of job stress, however, it has frequently been argued that occupational stress is very important.

THE BEGINNINGS OF JOB STRESS

Just as Selye revolutionized the study of *general* stress, one book has already done more to revolutionize the study of *job* stress than any other. Since *Organizational Stress: Studies in Role Conflict and Ambiguity* (Kahn et al. 1964) incited behavioral scientists with expertise in areas of human work to study job stress, it is often considered the pioneering work in the field. This is not to deny that some significant work had been done previously. The study by Friedman, Rosenman, and Carroll (1957) of the relationship of cardiovascular changes in tax accountants and the approach to tax deadlines, for example, was a commendable study of psychosocial job stress predating the Kahn book, but it did not have the same impact on the field. Given the historical importance of this book to the field of job stress, it is instructive to note that Kahn et al. do not even cite any of Selye's work, nor are Cannon or Brady cited. Thus, the work on job stress began with, and has had a continuing history of development independent from, the topic of general stress, in spite of assumptions that the two are closely related. The dominant activity has been a search for relationships between social psychological job characteristics and employee illness (psychological or physical).

Kahn et al. (1964), rather than following in the tradition of the mental health field, attempted a work they believed would be "complementary to therapy in much the same way that public health complements the conventional practice of medicine" (p. 7). The direction of this influential work away from traditional thinking about stress toward an independent approach to job stress was, therefore, at least partially intentional.

Table 4.1 outlines some selected major works in the history of job stress. Research on job stress has grown from its infancy since 1964, but it is still in its childhod. Consequently, it is now unlikely that a single, well-done

Table 4.1   A Selected History of Publications on General and Occupational Stress

Date	Author; titles	Comments
General stress		
1932, 1936	Cannon; *The Wisdom of the Body*	Book in semi-popular style by physiologist; developed the concept of homeostasis

Table 4.1 (continued)

1956, 1976	Selye; *The Stress of Life*	Book in semi-popular autobiographical style by medical researcher; led to widespread knowledge of general adaptation syndrome

Occupational stress

1964	Kahn, Wolfe, Quinn, Snoek, and Rosenthal; *Organizational Stress: Studies in Role Conflict and Ambiguity*	Book in academic style by social psychologists; reported theory behind and results of both a national survey and an intensive study of male employees
1976	McGrath; "Stress and Behavior in Organizations"	Chapter of industrial/organizational handbook in academic style by social psychologists; ignored health in developing a model of organizational stress and role performance and presented test of model using little league baseball players
1978-79	Beehr and Newman and Newman and Beehr; "Job Stress, Employee Health, and Organizational Effectiveness: A Facet Analysis, Model, and Literature Review" and "Personal and Organizational Strategies for Handling Job Stress: A Review of Research and Opinion"	Two-article series in academic style by industrial/organizational psychologists; reviewed empirical, scientific litrature on job stress and presented general model
1985	Beehr and Bhagat; *Human Stress and Cognition in Organizations: An Integrated Perspective*	Edited book in academic style by organizational psychologist and management researcher; a cognitive model focusing on uncertainty is developed and expanded by a variety of social science and organizational behavior-oriented researchers

Source: Compiled by the author.

project can have a large impact on the field the way the Kahn study did. As the field matures, this will probably become even more true.

A few observations can be made about the development of the field thus far. The first observation is that published research has increased at a dramatic rate. One of the indications of this is that until 1973, the heading "occupational stress" did not appear in the index of *Psychological Abstracts*, presumably because there was not enough written about the topic to justify a heading. From 1973 until 1976, there were only 41 abstracts listed under occupational stress, only seven of them in U.S. journals specializing in organizational behavior or organizational psychology. In recent years, there have been many abstracts on occupational stress in the abstracting service (Figure 4.1). A second sign of the relative lack of attention to the topic until the mid-1970s is the common college textbooks in industrial/organizational psychology and related fields that rarely mentioned social psychological job stress. Since then, a few texts have even included whole chapters on stress (Cummings and Dunham 1980; Davis and Newstrom 1985; Rowland and Ferris 1982).

Besides the rate of research on the topic, a second significant observation is that with the large numbers of studies in occupational stress, the emphasis has been on psychological consequences much more than on the physical consequences of stress. This coincides with the entry of many psychologically oriented researchers into the field. If one were interested in learning about the effects of stress on employees before 1964, one would almost have to investigate the general (non-job) stress literature. That literature, primarily by medical or physiological experts, did a relatively good job of operationalizing physical or physiological strains, but causal factors were generally limited to the study of physical stressors such as heat, cold, and so on. As behavioral scientists entered the area of job stress, they tended to measure more directly the stressors that are of interest at work, but they measured the strains less carefully. Projects that are strong on both ends of the stressor-strain formula are now needed to advance the field. An important article on measuring physiological strains has recently been published in *Personnel Psychology*, and it should aid behavioral scientists in designing their research (Fried, Rowland, and Ferris 1984).

A third observation is that the theories and knowledge about job stress have developed rather independently from the dominant theories and knowledge about stress in general. The work has proceeded more directly from social psychological theories (such as role theory) than from clinical psychology or medical theories. In some instances, job stress research has been almost an atheoretical search for effects of any aspect of work on employee health and well-being.

The remainder of this chapter is devoted to reviewing the primary views and studies of stress at work. It includes suggested approaches for the stress

Figure 4.1 Annual Entries under "Occupational Stress" in the Indices of *Psychological Abstracts* from 1964 through 1983

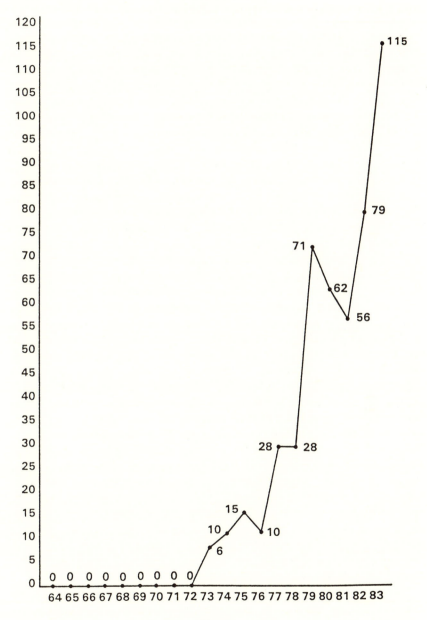

practitioner as well as recommendations for the development of thought and study in the field.

ROLES—A DOMINANT THEME IN JOB STRESS

Kahn et al. (1964), in a traditional social psychological fashion, framed their studies in role theory. This orientation, which was to be one of the dominant themes in job stress research over the next two decades, has been described briefly by Kahn et al. (1964) and in more detail by Sarbine and Allen (1969) and Stryker and Statham (1985). Role theory considers formal organizations to consist primarily of expectations that people, in their organizational roles, hold for and communicate to each other. These expectations define jobs or roles and determine what one is supposed to do at work. Since jobs or roles are defined by others' expectations, it is logical to assume that others' expectations are the key ingredient of job stress.

In role theory, each job in an organization is defined by two terms, "office" and "role." An office is simply a point in organizational space, with the organization comprising many interrelated offices. Role refers to a set of behaviors associated with an office. In the structure of the organization, each role is related to several others more or less closely, by virtue of the interdependence of the tasks required in each office. Offices that are very closely related to a given office and its associated role comprise the "role set" of the given role, which is labeled the "focal role." The interdependence of the roles in the role set leads the people performing the roles to expect certain behaviors of each other. These are the role expectations that strongly influence the definition of the role. If they communicate these expectations or some subset of them to the focal person, this set of expectations becomes the "sent role." The communication of the sent role constitutes an influence attempt, and this is called role "pressure." The focal person receives some of these communications or pressures and interprets them, resulting in the "received role." The received role, which may be more or less consistent with the sent role, depending on the accuracy of the communication process, results in psychological "role forces" within the person of some magnitude and direction. These experienced role forces may become stressful, depending on their nature. In summary, then, the role theory base of much of the thinking and research on organizational stress assumes that the organization is a social system and that jobs are defined by interactions with others in the organization. When these definitions and their accompanying pressures and forces take on certain characteristics, the employee experiences job stress.

Using role theory, Kahn et al. (1964) proposed two major types of role stressors that can easily occur in work organizations: role conflict and role ambiguity. There are several types of role conflict, including intra-sender conflict, inter-sender conflict, inter-role conflict, and person-role conflict

(Table 4.2). The essential characteristic of role conflict is that the focal person is sent two or more role messages that are mutually contradictory. Role ambiguity is the situation in which the focal person is sent role messages with information that is unclear, ambiguous, or deficient.

Table 4.2   Four Types of Role Conflict

Intra-sender conflict	One member of role set (e.g., supervisor) expects two or more behaviors that are incompatible.
Inter-sender conflict	Two or more members of role set (e.g., supervisor and a co-worker) expect behaviors that are incompatible.
Inter-role conflict	Expectations for behaviors in two roles (e.g., work role and role of parent) held by one person are incompatible.
Person-role conflict	Expectations for role behaviors are incompatible with person's own values.

Source: Compiled by the author.

Role ambiguity and role conflict have been the core job stressors investigated by researchers in the role theory tradition. In addition, role overload and a few other stressors have been introduced as role stressors, although it is often not clearly justified why other particular stressors are considered to fit with role theory. Examples include underutilization of skills, resource inadequacy, and lack of participation in decision-making (Beehr, Walsh, and Taber 1976; Gupta and Beehr 1979). Table 4.3 lists these role stressors and describes them in a way that explains their possible fit with role theory. The main reasons for including them in role theory approaches to job stress are that (1) they have often been used by researchers with role theory backgrounds and in conjunction with role stressors such as role conflict and role ambiguity, and (2) they can be described as emanating in part from expectations held by members of the focal person's role set.

Regarding role ambiguity and role conflict, the pioneering study by Kahn et al. (1964) found that role stressors tended to be more widespread among the male U.S. work force than might have been expected, with roughly one-third of the sample reporting that they experienced these stressors to an extent that bothered them. In addition, the existence of these role stressors was correlated with the presence of job-related tension, a potential strain. It should be noted that the measurement of job-related tension in the study was probably contaminated with perceptions of role stressors themselves, since the questionnaire was worded to ask whether people felt bothered (tension) *because of* role ambiguity and role conflict at work. This is

Table 4.3 Typical Role Stressor Names and Descriptions

Stressor	Description
Role conflict	Two or more role expectations are in conflict so that compliance with one makes compliance with the other(s) more difficult or impossible.
Role ambiguity	Information regarding role expectations is unclear or deficient.
Role overload	Sum of role expectations requires more work than can be done in the time available.
Underutilization of skills	Role expectations do not require or allow focal person to use his or her valued skills and abilities. It may be a type of role underload.
Resource inadequacy	Available organizational resources are inadequate for focal person to comply with role expectations. This may be a type of role overload; employee could get adequate amount of work done with more resources.
Nonparticipation	Focal person not involved in decisions affecting his or her part of the organization. Nonparticipation may be associated with role ambiguity, since participating in decisions might help the focal person to clarify role expectations.

Source: Compiled by the author.

apparently ignored, however, by most reviews and by occasional studies that use the same indices.

The role indices have also gotten a great deal of attention in organizational psychology and organizational behavior studies that were not clearly studies of stress. This may be because Rizzo, House, and Lirtzman (1970) and House and Rizzo (1972) developed some of the most popular role conflict and role ambiguity scales, developing a general theory of organizational behavior around them. They proposed that these two role constructs were related widely to a variety of important variables of traditional interest in the organizational sciences. There are therefore now many studies of role conflict and ambiguity that have little to do with job stress but that are often assumed to be studies of job stress because role ambiguity and role conflict were employed as variables. As noted by Jackson and Schuler (1985), there has been an unwarranted tendency to study role conflict and role ambiguity together and to expect them to behave in the same ways. This is obvious from their frequent inclusion in the same study as intended predictors of the same outcomes and with the expectation that the same third variables would moderate the relationship between these role indices and the outcomes.

Overall, the role constructs have generally been related to strains, indicating that they are indeed possible stressors in the workplace. Still, research using them has come to somewhat of an impasse with less new information about job stress obtained in recent years than before. One logical way of overcoming this impasse is to search for moderator variables of the stress (role variables)-strain relationship. Jackson and Schuler (1985), in a meta-analysis, have recently indicated the stressor-strain combinations most likely to be moderated by third variables. The use of theory-based moderators in empirical studies is a major new need. A second obvious way to increase the knowledge about job stress would be to abandon the role stress model and seek information about other types of stressors. It has been suggested (Love and Beehr 1981) that other social psychological theories may also prove useful for understanding work-related stress. Since there has been some success with the role stress model, however, a more prudent approach might be in order.

One such approach would be to examine different types of conflict and ambiguity besides the traditional *role* conflict and role ambiguity (Jackson and Schuler 1985). That is, job-related conflict and ambiguity may emanate from sources other than the people in the role set. It would be wise, therefore, for future research to be based outside role theory, even if conflict and ambiguity are kept as key variables.

Alternatively, staying with role theory, researchers might be encouraged to develop, measure, and test other types of role conflict and ambiguity. This could be accomplished through the measurement of more specific types. Kahn et al. (1964) described four basic types of role conflict (Table 4.2); this is an obvious theoretical starting point for the development of specific types of role conflict. The conflicts can be between role demands emanating from the same person in the role set (intra-sender conflict), between role demands emanating from two or more members of the role set (inter-sender conflict), between the demands of the work role and demands of another role in the person's life (inter-role conflict), or between demands of the work role and the expectations the person has for himself or herself as a person (for example, personal moral values). Still more specific types of conflict may be derived, and investigation of these would also be in keeping with the recommendation to broaden the base for studying work-related stress.

Of these four types of role conflict, one has come under relatively extensive consideration as a topic of research and theorizing. Inter-role conflict has been a frequently invoked concept in models and research on the stresses of women in the work force (Beutell and Greenhaus 1983; Hall 1972; Herman 1977; Sekaran 1983; Shamir 1983). The basic theme is that women tend to keep their non-work roles (such as mother and wife) when they enter the work force, and that these non-work roles tend to be more important to them than males' non-work roles are to males. Thus, they are pulled two ways (or more) more strongly than men are in our society. Inter-role conflict has therefore found a home in one rapidly growing area of interest in the organizational sciences (women in organizations).

There may be other specific areas characterized by certain of the subtypes of role conflict, but if so, they have not been studied as actively as the roles of women in the work force are today. One such topic, for example, might be the behaviors and reactions of managers in multinational corporations as they relate to person-role stress. Cross-cultural interactions may result in person-role stress if the manager is expected to behave in his or her work role in some way that violates his or her personal values (for example, a non-drinking Moslem manager who is expected to share three-martini lunches with U.S. business people).

Just as role conflict, as a work-related stressor, can probably be elaborated more than it typically has been in past research, role ambiguity may benefit from deeper consideration. Kahn et al. suggest many "areas" of ambiguity in work roles, such as ambiguity about the scope of employees' responsibilities, about why they are supposed to do certain activities, and about whose expectations are most important. Rizzo, House, and Lirtzman (1970) have provided descriptions of two types of role ambiguity in organizations: "the predictability of outcome or responses to one's behavior," and "the existence or clarity of behavioral requirements." Their scale contains items with face validity for each type of ambiguity, although these potential subscales have rarely been used separately, and their validity as separate scales is largely unknown. Pearce (1981) has labeled these two types of role ambiguity "unpredictability" and "information deficiency." She notes that although the two are included in the same scale (Rizzo, House, and Lirtzman 1970; House and Rizzo 1972), unpredictability is not conceptually the same as information deficiency. Consistent with the view proposed later in this chapter, Pearce focuses on unpredictability as the more central concept of interest in organizational psychology and organizational behavior. Beehr and Bhagat (1985) also use unpredictability as the concept of interest in role stress theory, and consistent with some of Pearce's reasoning, argue that this type of uncertainty can be integrated with expectancy theory of motivation to help explain stress in the work role.

A Note on Person-Environment Fit and Role Theory

Another orientation or approach to job stress is the person-environment (PE) fit theory of job stress (French and Kahn 1962; Caplan et al. 1980). Although many writings have used the term "person-environment fit" in describing *any* interaction between person characteristics and job or environmental characteristics leading to strains, the PE fit theory is actually much more specific. There are two basic types of fit or misfit that can occur between individuals and their jobs: fit between the resources of the job and the needs or preferences of the person, and fit between the individual's skills and the requirements of the job. Caplan's chapter in this volume provides further details on PE fit theory, but this simple description will suffice for the purpose of comparing role theory with PE fit theory.

PE fit theory considers four elements of work situations to be important in job stress: environmental resources, the person's needs, environmental requirements, and the person's skills. Role theory, on the other hand, has focused only on environmental (job) requirements. Furthermore, it has tended to focus on the perceived rather than on the objective requirements of the job. Basically, these requirements are the demands of the role as members of the role set have communicated them. Certain of the role stressors match PE fit theory somewhat (for example, role overload). Quantitative role overload can be described as having too much work to do in the time available. One way of interpreting this is to say that the incumbent's skills are not adequate for (do not fit) the requirements of the job. If the focal person were more highly skilled, he or she might be able to get more work done in the time available. A similar case could be made for qualitative overload and underutilization of skills as role stressors. Role overload may, therefore, be interpreted as an assumed case of poor fit between specific skills of the employee and the requirements of his or her job.

This analysis does not work as well for all role stressors, however. Role conflict and ambiguity are examples for which it is more difficult to propose PE fit assumptions, although some measures of perceived role ambiguity have included items asking about the likelihood of the employee receiving rewards or resources from the organization that might satisfy the employee's needs. In role theory studies, however, employees are not usually asked parallel questions specially designed to determine the degree to which the employee wants or needs this precise set of resources or rewards. This is an inherent difference between role stress and PE fit stress theories.

THE BEEHR-NEWMAN MODEL OF JOB STRESS

The Beehr-Newman (Beehr and Newman 1978) model of job stress is the result of a facet analysis developed with the ambitious aim of incorporation of all theories, models, and research designs on the general topic of job stress. As such, it is therefore a meta-model, one that encompasses others and is largely derived from them. The basic model is depicted in Figure 4.2. In it, stress is assumed to be a general area of study (McGrath 1976) having several facets. As described by Beehr and Newman (1978) and Newman and Beehr (1979) in their two-article series, the facet analysis or facet design is a nonrecursive model in which the most usual starting point is the assumption

Figure 4.2 The Beehr-Newman (1978) Meta-Model of Job Stress

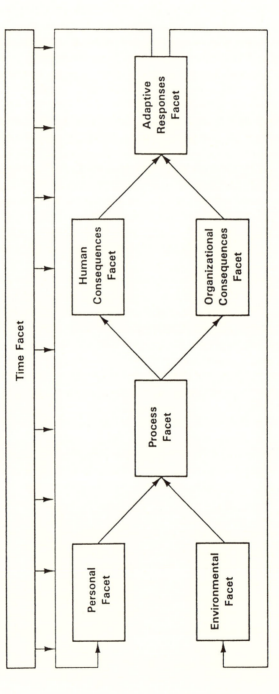

that elements of the person (employee) and of the employee's environment (job or work role) are causal in the stress process. These have therefore been placed at the left side of the model. Characteristics of the person and the job, alone or in combination, result in stress processes in the person, and these in turn result in consequences that are important to the person (human), the organization, or both. As a result of these important consequences (or in enlightened organizations and people, perhaps before the consequences even occur), adaptive responses may follow; these are aimed at reducing the negative effects of the stress.

The *environmental facet* includes job demands and task characteristics, role demands or expectations, organizational characteristics and conditions, and the organization's external demands and conditions. The *personal facet* consists of the psychological condition of the person (personality traits and behavioral characteristics), the person's physical condition, life stage, and demographic characteristics. The *process facet* contains both psychological and physical or physiological and neurological processes internal to the person experiencing stress. The *human consequences facet* includes the strains such as poor physical or physiological health, psychological reactions or health, and behaviors of the employee. The *organizational consequences facet* consists of all of the effects of job stress on any variable that is of importance to the organization's welfare or is valued by the organization's leaders. Many variables of traditional interest as criterion variables in industrial/organizational psychology are therefore included in this category (for example, job performance, absenteeism, and turnover). Included in the *adaptive responses facet* are responses by the individual, the organization, or third parties that are aimed at alleviating one or more of the negative effects of job stress. Finally, in the model, *time* is included in recognition of the likelihood that the duration of the stressors, strains, and even attempted adaptive reactions may have an effect. Beehr and Newman (1978) and Newman and Beehr (1979) did not focus on this idea, except for an expanded version of their model in which initial, secondary, and long-term effects of stress were proposed (Beehr and Newman 1978).

The Beehr-Newman model is general enough to include most, if not all, of the role stress literature regarding the work role. Objective role stressors have rarely been operationalized in the research (for exceptions, note Kahn et al., 1964; Sales 1970); instead, most of the role theory literature on job stress has employed subjective or perceived job stressors as variables. This type of perceived job stressor is a characteristic of the process facet in the model. The strains most often studied in the role-theory approach to job stress have been elements of the human consequences facet, although some of the outcome variables used in role stress research have been organizational consequences (especially absenteeism and turnover; Gupta and Beehr 1979).

The model is also general enough to cover PE fit theory. The objective person characteristics are included in the person facet; the objective environmental characteristics are included in the environmental facet; the subjective person characteristics and the subject environmental characteristics are included in the perceptions part of the process facet.

FROM ROLES TO GOALS

In 1981, Love and Beehr suggested four ways in which job stress research might proceed: (1) continue to search for additional psycho-social stressors, that is, ones that had not been discovered previously; (2) expand the types of social support that had been investigated as potentially helpful strategies for alleviating the negative effects of job stress; (3) search for an expanded set of outcomes (consequences of stress other than individual strains); and (4) use theories other than role theory to develop hypotheses and to guide research on job stress. In terms of the Beehr-Newman model, this means searching for more characteristics of the environmental facet (or of the process facet if the stressors and social support variables are measured subjectively) and searching for more characteristics of the human and (especially) organizational consequences facets that are involved in job stress. In addition, new theories might help guide research further into these or other facets.

There have been beginnings on some of these suggestions. Acute stress due to time-bounded stressful events at the workplace, has been studied as a stressor in the environmental facet (Eden 1982). New types of social support in the environmental facet have been suggested, including types of support varying according to the content of communication between the focal person and the supportive others, and according to whether or not the person offering support is also responsible for the focal person's stressors (Beehr 1985). In addition to individual strains, potential organizational outcomes such as likelihood of employee turnover have been studied in relation to job stress (Kemery et al. 1985). Finally, a model based on expectancy theory has been proposed as a guide to job stress research (Beehr and Bhagat 1985).

Beehr and Love (1983) later proposed a meta-model of organizational psychology that integrates variables and concepts from several other organizational psychology models focusing on goal and role characteristics. Their eleven propositions are incorporated into the model in Figure 4.3. Although not focusing on job stress, the model does include role ambiguity as a central variable in the lower half of the figure. For present purposes, it is important to note that several goal-related variables are included in the model, with variables related to one of the frequently studied job stressors, role ambiguity. In fact, two of the goal variables, participation in goal-setting and goal specificity, are proposed as direct and immediate precursors of role ambiguity. There is, therefore, a possibility that theories

Figure 4.3 The Beehr-Love (1983) Meta-Model of Human Performance in Organizations

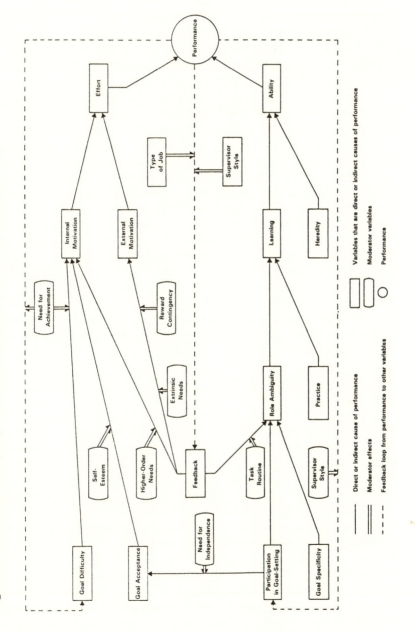

related to goals and goal-setting may be useful in examining the process of job stress.

Goal-related concepts can be found in PE fit theory. The fit between employee needs and the organization's resources can be interpreted as a fit between employee goals and the organization's ability and willingness to satisfy these goals (note that "needs" in PE fit theory of job stress often refers to conscious preferences similar to goals rather than to innate, bio- logically based requirements). The main point here is that goals and job stress may be related.

Besides goals, a second concept that has been dominant in the job stress literature is uncertainty. Beginning with Kahn et al. (1964) and continuing through a large number of studies until the present (Lyons 1971; House and Rizzo 1972; Schuler 1975; Beehr 1976; Jackson 1983), role ambiguity has been studied as a job stressor. It has obvious links to uncertainty, and uncertainty also has links to goals when it is defined as the inability to predict the outcomes of one's actions. Jackson, Schuler, and Vredenburgh (this volume) have noted that uncertainty is a handy concept for tying macro- and micro-organizational issues together, but the present discussion focuses only on micro-level stress phenomena. In the Beehr-Newman model, a person's uncertainty regarding the outcomes of his or her behavior is located in the process facet.

It has been suggested that more theory-guided work on job stress is desirable (Love and Beehr 1981; Jackson and Schuler 1985); what follows describes theory development that is focused on the process facet and is linked to employee goals and employee uncertainty regarding the means for reaching these goals.

Toward an Expectancy- and Goal-Oriented Theory of Job Stress

The idea that uncertainty regarding the means for reaching important goals may be stressful is not new. In fact, it can be found in a great many writings about stress, anxiety, and neurosis over the years, although the exact terminology may differ from author to author. In the job stress literature, the pioneering work by Kahn et al. (1964) described role ambiguity as, in part, a state in which employees are not sure what the consequences of their actions will be, that is, they are unsure of means-ends relationships at work. This can be rephrased to describe a situation in which the person is uncertain which of his or her behaviors (means) will lead to his or her goals (ends). Along these lines, Beehr, Walsh, and Taber (1976) later predicted that role ambiguity might reduce employee motivation in part by making it more difficult for employees to predict the consequences of their actions at work. They explicitly used assumptions derived from expectancy theory of motivation in developing their hypotheses. Pearce's (1981) review of role ambiguity research defined role ambiguity as this same type of unpredictability and linked it to expectancy theory.

Most recently, Beehr and Bhagat (1985) have proposed a new, cognitively oriented model of job stress that utilizes expectancy theory as its basis. The Beehr-Bhagat model maintains that much experienced job stress is a function of experienced or subjective uncertainty (Uc), importance (Im), and duration (D) of events in workers' lives (Fig. 4.4)

Expectancy theory was chosen as an integrating tool because it has been the dominant theory of employee motivation in organizational psychology for almost two decades (Vroom 1964; Lawler 1973; Mitchell and Bigland 1971), and because previous discussions of stressful role ambiguity in particular seemed to refer implicitly or explicitly to expectancies.

Uncertainty (Uc) in the model refers specifically to the uncertainty that one's efforts will lead to successful performance (effort-to-performance or $E \rightarrow P$ expectancy; Lawler 1973) and to the uncertainty regarding to whether one's performance will lead to valued outcomes (performance-to-outcome or $P \rightarrow O$ expectancy; Lawler 1973). Uc would be part of the process facet in the Beehr-Newman (1978) model.

Importance (Im) refers to the value that the person places on the outcome under consideration. Importance is moderately stable for many outcomes—it changes only very slowly for a given person. For example, the value that someone places on money or that he or she places on a sense of achievement is characteristic of the person for long periods of time. This must not be overstated, however, because adult employees' values probably do change as work life progresses through some developmental stages (Schein 1980). Nevertheless, since Im is relatively stable, it would be found in the person facet of the Beehr-Newman (1978) model. Duration (D) refers to the length of time during which the person experiences the job stresses leading to one or both types of uncertainty. Duration obviously fits into the time facet in the Beehr-Newman (1978) model. It is proposed that greater Uc (of $E \rightarrow P$ and/or $P \rightarrow O$), greater Im of the outcomes, and longer D of the situation will result in more serious consequences of job stress (will result in greater job strain).

Job stress is therefore a cognitive state and is a multiplicative function of

Figure 4.4 The Beehr-Bhagat (1985) Cognitive Model of Human Stress in Organizations

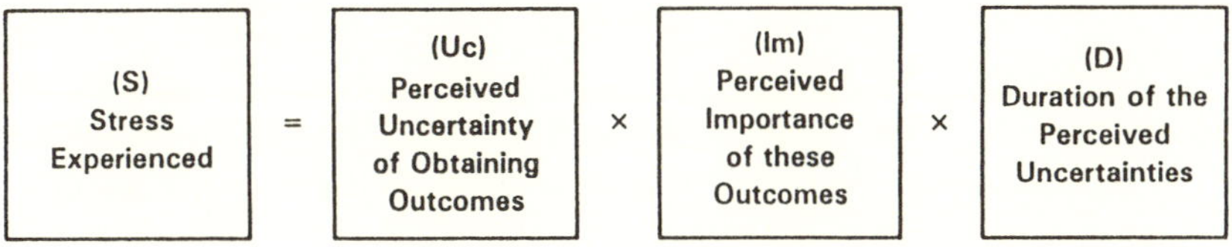

(S) Stress Experienced	=	(Uc) Perceived Uncertainty of Obtaining Outcomes	×	(Im) Perceived Importance of these Outcomes	×	(D) Duration of the Perceived Uncertainties

Uc, Im, and D. The function is proposed to be multiplicative on the grounds that only if any of the three elements of the model is zero, then the amount of experienced stress would also be zero. The model focuses on decision-making and therefore includes McGrath's (1976) "response selection" concept. Decisions might include, for example, deciding whether and how to answer a letter, whether to go to work when one feels slightly ill, or whether to reprimand a subordinate for being late.

The model is goal oriented in the sense that expectancy theory is goal oriented; that is, expectancy theory predicts employees' motivations to engage in behaviors that they anticipate will reach some "goal" (valued outcome). Typical organizational research on expectancy theory is concerned with making predictions about employee behaviors based on a combination of valences and *levels* of expectancies. In the stress model proposed by Beehr and Bhagat (1985), however, the clarity or *certainty* of the expectancies is the focus. Instead of the employees' subjective estimates regarding $E \rightarrow P$ and $P \rightarrow O$ linkages, the degree to which employees are certain about these estimates is central to this approach.

Table 4.4 contains proposed relationships between three stressors and the types of uncertainty ($E \rightarrow P$ or $P \rightarrow O$), as examples showing the link between role theory approaches to job stress and the Beehr-Bhagat model. In the table, role ambiguity, role overload, and underutilization of skills are three commonly studied role stressors (Kahn et al. 1964; French and Caplan 1973; Beehr and Newman 1978). These three stressors may be stressful because they are accompanied by uncertainty of $E \rightarrow P$ or $P \rightarrow O$. Table 4.4 proposes the type of uncertainty with which each of the three role stressors is most likely to be linked. Role ambiguity, overload, and under-

Table 4.4   An Expectancy Framework for Understanding the Uncertainty Inherent in Stress

Stressors: Perceived demand characteristics (examples of stressors)	Uncertainty regarding an expectancy	
	Effort-to-performance expectancy $(E \rightarrow P)$	Performance-to-outcome expectancy $(P \rightarrow O)$
Ambiguity	Uncertainty	Uncertainty
Overload	Uncertainty	
Underutilization of skills		Uncertainty

Source: Beehr, T. A. and Bhagat, R. S. 1985. *Human Stress and Cognition in Organizations: An Integrated Perspective* (New York: John Wiley & Sons). Reprinted by permission of John Wiley & Sons.

utilization are usually measured subjectively (via employee perceptions) in the research on work role stress, but these perceptions are in part due to objective role characteristics (Kahn et al. 1964). Thus, role set members may not send clear messages regarding their role expectations (role ambiguity), resulting in an uncertain $E \rightarrow P$ expectancy. The person may not know in this case how to direct his or her work efforts if there is ambiguity regarding the performance expected in the role. In some situations members of the role set may also send ambiguous (or no) messages regarding the outcomes that will result from good or bad performance. This would result in an uncertain $P \rightarrow O$ expectancy. Pearce (1981) has noted that questions asking about each type of uncertainty have been included in role ambiguity measures; therefore it appears that previous research on role ambiguity may have unknowingly studied a conglomeration of these two uncertainties and more objective (more directly environmentally based) role ambiguity.

Also in Table 4.4, role overload is proposed to result in an uncertain $E \rightarrow P$ expectancy. When the objective role demands result in a situation in which the individual is uncertain of his or her ability to meet the required performance standards, he or she experiences stress. With role overload, the focal person understands clearly what the definition of good performance is but is uncertain of meeting the demands, even if he or she tries hard. If the person does meet the expected performance standards, however, he or she may be quite certain of receiving pay, promotions, or other outcomes ($P \rightarrow O$ expectancy).

Underutilization of skills is the third role stressor used as an example in Table 4.4. Underutilization occurs when the person's job does not require or does not even allow the use of some skills that the person has, values, and would like to use at work. These skills may have been acquired from formal or informal training or education or simply from experience. Examples regarding underutilization usually describe rather menial work situations, such as assembly-line work, that require little complex skill or ability. The table proposes that the employee in this case may experience $P \rightarrow O$ uncertainty. Underutilization is a good example because it rounds out the discussion of role stressors and uncertain expectancies by proposing an uncertain $P \rightarrow O$ only, which was not the case for either of the other two examples, and because the particular outcome (O) is different from outcomes typically used as examples of outcomes. In this case the outcome is intrinsic rather than extrinsic. The outcome might be, for example, a sense of achievement or worthwhile accomplishment; the person is uncertain that successful performance on the job will lead to a sense of accomplishment because the task is so simple that it does not require valued, high-level skills. Intrinsic motivation in the workplace is thought to be dependent in part on the use of a variety of complex skills in completing challenging tasks (Hackman and Oldham 1980; Schein 1980).

In summary, the Beehr-Bhagat model of job stress proposes that uncertainity of $E \rightarrow P$ expectancies, $P \rightarrow O$ expectancies, or both are responsible for the experienced stress, so long as the outcome is important and especially if the uncertainty is of great duration; the key elements are Uc, Im, and D.

One of the biggest potential obstacles to implementing research using this model is the development of adequate measures of the elements, especially uncertainty. A start has been made, however, as items from published role ambiguity scales and newly created items have been pretested iteratively in a series of three studies of college students who have jobs (Beehr 1984). Using item analysis and face validity as the primary techniques of questionnaire development, preliminary scales measuring the uncertainty of $E \rightarrow P$ and $P \rightarrow O$ expectancies are now available. The ten best items (those with the best item-total correlations) for each type of uncertainty are presented in Tables 4.5 and 4.6. The next step will be to use them in future job stress studies to test their validity and explanatory power.

As a guide to occupational stress practitioners, the model suggests that job stress treatments will be successful to the extent that they reduce employee $E \rightarrow P$ or $P \rightarrow O$ uncertainties, the importance of the outcome to the employees, *or* the duration of the uncertainties. Since stress is a multiplicative function of these three characteristics, it is not necessary to reduce all three in order to have a big impact.

Path-goal leadership theory maintains that supervisors are effective to the extent that they influence employee expectancy levels (House 1971; Schriesheim and DeNisi 1981). If they can influence expectancy *levels*, they also may be able to influence the *certainties* of employee expectancies. Reducing employee uncertainty through supervisory training is therefore a logical approach to stress treatment. Supervisors could be trained to assess subordinates' expectancies during interactions with subordinates; if uncertainty exists, supervisors could work with subordinates to clarify $E \rightarrow P$ and $P \rightarrow O$ paths. On a larger scale, people in the personnel department could assess employees' uncertainties via questionnaires such as those in Tables 4.5 and 4.6, and work to increase clarity when needed.

Reducing uncertainties quickly diminishes the influence of duration in the stress model, but it would be a more difficult task to reduce the importance the employee places on the outcomes involved. Reducing uncertainties seems to be the most promising approach.

Overall, the Beehr-Bhagat model is cognitive and goal oriented. It is cognitive because its primary concept, uncertainty, involves perceptions and internal states, and because its grounding is a cognitive theory of motivation, expectancy theory. It is goal oriented because outcomes that are positively valued by the employee (and therefore may be employee goals) are a central part of the proposed stress process. These positively valued outcomes represent explicit or implicit personal goals of the employee.

Table 4.5   The Ten Best Expectancy-to-Performance ($E \rightarrow P$) Uncertainty
Items (Alpha = .82)

Items in order from best to tenth best

The amount of work I get done depends on how hard I work.

If I did not try as hard as I do, my job performance would suffer.

My job performance would not improve even if I worked more hours.

My job performance would not change regardless of how hard I work.

I could do better work if I worked more hours at my job.

The quality of my work is related to how hard I try.

If I were not corrected for my mistakes, my job performance would suffer.

People where I work could do better work if they tried.

I know what I am supposed to try to do at work.

If I loafed at work, my work would suffer.

Response categories:

(Item 9)   Strongly disagree, disagree, slightly disagree, neither agree nor
disagree, slightly agree, agree, strongly agree;

(Other items)   Very unsure, unsure, a little unsure, neither sure nor unsure,
a little sure, sure, very sure.

Questionnaire directions for "sureness" scale:

For the following questions please give two answers. First, circle T or F to
indicate whether you think the statement is true or false. Then circle a
number from 1 to 7, indicating how sure you were in answering true or false.

Example: I will graduate in four years.   T   F   1   2   3   4   5   6   7

Scoring: Uc scoring involves only the number circled and not T or F.

Source: Compiled by the author.

SUMMARY AND CONCLUSIONS

It is apparent that definitions of the elements of job stress offered by
different experts in the field are in conflict. Therefore, it is necessary to
define terms as they are being used. In the present chapter, the focus is on
social psychological stress in the workplace, and the following terms and

Table 4.6   The Ten Best Performance-to-Outcome ($P \rightarrow$ °) Uncertainty
Items (Alpha = .84)

Items in order from best to tenth best

People where I work would get more rewards if they performed their work better.

My co-workers will think highly of me if I do my job especially well.

Doing a good job will get me a promotion.

I will receive recognition when I perform well in my job.

If I did better work my pay would increase.

People where I work would lose out if they did poor work.

My job performance will result in a particular reward.

Pay increases have nothing to do with the quality of my work.

Doing a good job will get better pay for me.

The harder I work the more accomplishment I will feel.

Response categories:

Very unsure, unsure, a little unsure, neither sure nor unsure, a little sure, sure, very sure.

Questionnaire directions for "sureness" scale:

For the following questions, please give two answers. First circle T or F to indicate whether you think the statement is true or false. Then circle a number from 1 to 7 indicating how sure you were in answering true or false.

Example: I will graduate in four years.   T   F   1   2   3   4   5   6   7

Scoring: Uc scoring involves only the number circled and not T or F.

Source: Compiled by the author.

---

definitions are used: (1) *stress* is a general area of study; (2) *stressor* refers to environmental stimuli thought to be causal; and (3) *strain* is the person's (aversive) physiological, behavioral, or psychological response to stressors.

Although the history of serious, intensive research on job stress is relatively short, there is some evidence already that job stress may be quite widespread. There are considerable difficulties, however, in developing strong evidence for (or against) this belief. The research on job stress shows only very superficial and tenuous linkages to the research and body of knowledge on human stress in general, although it is often assumed that they are directly related. Kahn et al. (1964) reported a set of studies widely recognized as the pioneering work on job stress. It proposed role theory as a framework for thinking about job stress and investigated two particular role stressors: role conflict and role ambiguity. Since the publication of that book, research on job stress has increased at a growing rate. Role-theory approaches to job stress have led to a large amount of research and have resulted in important knowledge about the phenomenon, but it may be time to take a fresh look at the topic from some other points of view to see whether they also can add to the knowledge of employee reactions to stress.

Jackson and Schuler (1985) have recommended that job stress researchers investigate work-related ambiguity, and that conflict emanating from sources other than the role set be used as a point of departure from the traditional role-theory approach to the topic. A second way to gain new knowledge about job stress would be to stay within role theory for hypotheses but to investigate other types of role ambiguity, role conflict, and so on. This would mean fine-tuning the definitions of these role stressors and investigating them in more depth. The Beehr-Newman (1978) meta-model can accommodate each of these new approaches to the investigation of job stress as well as the one most advocated in this chapter, the cognitive model of job stress proposed in the Beehr-Bhagat (1985) model.

Instead of roles as the basic building blocks for research on job stress, the Beehr-Bhagat model proposes expectancy theory as the basis for investigation. It is assumed that the valued outcomes in expectancy theory models are often the goals of the individual employees; thus this approach may be seen as moving from role theory, in which the demands of others are the major causal variables, toward a goal-oriented approach in which the person's own aims and desires are seen as primary determinants. In that way, this theory recommends viewing the individual worker less as someone reacting to his or her environment and more as someone who is capable of being proactive and able to seek goals of his or her own. Obviously, either of these approaches (role or expectancy theories) by itself and in pure form may be deficient for understanding human behavior in organizations; role stress researchers have had too strong a tendency to assume a passive, reacting person, however, and therefore assuming a more proactive person is probably a move in the right direction. Eventually a happy medium might be struck in which people are seen as reactive, proactive, or both at various times and in various ways. It is possible that some third theory (neither expectancy theory nor role theory) will aid in such an integration. A possibility, for example, might be to use an information-processing approach (Salancik and Pfeffer 1977) to hypothesize that socially derived information helps to account for both the perceived roles of the individual and the goals he or she chooses. This suggestion is premature, however, since the expectancy-based model of Beehr and Bhagat (1985) has not yet been explored adequately.

In summary, role theory has produced a large amount of valuable information about job stress, but more innovative use of role theory or the use of other theories is now necessary in order to continue the rapid growth of understanding the phenomenon. This chapter proposes a shift to expectancy theory and a more goal-oriented, proactive view of employees as one means to accomplish this.

REFERENCES

Axelrod, W. L. and J. Gavin. 1980. "Stress and Strain in Blue-Collar and White-Collar Management Staffs." *Journal of Vocational Behavior* 17: 41-49.

Beehr, T. A. 1976. "Perceived Situational Moderators of the Relationship between Subjective Role Ambiguity and Role Strain." *Journal of Applied Psychology* 61: 35-40.

_____. 1984. "Psychometric Development of a Measure of the Uncertainty of Effort-to-Performance and Performance-to-Outcome Expectancies." Unpublished manuscript.

_____. 1985. "The Role of Social Support in Coping with Organizational Stress." In *Human Stress and Cognition in Organizations: An Integrated Perspective*, edited by T. A. Beehr and R. S. Bhagat (New York: Wiley), pp. 375-98.

Beehr, T. A. and R. S. Bhagat. 1985. *Human Stress and Cognition in Organizations: An Integrated Perspective* (New York: Wiley).

Beehr, T. A. and K. G. Love. 1983. "A Meta-Model of the Effects of Goal Characteristics in Human Organizations. *Human Relations* 36: 151-66.

Beehr, T. A. and J. E. Newman. 1978. "Job Stress, Employee Health, and Organizational Effectiveness: A Facet Analysis, Model and Literature Review." *Personnel Psychology* 31: 665-99.

Beehr, T. A., J. T. Walsh, and T. D. Taber. 1976. "Relationship of Stress to Individually and Organizationally Valued States: Higher Order Needs as a Moderator." *Journal of Applied Psychology* 61: 41-47.

Beutell, N. J. and J. H. Greenhaus. 1983. "Integration of Home and Nonhome Roles: Women's Conflict and Coping Behavior." *Journal of Applied Psychology* 68: 43-48.

Brady, J. V. 1958. "Ulcers in 'executive monkeys.' " *Scientific American* 199: 95-100.

Cannon, W. B. 1932. *The Wisdom of the Body* (New York: K. W. Norton & Co.).

Caplan, R. D., S. Cobb, J. R. P. French, Jr., R. V. Harrison and S. R. Pinneau. 1975; 1980. *Job Demands and Worker Health: Main Effects and Occupational Differences* (Washington, D.C.: U.S. Government Printing Office; Ann Arbor, MI: Institute for Social Research.

Cummings, L. L. and R. B. Dunham. 1980. *Introduction to Organizational Behavior: Text and Readings* (Homewood, IL: Richard D. Irwin).

Davis, K. and J. W. Newstrom. 1985. *Human Behavior at Work: Organizational Behavior*, 7th ed. (New York: McGraw-Hill).

Dubrin, A. J. 1974. *Fundamentals of Organizational Behavior* (New York: Pergamon Press).

Eden, D. 1982. "Critical Job Events, Acute Stress, and Strain: A Multiple Interrupted Time Series." *Organizational Behavior and Human Performance* 30: 312-39.

French, J. R. P., Jr. and R. D. Caplan. 1973. "Organizational Stress and Individual Strain." In *The Failure of Success*, edited by A. J. Marrow (New York: AMACOM).

French, J. R. P., Jr. and R. L. Kahn. 1962. "A Programmatic Approach to Studying the Industrial Environment and Mental Health." *Journal of Social Issues* 18: 1-47.

Fried, Y., K. M. Rowland and G. R. Ferris. 1984. "The Physiological Measurement of Work Stress: A Critique." *Personnel Psychology* 37: 583-615.

Friedman, M., R. Rosenman, and V. Carroll. 1957. "Changes in the Serum Cholesterol and Blood Clotting Time of Men Subject to Cyclic Variation of Occuptional Stress." *Circulation* 17: 852-61.

Gaines, J. and J. M. Jermier. 1983. "Emotional Exhaustion in a High Stress Organization." *Academy of Management Journal* 26: 567-86.

Greenwood, J. W. 1978. "Management Stressors." In *Reducing Occupational Stress* (Cincinnati, OH: NIOSH Research Report).

Gupta, N. and T. A. Beehr. 1979. "Job Stress and Employee Behaviors." *Organizational Behavior and Human Performance* 23: 373-87.

Hackman, J. R. and G. R. Oldham. 1980. *Work Redesign* (Reading, MA: Addison-Wesley).

Hall, D. T. 1972. "A Model of Coping with Role Conflict: The Role Behavior of College Educated Women." *Administrative Science Quarterly* 17: 471-86.

Harrison, R. V. 1985. "The Person-Environment Fit Model and the Study of Job Stress." In *Human Stress and Cognition in Organizations: An Integrated Perspective*, edited by T. A. Beehr and R. S. Bhagat (New York: Wiley), pp. 23-55.

Hennigan, J. K. and A. W. Wortham. 1975. "Analysis of Workday Stresses on Industrial Managers Using Heart Rate as a Criterion." *Ergonomics* 18: 675-81.

Herman, J. B. 1977. "Working Men and Women: Inter- and Intra-Role Conflict." *Psychology of Women Quarterly* 14: 319-25.

House, R. J. 1971. "A Path Goal Theory of Leadership Effectiveness." *Administrative Science Quarterly* 16: 321-38.

House, R. J. and J. R. Rizzo. 1972. "Role Conflict and Ambiguity as Critical Variables in a Model of Organizational Behavior." *Organizational Behavior and Human Performance* 7: 467-505.

Ivancevich, J. M. and M. T. Matteson. 1980. *Stress and Work: A Managerial Perspective* (Glenview, IL: Scott, Foresman, & Co.).

Jackson, S. E. 1983. "Participation in Decision Making as a Strategy for Reducing Job-Related Strain." *Journal of Applied Psychology* 68: 3-19.

Jackson, S. E. and R. S. Schuler. 1985. "A Meta-Analysis and Conceptual Critique of Research on Role Ambiguity and Role Conflict in Work Settings." *Organizational Behavior and Human Performance* 36: 16-78.

Jamal, J. 1984. "Job Stress and Job Performance Controversy: An Empirical

Assessment." *Organizational Behavior and Human Performance* 33: 1-21.

Kahn, R. L. and R. P. Quinn. 1970. "Role Stress: A Framework for Analysis." In *Occupational Mental Health*, edited by A. McLean (New York: Rand McNally).

Kahn, R. L., D. M. Wolfe, R. P. Quinn, J. D. Snoek, and R. A. Rosenthal. 1964. *Organizational Stress: Studies in Role Conflict and Ambiguity* (New York: Wiley).

Kemery, A., R. Bedeian, S. Mossholder, and D. Touliatos. 1985. "Outcomes of Role Stress: A Multisample Constructive Replication." *Academy of Management Journal* 28: 363-75.

Landy, F. J. and D. A. Trumbo. 1980. *Psychology of Work Behavior* (Homewood, IL: Dorsey).

Lawler, E. E., III. 1973. *Motivation in Work Organizations* (Monterey, CA: Brooks-Cole).

Love, K. G. and T. A. Beehr. 1981. "Social Stressors on the Job: Recommendations for a Broadened Perspective." *Group and Organization Studies* 6: 190-200.

Lyons, T. 1971. "Role Clarity, Need for Clarity, Satisfaction, Tension and Withdrawal. *Organizational Behavior and Human Performance* 6: 99-110.

Mason, J. W. 1975a. "A Historical View of the Stress Field: Part 1." *Journal of Human Stress* 1 (March): 6-12.

_____. 1975b. "A Historical View of the Stress Field: Part 2." *Journal of Human Stress* 1 (June): 22-35.

McCormick, E. J. 1976. *Human Factors in Engineering and Design* (New York: McGraw-Hill).

McGrath, J. E. 1976. "Stress and Behavior in Organizations." In *Handbook of Industrial and Organizational Psychology*, edited by M. D. Dunnette (Chicago, IL: Rand McNally).

McLean, A. 1974. *Occupational Stress* (Springfield, IL: Charles C. Thomas).

Mitchell, T. and A. Bigland. 1971. "Instrumentality Theory: Current Uses in Psychology." *Psychological Bulletin* 76: 432-56.

Moser, M. 1977. "Hypertension: A Major Controllable Public Health Problem—Industry Can Help." *Occupational Health Nursing* (August): 19-26.

Newman, J. E. and T. A. Beehr. 1979. "Personal and Organizational Strategies for Handling Job Stress: A Review of Research and Opinion." *Personnel Psychology* 32: 1-43.

Payne, R. and B. C. Fletcher. 1983. "Job Demands, Supports, and Constraints as Predictors of Psychological Strain among Schoolteachers." *Journal of Vocational Behavior* 22: 136-47.

Pearce, J. L. 1981. "Bringing Some Clarity to Role Ambiguity Research." *Academy of Management Review* 6: 665-74.

Putt, A. M. 1970. "One Experiment in Nursing Adults with Peptic Ulcers." *Nursing Research* 19: 484-94.

Rizzo, J. R., R. J. House, and S. I. Lirtzman. 1970. "Role Conflict and Ambiguity in Complex Organizations." *Administrative Science Quarterly* 15: 150-63.

Rowland, K. M. and G. R. Ferris, eds. 1982. *Personnel Management* (Boston, MA: Allyn and Bacon).

Salancik, G. R. and J. Pfeffer. 1977. "An Examination of Need-Satisfaction Models of Job Attitudes." *Administrative Science Quarterly* 22: 427-56.

Sales, S. M. 1970. "Some Effects of Role Overload and Role Underload." *Organizational Behavior and Human Performance* 5: 592-608.

Sarbine, R. R. and V. L. Allen 1969. "Role Theory." In *The Handbook of Social Psychology*, Vol. 1 (2nd edition) edited by G. Lindsey and E. Aronson (Reading, MA: Addison-Wesley), pp. 488-568.

Schein, E. H. 1980. *Organizational Psychology*, 3rd ed. (Englewood Cliffs, NJ: Prentice-Hall).

Schriesheim, C. A. and A. S. DeNisi. 1981. "Task Dimensions as Moderators of the Effects of Instrumental Leadership: A Two Sample Replicated Test of Path Goal Leadership Theory." *Journal of Applied Psychology* 66: 589-97.

Schuler, R. S. 1975. "Role Perceptions, Satisfaction, and Performance: A Partial Reconciliation." *Journal of Applied Psychology* 60: 683-87.

Sekaran, U. 1983. "How Husbands and Wives in Dual-Career Families Perceive Their Family and Work Roles." *Journal of Vocational Behavior* 22: 288-302.

Selye, H. 1956; 1976. *The Stress of Life* (New York: McGraw-Hill).

_____. 1974. *Stress without Distress* (New York: Lippincott).

_____. 1975. "Confusion and Controversy in the Stress Field." *Journal of Human Stress* 1 (June): 37-44.

_____. 1980. *Selye's Guide to Stress Research* (New York: Van Nostrand Reinhold).

Shamir, B. 1983. "Some Antecedents of Work-Nonwork Conflict." *Journal of Vocational Behavior* 23: 98-111.

Stryker, S. and A. Statham. 1985. "Symbolic Interaction and Role Theory." In *Handbook of Social Psychology*, vol. 1, 3rd ed., edited by G. Lindsey and E. Aronson (New York: Random House), pp. 311-78.

Vroom, V. H. 1964. *Work and Motivation* (New York: John Wiley & Sons).

Warshaw, L. J. 1979. *Managing Stress* (Reading, MA: Addison-Wesley).

Weiss, J. M. 1968. "Effects of Coping Responses on Stress." *Journal of Comparative and Physiological Psychology* 65: 251-60.

5

PERSON-ENVIRONMENT FIT IN ORGANIZATIONS: THEORIES, FACTS, AND VALUES

ROBERT D. CAPLAN

The theory described here may provide a useful framework to help organizational members in evaluating the consequences of different decisions that they might make regarding alterations in control and PE fit, which are valued stakes in organizations. Some of these consequences may have to do with emotional well-being and some with performance.

The first part of this chapter describes the concepts, basic hypotheses, and findings relating to the theory. The second part deals with areas where future research is needed. Those areas have to do with conditions under which person-environment (PE) fit is most likely to lead to improvements in well-being, and with the fact that cognition allows humans to focus on past, present, and anticipated levels of PE fit. Throughout the chapter examples are provided that link the theory to the workplace.

Social control and power are distributed unequally among members of work organizations. Thus, the line worker has less control than the line manager. This observation holds across cultures as diverse as those of the United States and Yugoslavia or of Israel and Italy (Tannenbaum et al. 1974). One of the consequences of this uneven distribution of power is that those with the most control have the best PE fit (French, Caplan, and Harrison 1982). PE fit refers to the match between the needs and abilities of the employee and the corresponding resources of and demands from the work environment.

Control, whether exerted by the simple operation of a lever on an assembly line or by the more complex operation of participation in a work group, is a process for improving PE fit. As will be explored here, improving PE fit can be achieved by changing characteristics of the person, the job environment, or some combination of both.

Many people find an anecdote helpful in introducing the idea of PE fit. The following anecdote will be used to illustrate a number of concepts that form the basis for a dynamic theory of person-environment fit.

When Susan Green first interviewed for the job at Weslake Corporation, she was fresh out of an MBA program. She wanted good pay, a good career ladder, and a job that would provide an opportunity to learn, but not too much responsibility. At the time of the interview, the employer was willing to offer a good compensation package for the right applicant. The right applicant was one who was flexible enough to adopt the company's way of doing things, was bright, and would be content to work under someone's tutelage for a while before taking on more supervisory responsibility. The fit was good, and Susan Green was hired.

Three years later Susan Green wanted more responsibility, but Weslake Corporation did not have the type of role she was seeking. The compensation package was still attractive, and the employer valued Green's productivity and contribution to the organization very much. But Susan Green began to feel very dissatisfied, particularly as others were promoted and she was not. Her productivity started to decline, and one day she came in and gave her employer 30 days notice that she was leaving the company to take another position with a competitor as a division manager. The people at Weslake were shocked by the news—her superior felt let down. Her boss had never known she felt so strongly about wanting more responsibility. Thirty days later she started work with the competitor. Her new level of responsiblity was what she had wanted at Weslake and could not get there. She was pleased with her new level of responsibility, but she was nervous because, although she liked a bit of ambiguity in her life, there was usually too much at the beginning of a new job.

Whether employer or employee, each of us may identify with one or more components of this anecdote. The anecdote illustrates that the closeness of fit between an employee and an organization is a matter of transactions (Lazarus and Launier 1978) between the person and the environment. Studying only the nature of the employee (Susan's need for and ability to take on responsibility) or only the nature of the organization (her boss's perception of her needs and abilities, and her boss's demands) does not provide a sufficient diagnosis of the situation. The anecdote suggests that employee and employer bring to the situation perspectives that do not necessarily overlap. What the employee views as *needs* to be fulfilled by the job and organization, the employer may view as *resources* to be given up. What the employer may view as *demands* made on the employee, the employee may view as *efforts to be expended*. Researchers do not understand what effects these different perspectives may have on the motivation of the employee. The perspectives may relate to a difference between being the driver and being driven: but the implications for productivity morale are unknown.

BEHAVIOR IN ORGANIZATIONS: A SET OF ASSUMPTIONS

At the outset, some assumptions will be made about the nature of people and their behavior in organizations. These assumptions suggest that learning how *change* in PE fit influences human well-being is a worthy endeavor.

1. There is a basic set of needs shared by all humans. These include those for (the list is is not intended to be exhaustive): physiological maintenance, safety and security (for example, job security), order or meaning, predictability and stability, belongingness and love, esteem, efficacy or control, and creative use of one's abilities (in its ultimate form, self-actualization; Maslow 1943).

2. There are *individual differences* that overlay these basic needs. For example, some people are particularly concerned with maintaining good physical health whereas others are not so concerned. Similarly, some persons are particularly interested in exercising social power, whereas others are less so (Winter 1973).

3. When supplies to meet needs are inadequate to serve everyone and hence, to produce good PE fit, control and power become important determinants of allocation (Pfeffer 1978).

4. Social (and hence, organizational) structures are created to regulate the extent to which certain basic needs will be met and to regulate the opportunities for individuals to satisfy their own unique patterns of needs. These structures include reward systems. The systems distribute rewards aimed at the total organization (for example, basic profit sharing), subgroups (unit performance rewards, union contracts), and individuals (for example, commissions, promotions, or merit increases in salary). Among the rewards are opportunities and supplies to improve PE fit. PE fit and the alleviation of stressors in general appear to increase emotional as well as physical well-being (Campbell 1974; French, Caplan, and Harrison 1982; Gardell 1971; Wall and Clegg 1981; and House et al. 1986). Consequently, organizations implicitly distribute mental health as a reward.

PE FIT AND PERFORMANCE

There do not appear to be studies of how PE fit specifically influences job performance, although at least one theory explicitly deals with this link (McGrath 1976). Studies of job stressors and of participation, which is discussed later as a mechanism for increasing PE fit, do lead to the hypothesis that improvements in PE fit will lead to increases in performance. Low levels of employee job stress have been related to high levels of performance, as measured by supervisory ratings (Jamal 1985), particularly among highly committed employees. Experimental increases in participation have been shown to reduce employee intention to turnover (Jackson 1983). And a five-year study of survey and performance data from 34 corporations found that participative corporate culture and good organization are both associated with organizational performance (Denison 1984). Organizational performance was assessed using Standard and Poor's COMPUSTAT listings and dealt with returns on investment and on sales.

Nevertheless, the attainment of good fit will probably involve some cost. This theory cannot generate the values that ought to be assigned to the attainment of PE fit. But this theory and supporting research can provide some additional tools by which members of organizations can assess the costs and benefits of good PE fit. With such assessment, the act of distributing well-being in organizations might become more explicit. This is seen as desirable on the grounds that when human well-being is at stake, it is good to know fully all the other stakes. The decision to enact one policy or another, and to pursue particular consequences, however, is ultimately a question of values and choices among values.[1] PE fit theory can provide a conceptual framework for evaluating how these choices result in consequences of interest to organizational members.

PE FIT THEORY

Overview

A number of theories about human stress (Pervin 1968; French, Rodgers, and Cobb 1974; Stokols 1979; Levi 1972; McGrath 1976) state that emotional well-being and performance are a function of characteristics of the person and the environment (Lewin 1935; Murray 1938). This interactionist perspective has generated considerable research in the field of social psychology (Magnusson 1982; Sarason, Smith, and Diener 1975) and in the area of occupational stress (French, Caplan, and Harrison 1982; Harrison 1976).

This chapter examines one line of this research, PE fit theory (French, Rodgers, and Cobb 1974), in terms of its application to the workplace. The text begins with an overview of the formal assumptions and requirements of the theory. There is then a review of some of the tests of the theory. Next, there is a discussion of some potential criticisms of the theory. The chapter concludes with a discussion of several potential extensions of the theory. One is that an employee's thoughts about past, present, and future prospects for good PE fit may influence his or her well-being. Another extension is that perceptions that employees can control PE fit influences their well-being, and another deals with the role of social support from others at work in influencing adjustment and allowing employees to tolerate deviations from perfect PE fit.

Conceptual Distinctions

From assumption 1, we begin with the concept of needs and will distinguish such needs (for example, for creative endeavor, for security, and so on) from abilities (being able to follow instructions, being able to work as part of a team, and so on). This distinction leads to two types of person-environment (PE) fit, as shown in Figure 5.1. One type is the fit between an employee's needs and the job's supplies or resources for meeting those needs (*needs-supplies fit*). For example, Susan Green had a need for responsibility and Weslake Corporation had inadequate supplies (opportunities) for meeting her needs. A second type is the fit between the job's demands and the person's abilities (*demands-abilities* fit). The case of Ms. Green did not provide information about the match between her *abilities* to discharge responsibility and the company's demands for such performance. With additional information, however, we could evaluate Ms. Green's demands-abilities fit.[2]

PE fit theory also contains the distinction between objective and subjective fit. *Subjective fit* is what is perceived by the person. For example, we might obtain some ratings from Susan Green as to what she *perceived* to be the demands for the discharge of such responsibility. *Objective fit*, by definition, is not influenced by biases of human perception and *can* (but need not) include facts about the job environment and the person that are not perceived by the person. For example, we might obtain some objective measure of Susan Green's ability to discharge responsibility as assessed by some validated situational test. We might also have some validated, standardized method of assessing demand for responsibility (for example, an index based on the number of subordinates under Ms. Green, the amount of capital she is responsible for, and so on). The question of what constitutes a truly objective measure is a philosophical as well as pragmatic one. It is safe to assume, however, that asking Susan Green's immediate superior to make these ratings would not necessarily produce more objective ratings than would be obtained from Ms. Green herself. Rather, we would simply elicit another set of subjective views.

As shown in Figure 5.1, objective fit is hypothesized to influence subjective fit. The relationship is generally expected to be imperfect. This imperfection can be due to a number of sources. For example, people have a limited capacity to process all the information about their jobs, their organizations, and their own needs and abilities (Miller 1960). There may also be limits to people's opportunities to gain access to information. For example, it may be difficult to gain information about one's performance relative to another's, or information on what *really* was decided by the upper echelon. Some of these difficulties may arise because the information does not exist. In other cases, certain members of the organization may wish to restrict the dissemination of information in order to control others and make others dependent on them as sources of expertise (Crozier 1964).

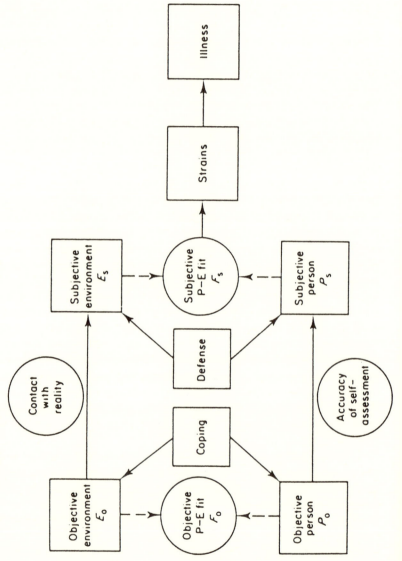

Figure 5.1 A model describing the effects of psychosocial stress in terms of fit between the person and the environment. Concepts within circles are discrepancies between the two adjoining concepts. Solid lines indicate causal effects. Broken lines indicate contributions to interaction effects (Harrison 1978).

Another potential source of distortion between objective and subjective fit is the psychological process of denial. Organizational members may be motivated to distort their own needs and abilities and the demands and resources of the organization in order to fit comforting preconceptions about self and the organizational environment. For example, did Susan Green's superior show shock at her leaving because her action violated the superior's preconception of Ms. Green's preference for responsibility? Did her superior deny that Susan Green was changing in her need for responsibility because it was comforting for the superior to think of the "old, recent-MBA Green" rather than the "new" Susan Green? Did the superior then create the illusion of perfect fit between *Green's demands* for responsibility from the superior and the *superior's ability* to provide opportunities for the exercise of such responsibility?

Note that changes in objective fit can either decrease or increase the correspondence between objective and subjective fit. Similarly, changes in subjective fit can also increase or decrease this correspondence. In the original formulation by French and his colleagues (1974) "coping" was used to refer to changes in objective P and E, whereas "defense" referred to changes in subjective P and E. Such definitions are free from any implication that defensive behaviors are more primitive or undesirable than coping behaviors. And indeed, the literature suggests that defense mechanisms (such as denial) can be quite adaptive in some circumstances (such as when one *must* cope with an unpleasant emergency) and not in other circumstances (for example, when one has increasing evidence that the organization is about to eliminate one's division and all the people in it without transfers; Lazarus 1983).

In extreme environments (such as PE fit for job security when the employer has just announced bankruptcy proceedings) there may be little or no distinction between objective and subjective PE fit. Consequently, either objective or subjective PE fit may be equally predictive of the person's well-being. In the conditions found in everyday life, such as those of responsibility, workload, and task complexity, however, subjective fit is hypothesized to be the stronger predictor of how people *respond* to poor PE fit. Such responses include affect (for example, anxiety, depression, dissatisfaction), physiological states (for example, heart rate, blood pressure, serum cholesterol level), and cognitive states, such as reduced (or heightened) vigilance. There are also behavioral indicators of strain, including the ingestion of drugs such as nicotine and alcohol. The persistence of medically and socially undesirable responses (referred to conveniently as "strains") is hypothesized to result in illness such as coronary heart disease, ulcers, or clinically diagnosed depression. In many cases, organizations have taken specific steps to deal with the reduction of such strains (Foote and Erfurt 1981).

Commensurate Dimensions

A special requirement of PE fit theory is that P and E be assessed along commensurate dimensions, so that the relevance of P and E to each other is explicit. Thus, one might ask an engineer, "How many hours of reading material do you receive per week?" (E) and, "How many hours of reading are you able to do per week?" (P).[3] This requirement makes it possible to use conceptually meaningful measurement scales to assess the discrepancies between P and E, and between the objective and subjective components of fit.

Three Basic Curves

In order to study PE fit in organizations systematically and empirically, one needs to become familiar with three basic curves that can describe the relation between the PE fit of employees and their levels of strain or well-being. These curves are shown in Figure 5.2. The curves have both substan-

Figure 5.2   Three hypothetical shapes of the relationship between PE fit and strain. Curves B and C can also be drawn as their mirror images to depict functions that are their respective opposites.

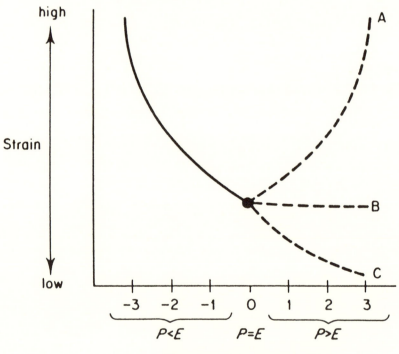

tive and methodological importance. Curve A, which is U-shaped, represents the condition in which excess as well as deficit in the environment decreases well-being. Excess elements may threaten one need and deficit elements may threaten another. For example, too much work load may threaten an employee's need to achieve, and too little may threaten the employee's need for change or sensory stimulation.[4]

Curve B shows an asymptotic relation. It represents the case where either an excess of E (demands, resources) but not a deficit, or an excess of P (needs, abilities), but not a deficit, can decrease well-being. For example, persons with a low need for autonomy and a high need for guidance (Burger and Cooper 1979) may feel threatened by too much opportunity for participation in decisions. Reducing this excess will reduce the strain people experience up to the point where the opportunity for participation meets their need. If the person has the option of choosing when and when not to participate, increases in opportunity for participation beyond the point of PE fit may have few additional strain-reducing effects.

Curve C represents the case where the absolute amount of one PE fit component (such as P's ability to handle customer complaints) relative to the other (such as E's supplies of complaining customers) has a linear effect on strain. For example, in some work situations, the more work one has *relative* to the amount one wants, the more strain there is. This is not the same as merely examining the amount of work load the person has per se, for in that case the need for work load is not considered.

There are many other PE fit curves that represent modifications of the three forms just described. For example, the U-shaped curves can be broadened at the base to represent the assumption that there is an interval of tolerance surrounding P = E, and that a certain amount of poor PE fit will be tolerated. Strain begins to increase only beyond the boundaries of that interval. For U-shaped curves, the nadir can also, in theory, be slightly beyond the point of P = E. This might be the case for persons who enjoy challenge and like to have slightly more demands posed than their abilities can handle (Kobasa's "hardy people"; Kobasa and Puccetti 1983). A more detailed discussion of such variants in these curves can be found elsewhere (Kahana 1978; Kulka 1979).

Figures 5.3 and 5.4 provide an illustration of an actual set of PE fit curves. These findings come from a study of a random subsample of 318 men selected from 23 occupations (Caplan et al. 1980). The dimension of fit is job complexity. A multi-item index of complexity was built for this study. The index was based on research (Kohn 1969) that identified several symptoms of a complex environment. These symptoms include dealing with people, working on multiple tasks in various stages of completion, having work that changes from day to day, and not being able to predict exactly how each day will go.

Figure 5.3 shows that depression (as measured by a self-report index) was

Figure 5.3 Relationship between Job complexity, PE fit, and depression. Eta, an index of percent of variance accounted for in the dependent variable, equals 0.26 (p < .002). N = 318 men from 23 occupations. From Caplan et al. 1980, p. 91.

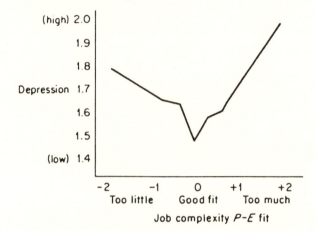

Figure 5.4 Relationships between scores on depression and scores on job complexity − E and job complexity − P. Etas = 0.14 and 0.19 (both nonsignificant), respectively. N = 318 men from 23 occupations. From Caplan et al. 1980, p. 90.

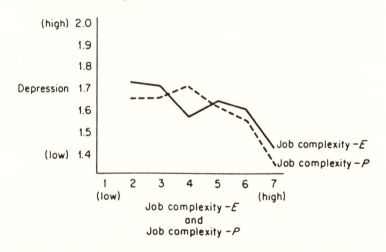

high for persons in jobs with too little complexity as well as in jobs with too much complexity, and lowest in jobs where PE fit was best. The measures of the amount of complexity desired (P) and the amount present (E) did not vary significantly with depression.

Research on PE Fit

Considerable research has been based on a person-environment inter-actionist approach to social psychology (Magnusson 1982; Sarason, Smith, and Diener 1975; Lazarus and Launier 1978). The first real test of a PE fit theory using commensurate measures of P and E, however, appears to be Pervin's (1967a, 1967b) study of adaptation among university students. Poor fit between the amount of structure in the educational approach of universities and the student's need for structure was associated with academic dissatisfaction and with dropping out of school for nonacademic reasons. Since Pervin's research, several major tests of PE fit theory have been conducted. The studies have been conducted in a variety of settings, including 23 occupations (Harrison 1978; Caplan et al. 1980; French, Caplan, and Harrison 1982), 52 industrial plants in five countries (Tannen-baum and Kuleck 1978), whole community (the Tecumseh project; House 1972), among high school students (Kulka, Klingel, and Mann 1980; Kulka 1976), and among the elderly (Kahana, Liang, and Felton 1980). With little exception, commensurately measured P and E contributed significantly to the variance explained in emotional and somatic symptomatology beyond that accounted for by P or E alone. Only the Pervin studies, however, have examined performance and leaving organizations as behavioral conse-quences of poor PE fit. This deficiency needs to be corrected.

Why does research deal only with subjective fit despite the inclusion of objective fit in the model?. Studies have dealt almost exclusively with sub-jective, rather than objective, measures of PE fit. Is there any evidence that these measures reflect objective conditions?

Some evidence comes from the above-cited study of 23 occupations. Those occupations ranged from machine-paced assembly-line work to family medicine, and from fork-lift driving to air traffic control (French, Caplan, and Harrison 1982; Caplan et al. 1980). The results showed that the PE fit measures varied in ways that were meaningful because of the objec-tive nature of such a diverse set of occupations.

For example, the more selective the objective entry requirements of a job (the requirements in terms of P, abilities and needs), the more likely it is that people in selective jobs would show good PE fit regardless of the level of job demands (E). This is particularly evident when one compares groups as different from one another as family physicians and machine-paced assembly-line workers on both P and E. The measures of P and E on work load indicated that family physicans and machine-paced assembly workers both reported very high levels of work load (E), but that the fit with desired levels of work load (P) was good only for the family physicians. These results would be expected, given the rigid ability requirements for entering medical practice and the minimal screening for becoming an assembly-line worker. Further, the measures of PE fit on complexity showed that the assemblers had attained and wanted lower levels of job complexity than was the case for the family physicians. The data indicated that the discrepancy between the desired and actual amount of complexity was four times as great for the assembly-line workers as for the physicians.

Additional analyses indicated that measures of job satisfaction, anxiety, depression, and somatic complaints varied significantly by occupational title. An occupational title can be viewed as a rough indicator of objective differences in job demands. Multivariate analyses showed that the effects of occupational title on well-being were substantially represented by the effects of the self-report measures of job demands and PE fit on well-being. These findings suggest that subjective measures of fit *do* reflect objective conditions of work.

More generally, a longitudinal study of German blue-collar workers found that objectively measured job stressors influence the development of perceived stressors and subsequent psychosomatic complaints (Frese 1985). The stressors included role ambiguity and conflict, organizational problems such as not getting materials, and environmental stressors such as noise. The study's results also suggest that the positive link between perceived job stressors and somatic complaints operates independently of employee tendencies toward overestimating or underestimating the level of job stressors. Other observational and experimental studies have also reported positive associations between self-reports and objective measures of work conditions, although the number of studies exploring this question are few (French and Caplan 1972; Jackson 1983).

This brings us to a second issue; do we need measures of objective fit if the subjective measures appear to be reasonably valid? For one thing, we do not know conclusively how objective and subjective PE fit are related. This lack of knowledge, however, is not a simple oversight. Although social scientists have been called upon in the past to develop objective measures of stress (Kasl 1978), this is not a trivial technical problem.[5] Nevertheless, the ability to distinguish operationally between objective and subjective environment is critical for the further development of theory and for practical as well as ethical reasons.

For example, there may be conditions in which the objective fit of a set of employees is good, but they are given inadequate feedback about their performance, and consequently suffer low self-esteem. Under such circumstances, changing perceptions of the group's subjective PE fit, without changing objective fit, would be highly desirable and humane. On the other hand, if people have poor objective fit, then attempting to convince them that "everything is ok" without improving objective fit is unethical.

Discrepancies between objective and subjective fit will also have other unpleasant consequences for organizations and their members. When employees mistakenly *underestimate the demands* made on them, they may experience temporarily good fit and resultant job satisfaction, but eventually the facts will catch up to them, and they may lose their jobs. When employees *underestimate* their own abilities, they may deny themselves the opportunity for full actualization of their skills and their organization may similarly suffer. When employees *overestimate* their own abilities, they may take on more than they can handle, producing burnout and eventually causing the organization to lose valued members. The reader can deduce other such consequences for the employee and organization from the various combinations in which objective P and E do not match subjective P and E.

Once the correspondence between objective and perceived PE fit is understood, another major problem in organizations can be reduced substantially, that of acceptance of innovation. Organizations probably can provide numerous examples of plans and designs that looked good "objectively" but turned sour when they were presented to those responsible for accepting and implementing the changes. Neither theory nor research on the *rules* of correspondence between objective and subjective fit exists; they would represent a major contribution to our understanding of human behavior.

An interim practical solution. It may be some time before such rules of correspondence are discovered. Meanwhile, organizations will continue to face the problem of how to engineer changes in the objective environment and in the person that will result in a subjectively good person-environment fit. One solution is to use participation (Coch and French 1948; French, Israel, and Aas 1960; Kanter 1982), a social process that will be referred to from time to time in this chapter because of research linking it to good PE fit.

To ensure acceptance of changes in objective PE fit, participation should involve those who are to be affected by the objective change. The participants would take part in making the decisions regarding the nature of the change and how it should be implemented. Deciding *who* will be affected by the decision and should, therefore, be included or represented in the participative process, is itself critical. If this decision is made incorrectly, both key horizontal and vertical elements of the organization may be omitted, and persons who are perceived by constituencies as illegitimate or irrelevant to the process may be included.

By using participation, one can, in principle, include in the decision-making process persons who are most likely to have information about the objective needs of the employees and the nature of the environment. Participation by itself, however, is not adequate for ensuring that objective solutions to PE fit will match perceptions of what constitutes good fit. Participation will lead to high-quality decisions only when those participating are offered the same resources we would expect to give to any key decision-maker. These are: access to information and expert consultants, adequate time, and objective and psychological empowerment to make and carry out the decisions. Unless such conditions can be met, it is unlikely that the decisions will be good for both the individual and the organization (Kanter 1982; Locke and Schweiger 1979).[6]

Part of the value of participation can be found in checking perceptions about what the objective demands and supplies are and what one's abilities and needs are. This checking is likely to be effective when one participates with peers in this process. Numerous studies suggest that objective information about the self and the environment is much more likely to be accepted when it comes from peers than from others. Peers have a credibility because of shared bases of power and perception, which nonpeers, particularly superiors, lack (Tripathi, Caplan and Naidu 1986; Lewin 1947; Baekelund and Lundwall 1975). Although studies have been done on the value of peer support in changing behavior and perceptions, there is a need to explore the effect of peer-group feedback in closing the gap between objective (or, at least, consensually held) PE fit and subjective PE fit.

Improving People's PE Fit: Should One Change P or E?

French and his colleagues described the theory of PE fit as a theory of "adjustment." As has been noted elsewhere (Caplan 1979b), the theory makes no assumptions about how such adjustment is to take place.

Certain parties in the organization may be trained or motivated to achieve PE fit in the work force by tailoring the employee's abilities to the demands of the organization. Other parties (such as experts in training or selection) may be trained to or motivated to achieve PE fit by altering the organization's resources to meet the needs of the employee. It may be natural for most employees, from executives to line workers, to prefer to attain their *own* PE fit by having the environment change (essentially, "let them change, not me").

As a case in point, consider a recent survey that asked members of management and union for their views on how stress should be reduced in organizations. The results indicated that each group thought the other should change (see Chapter 7 in this volume). Management personnel preferred that their employees deal with stress by changing P (biofeedback, meditation, retraining, and so forth). Union members preferred that management give up some of its control and power to the employees, rather than having the employees develop psychic stoicism. Such differences in perspective indicate that issues of power, among other motives, can influence people's preferences for how PE fit should be achieved in organizations. The theory may be cool, but the way it is played out in organizational life can get quite heated.

The PE fit theory does not preclude adjustments via changes in *both* P and E. Keep in mind, however, that one person's E is another person's P, and that changes in the adjustment of one person will influence the well-being of others. The stake that people have in each other's adjustments is a result of their interconnectedness as members of interdependent organizational subsystems (Katz and Kahn 1978). Consequently, it is short-sighted to adopt one perspective (such as adjustment via changing P) to the exclusion of the other perspective (via changing E).

Who Is Responsible for Changing PE Fit?: Research on the Antecedents of PE Fit in the Workplace

Although the PE fit theory deals with the adjustment of individuals, the theory does *not* suggest that the achievement of PE fit is a matter of individual responsibility. On the contrary, research on PE fit, on its antecedents, and on how to change PE fit suggests that the collective mechanism of participative decision-making is a potentially effective way of improving person-environment fit.

This conjecture has been examined in two Institute for Social Research studies, one a survey of 23 occupations, some results of which were described earlier, and the other a field experiment. The results of interest from the survey (Caplan et al. 1980) are summarized in Figure 5.5. They show that although low participation and poor person-environment fit were associated with boredom, all of the effects of participation on boredom operated statistically via participation's effects on PE fit. The dimensions of poor fit included responsibility for others (that is, for their performance and well-being) and job complexity. The findings were based on cross-sectional survey data, so our interpretations of participation as the cause of improved PE fit required further testing. For this reason, a field experiment in participation was conducted by Douglas Campbell (1974), a student of John R. P. French. The experiment was part of a program of research that French and his colleagues had been conducting with the support of NASA.

The first stage of the experiment required that the participants, NASA engineers, become informed about their own PE fit. PE fit data was collected by standardized self-report questionnaires from several teams of engineers. Half the teams were randomly assigned to the participation condition. Survey data from each group in that condition were fed back to each group, the survey feedback method of organizational development (Mann 1957). The other teams served as control groups and received no such information. In the experimental groups, a series of ten weekly group meetings followed. These meetings were designed to help the engineers, in a participative manner, to identify problems of poor PE fit in its work that each group felt was stressful, and to work out solutions.

One set of multivariate regression analyses treated the data as a longitudinal survey. Those analyses showed that antecedent improvement in PE fit on participation was one of the strongest predictors of subsequent improvement in fit on the amount of responsibility one has for the well-

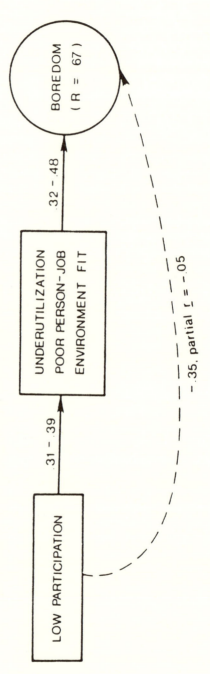

Figure 5.5 Summary of first-order correlations among participation, person-environment fit, and boredom. Arrows represent hypothesized directions of effect. The dashed arrow indicates a derived relationship.

being of others and fit on work load. Thus, the previously cited cross-sectional findings were replicated and their cause-effect interpretation was confirmed. On the other hand, there were few significant changes in PE fit as a result of the intervention. Indeed, the PE fit and job satisfaction of the experimental groups occasionally got *worse* rather than better compared to the unchanged state of the control groups.

The failure of the intervention appears to be due to its enactment in only parts of a large and highly interconnected organization rather than throughout the total organization (Blake and Mouton 1964, 1985; French and Bell 1973). The changes identified as useful by the engineers ran into frustration. Many attempted adjustments involved agreement by other interdependent units that were not included in the intervention. These other units did not have the flexibility delegated to the experimental teams and were understandably unable to go along with the proposed changes.

As a whole, these findings suggest that participation is a mechanism for improving well-being. There are, nevertheless, limits to its effectiveness. Those limits, in part, include the extent to which participative decision-making is a systemic property of the total organization or of selected units only (Likert 1967). As noted earlier, the decision as to *who* to include in the participative process is the first and most fundamental step. The NASA experiment illustrates this clearly.

SOME FUTURE DIRECTIONS FOR ACADEMIC RESEARCH AND IMPLICATIONS FOR MANAGEMENT

Compared to measures of P or E alone, measures of PE fit have doubled the amount of variance explained in well-being (Harrison 1978). On the other hand, PE fit has explained only an additional 1 percent to 5 percent variance in strain. Given the complexities of measurement and curve fitting inherent in testing the theory of fit (Harrison 1976), these findings are encouraging. The percentage of variance that PE fit can explain in strain must be increased, however, if the theory is to receive more serious attention in stress research, and if the measurement instruments are to be useful to organizations intent on monitoring the quality of PE fit. There are several areas of development in the theory that might increase its ability to explain human well-being in organizations. These areas deal with the topics of time frames, dimensions of PE fit, generic types of PE fit, and other moderators of the effects of PE fit on well-being, including cognition and social support.

Time Frames and Dimensions of PE Fit

Time and space form essential properties of human organizations (Katz and Kahn 1978). Time is a particularly key element that makes itself known through concepts such as scheduling, synchronizing, and allocation of resources (McGrath and Rotchford 1983). Although some hypotheses have been offered about how anticipated and current stressors influence emotion and well-being (Lazarus 1966; Campbell, Converse, and Rodgers 1976), little is actually known about how and why such time frames influence well-being. Similarly, PE fit theory has focused largely on how current fit influences well-being, ignoring the potential effects of cognitions about past and anticipated levels of fit.

It would seem worthwhile to examine cognitions about PE fit over time because people appear to have preferences for focusing on one time frame or another, depending on the circumstances. Organizations and their members appear to have a stake in perceptions of past, current, and anticipated PE fit. Thus, after a tough negotiation between the union and management, one may hear from all parties that they should "bury the past" (reduce the salience of *past* stressors). Similarly, in hard economic times, employees may be encouraged (and may wish) to concentrate on the imagery of a brighter future.

To take another example, significant changes in the structure of large organizations are estimated to take three or more years (Likert 1967) before they manifest themselves in stable changes in production and in financial security for the work force. In the interim, there is the phenomenon of hope, an intangible expectation of goods yet to be delivered, which must keep the organization going and its members in reasonably good spirits. Consequently, the ability to manage the expectations for future PE fit can be an important priority for some organizations.

An extension of PE fit theory was generated to examine some of the basic issues related to this topic of time frames. The theory, which is detailed elsewhere (Caplan 1983), suggests that the meaning of current fit may depend on perceptions about past and future fit. As an illustration, suppose that three employees all report slightly less complexity in their jobs than they desire. Without any other information about them, we should predict that all three employees will share the same level of job dissatisfaction and interest in leaving the employer. Now suppose we are told that the first employee had a much worse fit on complexity in the past, and the second employee had a much better fit on complexity in the past, and the third employee had the same level of complexity in the past. Under such circumstances the three current and similar levels of lack of PE fit on complexity conceal *improvement*, *worsening*, and *stability* of PE fit, respectively, for these three employees. Do we still want to assume that these employees all have the same level of dissatisfaction?

The reader can further extend the preceding exercise by adding cases in which the employees differ from one another in their *anticipations* of PE fit as well in their recollections of past fit. The point is that studies that are able to assess past, present, and future PE fit should do much better in predicting the well-being of employees than those that focus only on current fit.

We have made one preliminary test of this theory by examining the effects of thoughts about past, present, and anticipated fit on symptoms of somatic and emotional well-being (Caplan, Tripathi, and Naidu 1985). The symptoms included those associated with anxiety, depression, dissatisfaction, influenza, and other somatic complaints. The setting, respondents, and the types of stressor examined are not those typically encountered in work organizations, but the findings suggest some themes that may be worth pursuing in work organizations in general.

The setting was a major university in India, the 207 respondents were undergraduate students, and the stressor was the yearly examination that forms the sole basis of evaluation in most of India's universities. By way of mild analogy (the exams are far more traumatic and the stakes higher), the student of administrative sciences may wish to think of the students as lower-level organizational members who are subject to year-end performance evaluations (French, Kay, and Meyer 1966).

In this study, my colleagues and I assessed past, present, and anticipated fit directly ("How well *did* you do?" . . . "would you do *now*" . . . and "do you think you *will* do?") rather than measuring the P and E components separately. For each time frame, the respondents were asked to rate their fit on two dimensions—cognitive and motivational. Cognitive fit refers to how well a person can remember details, organize information, and determine what is and is not important. Motivational fit refers to the amount of effort the person is able to muster in relation to the demands of the situation. The two dimensions of fit represent the essential elements of performance, ability (in this case, cognitive fit) and motivation (motivational fit), and were assessed by statistically reliable, multi-item indices.

The first question asked of these data was whether perceptions of past, present, and future stress are interrelated. The findings with regard to this question are summarized by the topological representation (Lewin 1935) in Figure 5.6. The findings indicated that fit across adjacent time frames was more likely to be interrelated than fit across nonadjacent time frames, but only for motivational fit. Links across all the time frames were about equal and higher for cognitive fit (r in the .40s) than for motivational fit (r ranged from the low .20s to low .40s; all statistics are significant unless noted otherwise in the text). Commensurate dimensions of fit were more likely to be related across time frames (for example, the link between cognitive past and cognitive present fit) compared to links between noncommensurate dimensions (for example, the link between cognitive past and motivational present fit). Noncommensurate dimensions were most likely to be related within the same time frame (for example, the link between cognitive past and motivational past fit).

As a set, these findings illustrate that (a) there are interconnections among different dimensions of fit, (b) there are interconnectons among time frames; and (c) the interconnectedness among time frames depends on the

Figure 5.6 Links among cognitive and motivational fit in three times frames (Caplan et al. 1985).

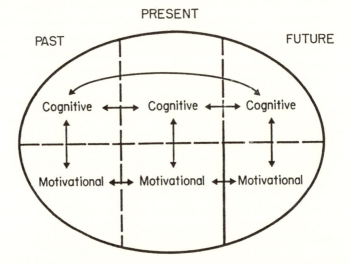

dimension of PE fit. A full interpretation of these links is detailed elsewhere (Caplan, Tripathi, Naidu 1985). Some organizationally related implications are considered below.

Implications regarding the ease with which ability and motivational fit can be changed. One of the findings represented by Figure 5.6 is that although thoughts about past, present, and future were correlated positively, they were more so for cognitive fit (a potential abilities fit) than for motivational fit. This suggests the hypothesis (which remains to be tested), that fit for abilities is perceived as more stable than fit for motivation or effort. It is possible that abilities and motivational PE fit differ *objectively* in how easily they are changed by both the person and by the organization. Abilities fit may be resistant to change to the extent that people perceive traits as unalterable—that is, perceive that their behaviors *are* trait-like.

If people perceive that their abilities are unalterable, they will resist attempts to change the technology they use, particularly if the proposed changes will require them to develop new patterns of abilities (Coch and French 1948). Organizations appear to recognize this resistance. Decision-makers prefer to avoid suggesting changes in P or E that might affect abilities fit and instead make use of changes in P or E that might effect motivational fit. For example, the development of new technology to fit employee needs is the choice of last resort, because both of these involve down time from productivity and are consequently expensive. More often, organizations (particularly large ones) make relatively frequent changes in their social organizations (reorganization) and in the provision of tangible (new compensation packages) and abstract commodities in order to convey social power, prestige, and the potential to exercise control (Katz and Kahn 1978; Pfeffer 1978). Under such circumstances, technology may become involved only insofar as it implies some social reward. (For example, there were anecdotes in the 1960s about providing top executives with "front office" computers. These executives did not know how to use the computers, but that did not matter. They could display proudly the impressive hardware in their office areas and let clients know that this was a "modern" organization. Today, computers are used less to provide motivational fit and more to represent a new level of demands-ability fit required by the organization).

When Are Abilities and Motivational Fit Achieved in Organizations?

It is hypothesized that a major achievement of good PE fit for abilities is probably accomplished in two stages, the first of which will be during personnel selection. Such selection will attempt to choose people who have potential for further training (that is, further adaptability) in order to minimize resistance to foreseeable and unforeseeable change. At the second stage, additional good fit for abilities will be produced by the organization by subjecting the person to training and socialization ("this is how we do things in this corporation"). Persons who might wish to achieve good fit by changing the organization (E) rather than their own abilities (P), and who are in subordinate positions, are likely to be selected out by this two-stage process. The preceding statement is not a prescription but rather a description of what is probably the typical behavior of organizations.[7]

Although motivational fit can, in principle, be accomplished by using selection, the criteria for selection remain elusive. The hypothesized turbulence of the social-psychological environment of organizations (compared to the relative stability of technology) means that the maintenance of motivation is more likely to be an ongoing process rather than one that can be handled by selection. If the maintenance of motivation were not a continual problem, organizations would not have to constantly plan how to distribute rewards more adequately in order to improve productivity and maintain commitment.

Implications of the spillover between cognitive and motivational fit. As represented by the model in Figure 5.6, motivational and cognitive fit were positively interrelated only within the same time frame; cognitive fit from one time frame and motivational fit from another were never interrelated (average r of .46 versus .20, respectively). This suggests that attempts to change one dimension of PE fit may have spillover effects onto other forms of fit within the same time frame. For example, changes in the organization that alter cognitive fit may lead, in some cases, to simultaneous alterations in motivational fit. Until skill in using technological innovations is achieved, the experience of poor performance may discourage employees and lead to psychological resistance. Once skill is achieved, there may be bursts of energy in applying the skill—a honeymoon period of innovation. Whereas the skill may remain over time, the enthusiasm to apply it may wane and need to be maintained. In summary, during initial periods of change in procedures, poor ability fit may generate poor motivational fit, and good ability fit may generate good motivational fit.

How do different time frames influence emotional well-being?. Research shows that people tend to view their past behavior, compared to their future behavior, as more uncontrollable, more inevitable, and more influenced by inherent traits or stable abilities such as intelligence and cognitive complexity (Janoff-Bulman and Brickman 1981; Fischoff 1975; Miller and Porter 1980). In contrast, people tend to think of their future behavior as more controllable and less influenced by inherent traits and stable abilities (Taylor 1983). It has been suggested that such beliefs are maintained because they enhance self-esteem (Brickman et al. 1982; Frankel and Snyder 1978). Perceptions of the past as being unalterable can lead us to believe that there are no better ways in which the past could have been relived, a palatable alternative to remorse. A belief that the future is malleable, should we wish to control it, is preferable to a sense of helplessness. To return to Susan Green's case, her employers may have viewed her ability to handle responsibility as stable, unchanged from when she was first hired; she may have viewed it as less trait-like and more controllable and unstable. Consequently, her anticipated lack of fit, rather than her past fit for responsibility, may have been a highly salient source of dissatisfaction for her.

These dynamics of time frames appear to be present in the study just described. Cognitive fit, compared to motivational fit, was a better predictor of well-being, regardless of time frame. Nevertheless, there were some differences. Cognitive fit was a better predictor of well-being when it dealt with the past or present rather than with the future. On the other hand, motivational fit performed best as a predictor of well-being when it dealt with anticipated fit. (The average multiple R using both dimensions of fit across all three time frames was a .32, the range being .23 to .51, with only the lowest coefficient being nonsignificant.)

These findings suggest that *motivational* occupational fit should be a more important determinant of current employee well-being when such fit deals with the employee's *anticipations* of future adjustment rather than with thoughts about present or past adjustment. *Abilities* fit should be a more salient predictor of well-being when it deals with *present* and *past time frames* rather than the future.

Additional research is needed to determine if these findings and their associated hypotheses generalize to work organizations. If they do, they would have the following implications. The well-being of organizational members and perhaps their commitment and productivity should be most influenced by perceptions of motivational fit and by other dimensions of PE fit that are perceived as unstable and controllable, if such perceptions deal with expectations about the future. Well-being and performance should also be influenced by recollections and perceptions of past and current ability fit (that is, how well their particular sets of skills match with those required to do the job), if those abilities are viewed by the employee as stable and uncontrollable or unalterable. This would suggest that helping employees think about their *past effort* will not influence their emotional well-being and performance as much as counseling them about their *past stable traits* in doing the job ("Recall that you are basically a dependable and creative person"). Similarly, helping employees think about their *future stable traits* should not be as likely to influence their emotional well-being and performance as much as helping them focus on their *anticipated effort* ("Think about how much you can achieve if you work at it").

Summary. The time frames that occupy organizational members' thoughts about PE fit remain a largely unexplored dimension of this field. This gap in knowledge exists even though social organizations operate in a world of traditions (precedents) and expectations (unrealized and sought-after futures). The study of time frames provides a potentially rich array of research areas dealing with how past and anticipated characteristics of the person and the environment influence the well-being and performance of organizational members.

Which Dimensions of PE Fit Should Be Examined in Organizations?

Cognitive and motivational fit are only two dimensions from a potentially larger array. Other studies of PE fit in work organizations have conceptualized fit along other dimensions, including quantitative work load, responsibility for persons, role ambiguity, and task complexity.

Overviews of the litrature on coping (Sutton and Kahn 1986; Lazarus and Folkman 1984; Rothbaum, Weisz, and Snyder 1982) suggest that there are three other basic dimensions that can describe an organizational member's relationship with the environment: control, predictability, and meaning. PE fit may be a useful concept with regard to each of these three dimensions in organizational settings. For example, people differ in how much control they prefer (Burger and Cooper 1979); more control is not always preferable to less. Control will be rejected when people feel that it is not legitimate for them to exercise such control (for example, because that is the union's responsibility"; French et al. 1960) or when excess control means excess responsibility for undesirable outcomes (Rodin, Rennert, and Solomon 1980; Bazerman 1982).

Similarly, there appear to be individual differences in the amount of predictability and meaning people want in their lives. This notion of fit has been studied under the rubric of "tolerance for ambiguity" (Frenkel-Brunswik 1949; Kahn et al. 1964; French, Caplan, and Harrison 1982).

Rothbaum and colleagues (1982) suggest that control, prediction, and meaning represent a hierarchy of methods for coping with the environment. As an illustration, if one cannot control one's superior in an organization, then the fall-back position is to develop methods for predicting the superior's behavior so that one is prepared for it in advance ("Here comes the boss, look busy!") If prediction fails, then perhaps one should attempt to derive a sense of passive control by focusing on the meaning of the ensuing events (Frankl 1962).

This notion of a hierarchy of coping options can be explored via PE fit theory. The relative powers of control, predictability, and meaning fit as predictors of emotional well-being may indicate the stage of coping occupied by a person or group within an organization. Changes in the relative saliencies of these dimensions of fit as predictors of well-being may indicate how organizational interventions are moving people up and down this coping hierarchy.

Types of PE Fit and Their Implications for Well-Being

The term "dimension" has been used to refer to the quality of fit that is being assessed. For example, responsibility and role ambiguity represent dimensions of PE fit. The term "type" will be used to refer to the *combination* of specific characteristics of the person and environment that are being examined to determine fit. For example, "ability-demand" and "need-supply" are *types* of fit.

Single dimensions of fit can be examined potentially in terms of more than one type of fit. For example, the *dimension* of responsibility fit can be examined in terms of the fit between *abilities* to handle responsibility and the *demands* of handling responsibility, or in terms of the fit between *needs* to have responsibility and the *supplies* or opportunities for assuming responsibility. Examples of how these types of PE fit are operationalized can be found in Kulka (1976).

Very little theory or empirical work has been generated on whether these different *types* of PE fit have different effects on well-being (as a singular exception, see Harrison 1978). To examine this topic, consider the following example. Suppose that the elements of PE fit for work load are measured for someone performing direct-data entry at a video display terminal. We will assume the person is processing claim forms for an insurance company. In this case the component measures of PE fit are constructed as follows:

PE Fit Component	Content
a. Demand (E)	How many total hours of key-entry *work* are *assigned* to you per day?
b. Opportunity/Resource/Supply*(E)	How many total hours of time per day are *available* to you to do the key-entry work assigned? (Available hours are those that are not taken up by other things you do, including rest periods and lunch.)
c. Ability (P)	After *how many* hours of key-entry work do you find that your performance begins to decline?
d. Need/Aspiration (P)	On the average, what is the *minimum* number of hours of key-entry work you feel you should do per day in order to feel *satisfied* with yourself?

*Resources, supplies, and opportunities are used interchangeably here as elements of the environment relevant to satisfying the needs and aspirations of the person. For ease of presentation, fit will be represented by the term "supplies" (as in needs-supplies fit and aspirations-supplies fit).

In this example, the four elements yield the following six types of fit:

a,b = demands-supplies fit (E,E)
a,c = demands-abilities fit (E,P)
a,d = demands-aspirations fit (E,P)
b,c = supplies-abilities fit (E,P)
b,d = supplies-aspirations fit (E,P)
c,d = abilities-aspirations fit (P,P)

The set of six types of fit provides a broad account of the nature of the person, the environment, and their relation. The first element, EE fit, is of consequence in determining whether or not the environment has provided its members with the types of resources required to meet the demands it imposes. For example, is there adequate time allotted by the environment to meet the demand? The last element, PP fit, is of consequence in determining whether the person has the capability required to meet the person's aspirations, or conversely, the motivation to perform, given the ability to do so. All the other combinations involve fit between P and E.

What are the differences that one might expect in well-being when PE fit varies for some of these types of fit as compared to others? The most basic hypothesis is that emotional well-being should be influenced by *demands-*

abilities fit when the employee has a strong need to satisfy others relative to the need to satisfy self, but by *needs-supplies* fit when the employee has a strong need to satisfy self relative to the need to satisfy others. The rationale is as follows: demands-ability fit is defined in terms of the requirements of others (E), whereas needs-supplies fit is defined in terms of the requirements of the person (P). It is assumed that demands-abilities fit will be more important than needs-supplies fit to persons with a strong need to satisfy others. (The logical exception would be PE fit between the *need* to satisfy others and the *opportunities* to do so.) It is similarly assumed that needs-supplies fit will be particularly important to persons with a strong need to satisfy themselves rather than others.

If these hypotheses are confirmed, they would suggest that the type as well as the dimension of fit are important conceptual determinants of well-being for people. Such findings would indicate that the language that people use to describe their job adjustment is a window into their motives, into how they want change in PE fit to be described to them by others, in order to satisfy their needs best. The person who describes a loss of responsibility for others (for example, a reduction in the number of subordinates one supervises) as a loss of "opportunity to supervise," rather than as a reduction in "demands on my abilities," may be making a significant motivational distinction regarding the meaning of the change.

Commensurate compared to noncommensurate types of fit. Demands-abilities and needs-supplies fit are commensurate types in that the E and P components are conceptually relevant to one another. Demands-needs and supplies-abilities PE fit are noncommensurate types. Demands-needs fit deals with an E measure relevant to the need to satisfy others ("How much do others expect of you?"), and a P measure relevant to the need to satisfy oneself ("How much do you expect from them?"). Supplies-abilities fit deals with an E measure relevant to the need to satisfy oneself ("How much do they provide you?"), and a P measure relevant to the need to satisfy others ("How much do you provide to them?").

The noncommensurate types of fit should have less predictive power than the commensurate types. This hypothesis is more than a purely academic exercise. Note that PE fit is an interactionist theory that emphasizes the importance of commensurate measurement. If commensurability is an important aspect of the theory, a test of the above conjecture should demonstrate it and point the way for more valid and, consequently, more useful measures of PE fit.

EE and PP fit. It is unlikely that the two forms of fit that are wholly characteristic of the environment (demands-supplies fit) and the person (abilities-needs fit) will have much of an effect on emotional well-being, although they may be of use for the diagnostic purposes described above. Demands-supplies fit may be a potentially necessary, but not sufficient condition for well-being. One expects that there will be certain resources available with which to meet demands. This is an enabling type of fit that must be met by the person's own abilities and aspirations. A similar argument can be made regarding the necessary, but not sufficient, quality of ability-aspiration fit.

If *both* abilities-aspirations fit and demands-opportunities fit are good, there will still be an insufficient set of conditions for promoting employee well-being. To illustrate this, suppose an employee aspires to a higher level of supervisory responsibility than for which there are opportunities. Then perfect fit between abilities and aspirations and between demands and opportunities will not be sufficient to promote maximum well-being. Consequently, although it is expected that ability-aspiration and demand-opportunity fit will have some positive effects on well-being, demands-ability and needs-opportunity fit should have much stronger effects. Such hypotheses are an agenda for future research aimed at validating distinctions among needs, abilities, demands, and supplies.

THE EFFECT OF CHANGES IN PE FIT ON WELL-BEING: POTENTIAL MODERATORS

Although PE fit theory is intended to deal with the dynamics of adjustment over time, very little attention has been paid to dynamic process. It is likely that this process of influencing well-being involves how much PE fit changes as well as the mechanisms by which it changes. The literature on stress suggests that the mechanisms might include whether or not the change in fit is controlled by the person (the particular acts of coping) and anyone else who is involved in the change (a matter of social support). These moderators can determine whether improvement in PE fit is equally satisfying under all conditions or, for example, only when self-controlled. The moderators can also determine whether people can *tolerate* PE misfit emotionally and physically.[8]

Control

It is likely that improvements in PE fit will produce stronger effects on well-being when people perceive that they have internal rather than external control over those changes. Even if fit improves, a sense of external control may detract from the sense of accomplishment (deCharms 1968). Thus, if Susan Green were to be promoted to a sought-after position of more responsibility, she might feel less satisfaction if she learned that the promotion was the result of someone "pulling rank" rather than her ability.

The exact costs and benefits of having control over changes in PE fit appears to be a complex area for study. In cases where a worsening in PE fit occurs, a sense of control may provide the person with the reassuring cognition that the event is controllable, and therefore avoidable in the future

(Janoff-Bulman 1979). On the other hand, if the employee is given and assumes a sense of control for changes in future fit, that will increase the risk that others will blame the employee for any worsening in PE fit.

It would be worthwhile to determine if the mechanism of participation in decision-making would help solve this apparent dilemma. It is hypothesized that in the event that participation results in poor PE fit, the responsibility for blame is shared, and therefore, diffused—a reduced cost for the individual employee. If good PE fit results, the sharing of responsibility should enable a large number of persons to make an internal attribution of contributing to the outcome. No research is known which tests these hypothesized relations among success and failure in changing PE fit, degree of participative decision-making, attribution, and well-being.

Other Cognitions

Closely related to the perception of control is a set of cognitions that Kobasa (1979) has labeled as "hardiness." These cognitions should enable employees who are facing a worsening in PE fit to persist in overcoming it, and to experience relatively low levels of emotional strain under those circumstances. One of these potentially moderating cognitions is a view of poor fit as an opportunity for positive growth, promoting challenge rather than threat (Antonovsky 1979). For example, Susan Green might have decided to view the lack of fit as a call to reeducate her employer about her skills in managing other employees.

Another potentially moderating cognition is that lack of fit provides an opportunity to derive some meaning from life that might not have presented itself in more fortunate circumstances (Frankl 1962; Taylor 1983; Bulman and Wortman 1977). Thus, Susan Green might have decided to "bite the bullet" and view her frustration as a lesson about the world of work (fortunately for Susan and for her new employer, she did not choose this option, and was able to cope at a higher level—the exercise of control).

Similarly, the *commitment to the process* of improving the poor fit rather than focusing on the outcome (Antonovsky 1979) should buffer the hypothesized effects of poor PE fit on well-being. This tactic was identified in Hindu philosophy more than 2,000 years ago under the rubric of "detachment" from outcomes. Commitment to the process should provide a buffer between poor fit and well-being by allowing the person to focus on the *methods* for pursuing a solution for the sake of the pursuit, rather than dwelling on the discrepancy between the goal and the current state. In the case of Susan Green, she no doubt could have derived considerable satisfaction from the mere act of being able to engage in charting her own career course *aside* from the result that it produced.

In sum, some of these cognitions might enable employees to persist in overcoming poor fit. Such cognitions might trigger a problem-solving approach (diagnoses, generation of alternative solutions, evaluation of alternatives, and so on). This would seem to be the case for the set of cognitions associated with hardiness.

There are conditions, however, where one has little control over a situation. Under such circumstances, searching for meaning (Rothbaum, Weisz, and Snyder 1982) and adopting emotion-focused coping (Folkman and Lazarus 1980), that is, attempting to repress unpleasant affect without attempting to alter the lack of PE fit (Baum, Fleming, and Singer 1983), may be more productive responses. Consequently, the controllability of the situation will determine whether or not a particular cognitive response will produce buffering or, if inappropriate, make matters worse.

Coping

As noted earlier, coping is defined in PE fit theory as behavior that changes the objective nature of PE fit. It is distinguished from cognitive responses in that it involves *more* than new ways of thinking about the problem, or denying that the lack of PE fit exists. Coping can involve attempts to alter the environment (such as getting others to reduce the work load) or attempts to change the objective self (such as training to increase one's level of skill). There is no research on the emotional and behavioral consequences of attempting to overcome poor PE fit by changing P as compared with E. Some basic research would be helpful. As was suggested earlier, people may be more resistant to adjusting by learning new skills than by changing their effort. Researchers of coping need to assess the effects on well-being of the mix of changes in E and P and their joint consequences for well-being. Adjustment by changing E may produce changes in P and vice vesa. For example, reducing work load (E) slightly to improve fit may promote an increased feeling of accomplishment and result in an increased level of aspiration (P).

Coping is expected to have direct and beneficial effects on well-being in addition to improving PE fit. This will be the case if the mere *act* of coping gives the person reassurance that the situation is potentially controllable, thus reducing the emotional strain produced by the poor fit for need for control. Anecdotal evidence suggests that when people are faced with an upsetting event or problem, they often feel better just working on its solution, even before the outcome of their efforts is known to them.

Social Support

The buffering hypothesis states with regard to social support that it will reduce the effects of stressors on strain (Cobb 1976). Thus, social support should reduce the effect of decrements of PE fit on outcomes such as anxiety and depression. Social support should buffer the effects of poor fit on emotional strain because of the possible effects of social support on two moderators just discussed—cognitions and the ability to cope. Socially supportive employees may help another employee view a problem in a more constructive manner (Caplan 1979a, 1979b). Such support can change, for example, a set of unhardy cognitions into a set of hardy ones ("view this as an interesting challenge"; "think about the process, not the outcome," and so on). Furthermore, social support from employees, particularly in the form of trust or referent power (French and Raven 1959), may make the person maximally responsive to advice and training from those employees who want to help the person develop increased abilities to cope (Caplan 1979a, 1979b; Janis 1983).

The literature is mixed in its support for the buffering hypothesis. Some studies find confirming evidence (Karasek, Kionstantinos, and Chaudhry 1982; LaRocco, House, and French 1980; Abbey, Abramis, and Caplan 1985; House and Wells 1978); others do not (Thoits 1982). A recent review of community-based, random-sample surveys concluded, however, that buffering occurred consistently in studies with good methodology and rarely in studies with poor measures or inadequate statistical methods of analysis (Kessler and Mcleod in press). It is conceivable that buffering will not take place when the recipient perceives the donor as having ulterior motives, such as social control (Tripathi, Caplan, and Naidu, 1986). Consequently, context as well as poor research methodology may play a role in explaining the mixed support for the buffering hypothesis.

Participation

In the study of 23 occupations, workers who reported social support from their supervisor or others at work were also more likely to report high levels of participation ($r = .25$ and $.33$ respectively, both $p < .001$; Caplan et al. 1980). This suggests that participation may increase social support, and may therefore indirectly buffer the undesirable effects of poor PE fit on well-being. French and his colleagues (1982) searched for a buffering effect of participation in the data on the 23 occupations, but found no support. On the other hand, Karasek (1979) found that job decision latitude, a concept that overlaps heavily with that of participation, did buffer the effects of job demands (primarily quantitative work load) on self-report measures of exhaustion and depression. Karasek's findings are based on a replication across random-sample surveys of the male work forces of the United States and Sweden. Unfortunately, Karasek's data did not include measures of PE fit.

Why did one study fail to produce buffering effects of participation whereas another study succeeded? The difference may lie in the difference between participation and decision-latitude concepts. Karasek's measure of decision latitude adds to participation a measure of how much a person's job requires high levels of skill and creativity and provides opportunities to learn new things. Putting both studies together, the implication is that participation may not buffer the deleterious effects of poor PE fit on well-beng, in jobs where there are no objective opportunities to be creative and constructive in the application of participation (see also French, Israel, and Aas 1960).

CONCLUSION

Person-environment fit theory reminds us that the behavior of people in organizations (and in other social settings) is a function of transactions between the person and the environment. This is *not* common sense. Research on the attribution of blame and responsibility clearly demonstrates that we tend to simplify the world by attributing the cause of success to ourselves (P) and the cause of failure to external circumstances (E). We also tend to view the mistakes of others as due to their own ineptitude.

These elements of our cognitive natures must make it very difficult, on a day-to-day basis, to appreciate that behavior usually is a function of person *and* environment. The search for adaptive solutions in organizations that takes into account the possibility of changing both P *and* E must, accordingly, be very counterintuitive. As a result, a search for solutions that consider changes in *both* P and E is probably achieved only with the greatest persistence and commitment to full and open problem-solving (Janis and Mann 1977).

Person-environment fit theory could provide a useful framework for examining the nature of human adjustment in this transactional mode, and this chapter has been concerned largely with the many questions that need to be addressed to enhance the constructive value of the theory. These questions have to do with the following:

1. Are there different consequences for well-being and productivity when one produces fit via changes in P, E, or in both?

2. Does it make a difference if the change in fit that is produced is under or not under the target person's control? How is the mechanism of participation related to such control?

3. When poor PE fit occurs, does it make a difference in the probability that good fit will be attained if the person views the task as a challenge or as an adversive demand?

4. Are well-being and productivity influenced only by current perceptions of PE fit, or do thoughts about past and future fit also have affective and motivational properties?

5. If one is to perform a diagnosis of PE fit in an organization, what are the most basic elements that should be examined? Are they, for example, fit with regard to control, predictability, and meaning? Or should they deal with quantity (load) and quality (complexity and responsibility, for example)?

6. If organizations attempt to promote well-being by making changes in the objective nature of the job environment and the objective nature of the person (abilities and skills), what types of principles can guide such efforts to ensure that objective improvements in fit correspond to perceptions that improvement has taken place? What are the ethical ways in which this correspondence can be attained?

7. Is it possible to develop a measure of PE fit that represents the fit of *all* the stakeholders in the organization, or a method for representing the values attained by different coalitions? In this way, one might address the consequences for the total organization of improving fit in particular components of an organization.

These questions represent a tall order for social research. The ability to generate useful answers will depend on the ingenuity of social scientists as well as the interest and cooperation of work organizations and their employees. The combined efforts of these parties will make such questions more than purely academic.

NOTES

1. The reader is referred to Hammond and Adelman (1976) for a practical illustration of how values, when made explicit, can be combined with facts to make value-maximizing choices.

2. One can also examine person-person fit. For example, there is the fit between one's aspirations and abilities.

3. One can also ask automobile mechanics the same question. An automobile mechanic once told the author that it was impossible to find time to read the continual stream of technical memos, updates, and modifications of service procedures from the automobile manufacturer.

4. In one organization the author visited, too little work load threatened the employees' needs for job security. Not being occupied fully was a sign that the employee was not needed and was a sure target for an impending reduction in the work force.

5. As an informal experiment, try to get a secretary to develop a daily objective measure of his or her work load. Require that the measure represent a *fair* assessment of all the aspects of the work load that influence well-being. Holes in the fabric will quickly appear. In my own attempt at such an experiment, I noted that three manuscripts of 30 pages do not represent the same amount of work load as one 90-page manuscript being reworked completely for the third time (doctoral students and journal contributors may be especially mindful of the agony of revision as compared to the joy of first insight). Such an example, however, is a relatively easy one compared to developing an objective measure of PE fit on supervisory responsibility or task complexity that is meaningful to both employee and investigator.

6. Note that participation may be rejected by employees when it is seen as the legitimate domain of the union (French et al. 1960); when the topic is viewed as relatively inconsequential to the person; when it is viewed as a manipulative ploy of superiors; and when explicit decision rules exist and some superior or delegate can be entrusted to make use of those rules (Vroom and Yetton 1973).

7. The selection process should be relatively unimportant in organizations with an array of technologies, low status differentials between occupations, and a sense of

commitment to the community. A case in point is the kibbutz (Leviatan 1984). Here members are mostly born into the community-organization. Birth confirms a right of membership, although each individuald has the right to decide whether or not to become a member upon adulthood. The kibbutz has introduced a variety of technologies, in part, so that people can move to the part of the organization that best fits with their abilities and preferences. The commitment of the kibbutz to the total community means that opportunities are created for the individual member to choose the organizational setting most appropriate to his or her needs. This system is successful largely because both the individual and the organization recognize their mutual interdependence. Although such a system hardly describes the typical organization, it is worth mentioning here. The kibbutz example should remind us that much of our knowledge about the nature of adjustment is based on culturally determined access to how organizations behave, rather than on some sampling from the total universe of organizations.

8. The topic of stress *tolerance* again raises the important distinction between value and fact. Fact can determine methods for increasing toleration of poor PE fit. Values will determine whether toleration is desirable (perhaps to weather a brief organizational storm), or *intolerance* is the more socially and individually appropriate response.

Acknowledgments—Preparation of this chapter was made possible in part by federal grant MH39675. Mary Jo Griewahn assisted in the preparation of the text.

REFERENCES

Abbey, A., D. J. Abramis, and R. D. Caplan. 1985. "Effects of Different Sources of Social Support and Social Conflict on Emotional Well-being." *Basic and Applied Social Psychology* 6:111-29.

Antonovsky, A. 1979. *Health, Stress and Coping* (San Francisco, CA: Jossey-Bass).

Baum, A., R. Fleming, and J. E. Singer. 1983. "Coping with Victimization by Technological Disaster." *Journal of Social Issues* 39, no. 2: 117-38.

Baekelund, F. and L. Lundwall. 1975. "Dropping out of Treatment: A Critical Review." *Psychological Bulletin* 82: 738-83.

Bazerman, M. H. 1982. "Impact of Personal Control on Performance: Is Added Control Always Beneficial?" *Journal of Applied Psychology* 67, no. 4: 472-79.

Blake, R. R. and J. S. Mouton. 1964. *The Managerial Grid: Key Orientations for Achieving Production through People* (Houston, TX: Gulf Publishing).

_____. 1985. "How to Achieve Integration on the Human Side of Merger." *Organizational Dynamics* 13: 41-56.

Brickman, P., V. C. Rabinowitz, J. Karuza, Jr., D. Coates, E. Cohn, and L. Kidder. 1982. "Models of Helping and Coping." *American Psychologist* 37, no. 4: 368-84.

Bulman, R. J. and C. B. Wortman. 1977. "Attributions of Blame and Coping in the 'Real World': Severe Accident Victims React to Their Lot." *Journal of Personality and Social Psychology* 35: 351-63.

Burger, J. M. and H. M. Cooper. 1979. "The Desirability of Control." *Motivation and Emotion* 3: 381-93.

Campbell, A., P. F. Converse, and W. L. Rodgers. 1976. *Quality of American Life: Perceptions, Evaluations, and Satisfaction* (New York: Russell-Sage).

Campbell, D. B. 1974. "A Program to Reduce Coronary Heart Disease Risk by Altering Job Stresses." Doctoral dissertation, University of Michigan, 1973. *Dissertation Abstracts International* 35: 564-B. University Microfilms no. 74-15681.

Caplan, R. D. 1979a. "Patient, Provider and Organization: Hypothesized Determinants of Adherence." In *New Directions in Patient Compliance*, edited by S. J. Cohen (Lexington, MA: D. C. Heath), pp. 75-110.

_____. 1979b. "Social Support, Person-Environment Fit, and Coping." In *Mental Health and the Economy*, edited by L. Ferman and J. Gordus (Kalamazoo, MI: W. E. Upjohn Institute for Employment Research), pp. 89-138.

_____. 1983. "Person-Environment Fit: Past, Present, and Future." In *Stress Research: New Directions for the 1980s*, edited by C. Cooper (London: Wiley), pp. 35-78.

Caplan, R. D., S. Cobb, J. R. P. French, Jr., R. V. Harrison, and S. R. Pineau, Jr. 1980. *Job Demands and Worker Health: Main Effects and Occupational Differences* (Ann Arbor, MI: Institute for Social Research). Originally published as HEW publication no. (NIOSH) 75-160, 1975.

Caplan, R. D., R. C. Tripathi, and R. K. Naidu, 1985. "Subjective Past, Present, and Future Fit: Effects on Anxiety, Depression and Other Indicators of Well-Being." *Journal of Personality and Social Psychology* 48: 180-97.

Cobb, S. 1976. "Social Support as a Moderator of Life Stress." *Psychosomatic Medicine* 38: 300-14.

Coch, L. and J. R. P. French, Jr. 1948. "Overcoming Resistance to Change." *Human Relations* 4: 512-33.

Crozier, M. 1964. *The Bureaucratic Phenomenon* (Chicago, IL: University of Chicago Press).

deCharms, R. 1968. *Personal Causation: The Internal Affective Determinants of Behavior* (New York: Academic Press).

Denison, D. R. 1984. "Bringing Corporate Culture to the Bottom Line." *Organizational Dynamics* 13:5-22.

Fischoff, B. 1975. "Hindsight = Foresight: The Effect of Outcome Knowledge on Judgment under Uncertainty." *Journal of Experimental Psychology: Human Perception and Performance* 1: 288-99.

Folkman, S. and R. S. Lazarus. 1980. "An Analysis of Coping in a Middle-Aged Community Sample." *Journal of Health and Social Behavior* 21: 219-39.

Foote, A. and J. C. Erfurt. 1981. "Effectiveness of Comprehensive Employee Assistance Programs at Reaching Alcoholics. *Journal of Drug Issues* 2: 217-32.

Frankel, A. and M. L. Snyder. 1978. "Poor Performance Following Unsolvable Problems: Learned Helplessness or Egotism?" *Journal of Personality and Social Psychology* 36: 1415-23.

Frankl, V. E. 1962. *Man's Search for Meaning* (Boston, MA: Beacon Press).

French, J. R. P., Jr. and R. D. Caplan. 1972. "Organizational Stress and Individual Strain." In *The Failure of Success*, edited by A. J. Marrow (New York: AMACOM), pp. 30-66.

French, J. R. P., Jr., R. D. Caplan, and R. V. Harrison. 1982. *The Mechanisms of Job Stress and Strain* (London: Wiley).

French, J. R. P., Jr., J. Israel, and D. Aas. 1960. "An Experiment in Participation in a Norwegian Factory." *Human Relations* 13: 3-19.

French, J. R. P., Jr., E. Kay, and H. H. Meyer. 1966. "Participation and the Appraisal System." *Human Relations* 19: 3-20.

French, J. R. P., Jr. and B. Raven. 1959. "The Bases of Social Power." In *Studies in Social Power*, edited by D. Cartwright (Ann Arbor, MI: Institute for Social Research), pp. 150-67.

French, J. R. P., Jr., W. Rodgers, and S. Cobb. 1974. "Adjustment as Person-Environment Fit." In *Coping and Adaptation*, edited by G. V. Coelho, D. A. Hamburg, and J. E. Adams (New York: Basic Books).

French, W. and C. Bell. 1973. *Organization Development: Behavioral Science Interventions for Organization Improvement* (Englewood Cliffs, NJ: Prentice-Hall).

Frenkel-Brunswik, E. 1949. "Intolerance of Ambiguity as an Emotional and Perceptual Personality Variable." *Journal of Personality* 18: 108-43.

Frese, M. 1985. "Stress at Work and Psychosomatic Complaints: A Causal Interpretation." *Journal of Applied Psychology* 70: 314-28.

Gardell, B. 1971. "Technology, Alienation and Mental Health in the Modern Industrial Environment." In *Society, Stress and Disease*, vol. 1, edited by L. Levi (London: Oxford University Press), pp. 148-80.

Hammond, K. R., and L. Adelman. 1976. "Science, Values and Human Judgment." *Science* 194: 389-96.

Harrison, R. V. 1978. "Person-Environment Fit and Job Stress." In *Stress at Work,* edited by C. L. Cooper and R. Payne (New York: John Wiley and Sons).

House, J. S. 1972. "The Relationship of Intrinsic and Extrinsic Work Motivations to Occupational Stress and Coronary Heart Disease Risk." Doctoral dissertation, University of Michigan. *Dissertation Abstracts International* 33: 2514A. University Microfilms no. 72-29094.

House, J. S., V. Strecher, H. L. Melzner, and C. Robbins. 1986. "Occupational Stress and Health among Men and Women in the Tecumseh Community Health Study." *Journal of Health and Social Behavior* 27: 62-77.

House, J. S. and J. A. Wells. 1978. "Occupational Stress, Social Support and Health." In *Reducing Occupational Stress: Proceedings of a Conference,* edited by A. McLean, G. Black and M. Colligan. U.S. Department of Health, Education and Welfare, HEW (NIOSH) publication no. 78-140, 8-29.

Jackson, S. 1983. "Participation in Decision Making as a Strategy for Reducing Job-Related Strain." *Journal of Applied Psychology* 68: 3-19.

Jamal, M. 1985. "Relationship of Job Stress to Job Performance: A Study of Managers and Blue Collar Workers." *Human Relations* 38: 409-24.

Janis, I. L. 1983. "The Role of Social Support in Adherence to Stressful Decision." *American Psychologist* 38: 143-60.

Janis, I. L. and L. Mann. 1977. *Decision Making: A Psychological Analysis of Conflict, Choice, and Commitment* (New York: The Free Press).

Janoff-Bulman, R. 1979. "Behavioral versus Characterological Self-Blame: Inquiries into Depression and Rape." *Journal of Personality and Social Psychology* 37: 1798-1810.

Janoff-Bulman, R. and P. Brickman. 1981. "Expectations and What People Learn from Failure." In *Expectations and Actions* edited by N. T. Feather (Hillsdale, NJ: Lawrence Erlbaum), pp. 207-37.

Kahana, E. 1978. "A Congruence Model of Person-Environment Interaction." In *Theory Development in Environments and Aging*, edited by M. P. Lawton (New York: Wiley).

Kahana, E., J. Liang, and B. J. Felton. 1980. "Alternative Models of Person-Environment Fit: Prediction of Morale in Three Homes for the Aged." *Journal of Gerontology* 35: 584-95.

Kahn, R. L., D. M. Wolfe, R. P. Quinn, J. D. Snoek, and R. A. Rosenthal. 1964. *Organizational Stress: Studies in Role Conflict and Ambiguity* (New York: Wiley).

Kanter, R. M. 1982. "Dilemmas of Managing Participation." *Organizational Dynamics* 11:5-27.

Karasek, R. A., Jr. 1979. "Job Demands, Job Decision Latitude, and Mental Strain: Implications for Job Redesign." *Administrative Science Quarterly* 24: 285-308.

Karasek, R. A., P. T. Kionstantinos, and S. S. Chaudhry. 1982. "Coworker and Supervisor Support as Moderators of Associations between Task Characteristics and Mental Strain." *Journal of Occupational Behaviour* 3: 181-200.

Kasl, S. V. 1978. "Epidemiological Contributions to the Study of Work Stress." In *Stress at Work*, edited by C. L. Cooper and R. Payne (New York: Wiley).

Katz, D. and R. L. Kahn. 1978. *Social Psychology of Organizations* (New York: Wiley).

Kessler, R. C. and J. D. McLeod. 1985. "Social Support and Mental Health in Community Samples." In *Social Support and Health*, edited by Sheldon Cohen and Leonard Syme (New York: Academic Press), pp. 219-240.

Kobasa, S. C. 1979. "Stressful Life Events, Personality, and Health: An Inquiry into Hardiness." *Journal of Personality and Social Psychology* 37: 1-11.

Kobasa, S. C. and M. C. Puccetti. 1983. "Personality and Social Resources in Stress Resistance. *Journal of Personality and Social Psychology* 45: 839-50.

Kohn, M. L. 1969. *Class and Conformity: A Study in Values* (Homewood, IL: Free Press).

Kulka, R. A. 1976. "Person-Environment Fit in the High School: A Validation Study. Doctoral dissertation, University of Michigan, 1975, 2 vols. *Dissertation Abstracts International* 36: 5352B. University Microfilms no. 76-9438.

——. 1979. "Interaction as Person-Environment Fit." *New Directions for Methodology of Behavioral Science* 2: 55-71.

Kulka, R. A., D. M. Klingel, and D. W. Mann. 1980. "School Crime and Disruption as a Function of Student School Fit: An Empirical Assessment." *Journal of Youth and Adolescence* 9: 353-70.

LaRocco, J. M., J. S. House, and J. R. P. French, Jr. 1980. "Social Support, Occupational Stress, and Health." *Journal of Health and Social Behavior* 21: 202-18.

Lazarus, R. S. 1966. *Psychological Stress and Coping Process* (New York: McGraw-Hill.

——. 1983. "The Costs and Benefits of Denial." In *The Denial of Stress*, edited by S. Breznitz (New York: International Universities Press), pp. 1-30.

Lazarus, R. S. and S. Folkman. 1984. *Stress, Appraisal, and Coping* (New York: Springer).

Lazarus, R. S. and R. Launier. 1978. "Stress-Related Transactions between Person and Environment." In *Perspectives in Interactional Psychology*, edited by L. Pervin and M. Lewis (New York: Plenum), pp. 287-327.

Leviatan, U. 1982. "Counterbalancing the Ill Effects of Hierarchy: The Case of the Kibbutz Industrial Organization." *Journal of Social and Biological Structure* 5: 141-59.

_____. 1984. "Research Note: The Kibbutz as a Situation for Cross-Cultural Research." *Organization Studies 5*, no. 1: 67-75.

Levi, L., ed. 1972. *Stress and Distress in Response to Psychosocial Stimuli* (Oxford: Pergamon Press).

Lewin, K. 1935. *A Dynamic Theory of Personality* (New York: McGraw-Hill).

_____. 1947. "Frontiers in Group Dynamics." *Human Relations* 1: 5-41.

Likert, R. 1961. *New Patterns of Management* (New York: McGraw-Hill.

_____. 1967. *The Human Organization: Its Management and Value* (New York: McGraw-Hill).

Locke, E. and D. Schweiger. 1979. "Participation in Decision Making: One More Look." In *Research on Organization Behavior*, edited by Barry M. Staw and L. L. Cummings (Greenwich, CT: JAI Press).

Magnusson, D. 1982. "Situational Determinants of Stress: An Interactional Perspective." In *Handbook of Stress Theoretical and Clinical Aspects*, edited by L. Goldberger and S. Breznitz (New York: The Free Press), pp. 231-53.

Mann, F. C. 1957. "Studying and Creating Change: A Means to Understanding Social Organization." *Resarch in Industrial Human Relations* 17: 146-67.

Maslow, A. 1943. "A Theory of Human Motivation." *Psychological Review* 50: 370-96.

McGrath, J. E. 1976. "Stress and Behavior in Organizations." In *Handbook of Industrial and Organizational Psychology*, edited by M. D. Dunnette (Chicago, IL: Rand McNally).

McGrath, J. E. and N. L. Rotchford. 1983. "Time and Behavior in Organizations." *Research in Organizational Behavior* 5: 57-101.

Meichenbaum, D. 1985. *Stress Inoculation Training: A Clinical Guidebook* (New York: Pergamon).

Miller, D. T. and C. A. Porter. 1980. "Effects of Temporal Perspective on the Attribution Process." *Journal of Personality and Social Psychology* 39: 532-41.

Miller, J. G. 1960. "Information Input Overload and Psychopathology." *American Journal of Psychiatry* 116: 695-704.

Murray, H. A. 1938. *Explorations in Personality* (New York: Oxford University Press).

Neale, M. S., J. S. Singer, and G. E. Schwartz. 1987. "A Systems Assessment of Occupational Stress: Evaluating a Hotel during Contract Negotiations." Chapter 7, this volume.

Pervin, L. A. 1967a. "Satisfaction and Perceived Self-Environment Similarity: A Semantic Differential Study of Student-College Interaction." *Journal of Personality* 35: 623-34.

_____. 1967b. "A Twenty-College Study of Student X College Interaction Using TAPE (Transactional Analysis of Personality and Environment): Rationale, Reliability, and Validity." *Journal of Educational Psychology* 58: 290-302.

———. 1968. "Performance and Satisfaction as a Function of Individual-Environment Fit." *Psychological Bulletin* 69: 56-68.

Pffefer, J. 1978. *Organizational Design* (Arlington Heights, IL: AHM Publishing Corp.).

Pinneau, S. R., Jr. 1975. "Effects of Social Support on Psychological and Physiological Strains." Doctoral dissertation, University of Michigan. University Microfilms no. 76-9491.

Rodin, J., K. Rennert, and S. K. Solomon. 1980. "Intrinsic Motivation for Control: Fact or Fiction?" In *Advances in Environmental Psychology. [Vol. 2]: Applications of Personal Control* edited by A. Baum and J. E. Singer (Hillsdale, NJ: Lawrence Erlbaum Associates).

Rothbaum, F., J. R. Weisz, and S. S. Snyder. 1982. "Changing the World and Changing the Self: A Two-Process Model of Perceived Control." *Journal of Personality and Social Psychology* 42, no. 1: 5-37.

Rotter, J. B. 1966. "Generalized Expectancies for Internal Versus External Control of Reinforcement." *Psychological Monographs: General and Applied* 80, whole no. 609: 1-28.

Sarason, I. G., R. E. Smith, and E. Diener. 1975. "Personality Research: Components of Variance Attributable to the Person and the Situation." *Journal of Personality and Social Psychology* 32: 199-204.

Stokols, D. 1979. "A Congruence Analysis of Human Stress." In *Stress and Anxiety*, vol. 6, edited by I. G. Sarason and C. D. Spielberger (Washington, D.C.: Hemisphere), pp. 27-53.

Sutton, R. I. and R. L. Kahn. 1986. "Prediction, Understanding, and Control as Antidotes to Organizational Stress. In *Handbook of Organizational Behavior*, edited by J. W. Lorsch (Englewood Cliffs, NJ: Prentice-Hall), pp. 272-85.

Tannenbaum, A., B. Kavcic, M. Rosner, M. Vianello, and G. Wieser. 1974. *Hierarchy in Organizations* (San Francisco, CA: Jossey-Bass).

Tannenbaum, A. S. and W. J. Kuleck, Jr. 1978. "The Effect on Organization Members of Discrepancy between Perceived and Preferred Rewards Implicit in Work." *Human Relations* 31: 809-22.

Taylor, S. E. 1983. "Adjustment to Threatening Events. A Theory of Cognitive Adaptation." *American Psychologist* 38: 1161-73.

Thoits, P. A. 1982. "Conceptual, Methodological, and Theoretical Problems in Studying Social Support as a Buffer against Life Stress." *Journal of Health and Social Behavior* 23: 145-59.

Tripathi, R. C., R. D. Caplan, and R. K. Naidu. 1986. "Accepting Advice: A Modifier of How Social Support Affects Well-Being." *Journal of Social and Personal Relationships* 3:213-28.

Vroom, V. H. and P. W. Yetton. 1973. *Leadership and Decision-Making* (Pittsburgh, PA: University of Pittsburgh Press).

Wall, T. P. and C. W. Clegg. 1981. "A Longitudinal Study of Group Work Design." *Journal of Occupational Behavior* 2: 32-43.

Winter, D. 1973. *The Power Motive* (New York: The Free Press).

6

MANAGING STRESS
IN TURBULENT TIMES

SUSAN E. JACKSON,
RANDALL S. SCHULER,
and DONALD J. VREDENBURGH

Why do organizational psychologists study stress? Because they believe stress is related to the way people at work feel and act. Like all psychologists, stress researchers seek to understand human behavior and experience. They are interested in a variety of processes and responses, including perceptions, emotions, cognitions, physiological changes, and overt behaviors. Historically, stress researchers have created a niche for themselves not by studying a unique set of feelings or behaviors but by studying people in unique types of circumstances, as in aversive situations. Volunteers in laboratory studies of stress may be given electric shocks or asked to watch repulsive films. People in field studies of stress are usually experiencing traumas such as the death of a loved one, their own impending death, major illnesses, surgery, natural disasters such as hurricanes and floods, or man-made disasters such as wars and nuclear accidents. In the past, at least, stress research meant studying people in situations that almost everyone agreed were "stressful."

More recently, the domain of our inquiry has broadened somewhat to include the study of nonaversive situations. Stress researchers now discuss concepts such as challenge, opportunity, and hardiness, and we have admitted events such as marriage, the addition of a child to one's family, and holiday celebrations to our list of "stressful" situations (Holmes and Rahe 1967). Parallel to this broadening view is an increasingly large nomological net of relevant constructs and operational variables. By the 1970s the number of stress-related studies had become unwieldy, and the number of relevant constructs was threatening to become unmanageable. The field had reached the point at which even the most cognitively complex person could barely keep track of the linkages holding together the many fragments. What was badly needed was a way to organize the pieces into a recognizable whole. Early work on this problem included identification of recurrent themes in the stress literature (Appley and Trumbull 1967; Lazarus 1966; McGrath 1970), and development of descriptive schemes and taxonomies (Beehr and Newman 1978). These were the first steps toward simplicity and clarity in a fragmented area of study. With this chapter, we hope to move our understanding of job stress one step further by presenting a theoretical framework for examining stress as a phenomenon that occurs across and within all levels in an organization. That is, we present a framework that links the individual's experience of job stress to work group processes and organizational conditions. Development of this framework required that we define stress in a way that would facilitate the integration of research conducted on individuals, groups, and organizations. By defining stress as uncertainty (McGrath 1976) it is possible to discuss stress as a phenomenon common to these three levels of analysis.

McGrath (1976) argued that perceived uncertainty is a key determinant of both physiological and behavioral stress reactions. McGrath's formulation of stress as uncertainty is gaining wide acceptance. For example, Schuler (1980) extended McGrath's work to define stress as a perceived dynamic state involving uncertainty about something important. Using a similar conceptualization, Beehr and Bhagat (1985) have shown how job stress research can be usefully reformulated and integrated by defining stress to be a function of the uncertainty of outcomes in a situation, the importance of those outcomes, and the duration of the situation. Beehr and Bhagat's argument is made convincing by the fact that several contributors to their edited volume were able to reformulate a variety of topics using an uncertainty framework. These topics include the person-environment fit model of job stress as discussed by Caplan in this volume (Van Harrison 1985), reactions to budget cuts (Jick 1985), dual-career couples (Gupta and Jenkins 1985), retirement (McGoldrick and Cooper 1985), and the career experiences of minority professionals (Ford 1985).

Like the authors cited above, we will argue that a better understanding can be gained of many phenomena that have been labeled "job stress" by focusing on the more narrow construct of uncertainty. Of course, not all phenomena that might be brought together under the label of "job stress" are covered by a definition of stress as uncertainty. But this narrowing of scope is counterbalanced by a significant gain in our ability to examine phenomena that cut across several levels of analysis. In other words, defining stress as uncertainty facilitates a systems-theory viewpoint. Such a perspective is particularly important, because it allows us to recognize and treat job stress as a true organizational phenomenon.

OVERVIEW OF THE UNCERTAINTY FRAMEWORK

In his excellent discussion of the development and use of psychological theories, McGuire (1983) describes four types of theories: guiding-idea, categorical or taxonomic, process, and axiomatic. Of these four types, axiomatic theories, which require the development of a small number of axioms that can be combined to yield more complex theorems, are the most sophisticated. The framework that will be presented here is not as sophisticated as an axiomatic theory. However, it does incorporate the elements of each of McGuire's three remaining types of theories, as described below.

Guiding Ideas Relevant to the Uncertainty Framework

McGuire (1983) describes guiding-idea theories as incomplete, partial depictions of the person. They are recognized as inadequate pictures of human behavior. Nevertheless, they are useful assumptions on which a set of integrated assertions can be built. Two guiding-idea theories form the foundation for the uncertainty framework: systems theory and an information-processing view of human nature.

Two primary assumptions comprising a systems perspective are (1) that any acting agent, such as a person, a group, or an organization, exists within and seeks survival through a surrounding environment; and (2) that any agent can be conceived of as a system embedded within other subsystems. In the context of organizational psychology, three subsystems or levels of analysis are typically recognized as agents: the individual, the group, and the organization. The systems-theory perspective is important to the uncertainty framework because it emphasizes the interdependence between uncertainty at any one level of analysis (the individual) and concurrent conditions at other levels of analysis (the group and the organization). Another important aspect of the systems theory is its explicit recognition that a system is *both* embedded in larger systems and composed of "smaller" subsystems. Subsystems within the same larger system are assumed to be interdependent. Thus, groups within organizations affect each other, in addition to affecting and being affected by the larger organization; individuals within groups are similarly linked. Furthermore, subsystems *within* the individual (such as cognitive and physiological systems) can be assumed to be interdependent. For stress researchers, this interface between a person's awareness and thoughts and the physiological subsystems has been of primary interest.

The second guiding idea underlying our uncertainty framework is a view of people as problem-solvers whose actions are both reasoned (Fishbein 1980) and goal oriented (Lewin 1951). This emphasizes the information-processing activities of a person that are initiated when a "problem" is posed (Howard and Scott 1965) that must be resolved before action can be taken. This view of people as problem-solvers helps define the boundary conditions for application of the uncertainty framework. Put simply, the necessary condition for activating the model is that a person be considering the question, "What will I do now?" When action is *not* needed, the uncertainty framework may not be relevant for understanding the person's responses. An important implication of this boundary condition is that uncertainty in and of itself is *not* viewed as a condition to be resolved, alleviated, or reduced whenever it exists.

The Taxonomic Component

Taxonomic theories are simplistic representations for organizing a large set of variables into a manageable number of categories (McGuire 1983). Recently, several such theories have been developed by stress researchers (Cooper and Marshall 1978; Beehr and Newman 1978). These provide useful checklists of independent and dependent variables to consider when conducting research on job stress. Such checklists are especially helpful when the research goal is to predict rather than explain phenomena.

The taxonomic component of the uncertainty framework is shown in Table 6.1. Like its forerunners, our taxonomy comprises organized lists of related variables. It is organized along two dimensions. The vertical dimensions represents three levels of analysis typically used for describing organizational behavior: the individual, the group, and the organization. The horizontal dimension of Table 6.1 represents time. Precursors of uncertainty are listed on the left and reactions are listed on the right. Uncertainty, which is a state that can be used to characterize the experiences of individuals, groups, and organizations, is the central linking variable between the environment and a system's reactions to it. The central position given the uncertainty construct reflects the assumption that a primary activity in human functioning is making choices.

The taxonomy presented in Table 6.1 is based on literature related to behavior that occurs in organizations. This includes the job-stress literature as well as literature related to organizational theory, small group performance, and personality theory. Reviewing all of these works here is impossible; however, the interested reader may wish to see Jackson et al. (1983) and Schuler, Jackson and Vredenburgh (1984).

The Process Component

Process theories attempt to map the intermediate steps that link together categories of variables (McGuire 1983). When process theories and taxonomies are combined, as is done in our uncertainty framework, the result can be a sophisticated representation of a complex domain of knowledge. The resulting representation can both facilitate integration of new knowledge and illuminate existing gaps in our knowledge (McGuire 1983).

Table 6.1 Taxonomic Component of the Uncertainty Framework

Units of analysis	Sources of uncertainty	Attributes of information that relate to uncertainty	Moderators of the uncertainty–reaction link	Short-term reactions to uncertainty	Longer-term consequences of uncertainty
Organization	Suppliers Competitors Creditors Government agencies Unions Customers and clients	(Un)availability Ambiguity Rate of change Pattern of change (predictability) Lack of consensus Novelty Number of elements	Time pressure Control Event labeling (e.g., threat or opportunity) Personality styles Past experience	Information seeking Information distribution Information distortion Use of rules/ heuristics Avoidance Anxiety	Structuring Strategy development Conflict or cooperation Learning Creativity Performance change Withdrawal
Group	Intra-organization groups Technology				
Individual	Task procedures Role Expectations Supervisors Peers Subordinates Nonwork				

Source: Compiled by the authors.

It may also serve as the basis on which axiomatic theories are eventually developed. The process component of the framework is illustrated by Figure 6.1. It describes a partial model of human activity that combines systems theory and an information processing view to provide a logic from which to develop testable hypotheses about the relationships among the variables included in our taxonomy (Table 6.1).

Figure 6.1   Process component of the uncertainty framework

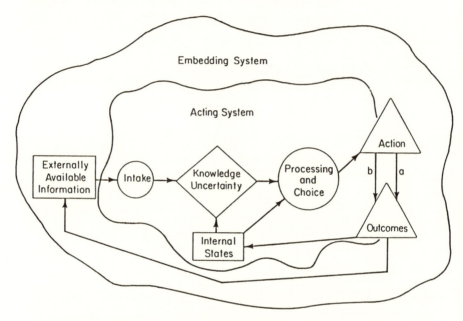

Uncertainty. As Figure 6.1 shows, the uncertainty construct is centrally positioned in the process model. It is the variable linking objective environmental conditions to the responses of individuals, groups, and organizations. Recent reviews of the psychological and organizational literature (Jackson et al. 1983) reveal how frequently the uncertainty concept and the closely related concept of ambiguity have been studied.

Because it has been used in a variety of research areas, definitions of uncertainty differ greatly. When the level is the organization, uncertainty is most often used to refer to an objective characteristic of the environment, such as the degree to which future events are unpredictable (Lorenzi 1980; Pfeffer and Salancik 1978) or the extent to which such unpredictability of the future leads to an inability to predict the outcomes linked to alternative courses of action (Hinings et al., 1974; Milburn and Billings 1976). These definitions emphasize the difficulties of problem-solving when information is unavailable. In contrast, others have defined uncertainty as a state of ambiguity, that is, a situation is unstructured or ill-defined and/or information is vague or untrustworthy (Burns and Stalker 1961; Galbraith 1977; Lawrence and Lorsch 1967; McCaskey 1979; Thompson 1967). Here the focus is on the difficulties uncertainty creates for identifying and formulating problems.

When the level of analysis is the group, the term *ambiguity* is used rather than *uncertainty*. Specifically, role ambiguity has been used to denote lack of clarity about: information about others' expectations for one's behavior, information about the consequences linked to one's behavior, and information about the means through which others' expectations can be fulfilled (Graen 1976; Kahn et al. 1964; Rizzo, House, and Lirtzman 1970).

Finally, when the level of analysis is the individual, both ambiguity and uncertainty are used to describe characteristics of information available to a person, with ambiguity used more often in the context of personality research (Ball-Rokeach 1973; Budner 1967; Frenkel-Brunswick 1949) and uncertainty used more often in the context of research on cognitive processes and decision-making (Beach and Mitchell 1978; Einhorn and Hogarth 1981).

The inconsistencies in the meanings given to uncertainty cannot be resolved here. For the purpose of our discussion, we use the following definition of uncertainty: *Uncertainty exists to the extent that knowledge about an event or condition that requires action or resolution is experienced as inadequate.*

The term "knowledge" is used to ground the experience of uncertainty in the acting system. That is, uncertainty is not viewed here as an objective environmental condition. Knowledge is assumed to result from the intake of available information. A systems-theory perspective implies that three types of relevant knowledge are (1) knowledge about current states, (2) knowledge about future states, and (3) knowledge about the cause-effect relationships between actions and future states.

Inputs and outputs of the process. Figure 6.1 represents inputs as boxes and outputs as triangles. In accordance with the guiding view of people as problem-solvers, information is the relevant input. Information may pertain to phenomena external *or* internal to the acting system. Several possible "sources of uncertainty" are listed in the second column of Table 6.1; they are varied. They include individuals, such as supervisors, as well as large social entities, such as businesses competing in one's industry. Despite this diversity, the sources of uncertainty can be described as information generators. The information generated can, in turn, be described as having various abstract attributes that are meaningful at all three levels of analysis. These are listed in Table 6.1 as "attributes of information that relate to uncertainty," which describe specific characteristics of information and define the particular nature (type) of uncertainty experienced. In general, the more characteristic these attributes are of the information generated by a source, the more uncertainty the source produces. Furthermore, the more sources characterized by uncertainty, the more total uncertainty there exists for a system or a unit of analysis.

Outputs are the immediate actions of, and subsequent outcomes for, the acting and embedding systems. Outputs are represented in Figure 6.1 as two distinct triangles to emphasize the importance of analyzing both short- and long-term changes in the system. In reality, of course, time is a continuous dimension and the distinctions between reactions and consequences are not always clear. Note also that outputs are positioned to span the boundary between the acting and embedding systems. This emphasizes two assumptions: (1) that actions are visible to both the acting and embedding systems, and (2) that actions can change the previously existing states of both the acting and embedding systems.

Intake and processing of information. The intake and processing elements are the least well-developed aspects of our model at this time. Their inclusion is intended to address two important issues. First, the experience of uncertainty is explicitly located in the acting system and the primary sources of uncertainty exist in an external, embedding system. This is comparable to distinguishing between "subjective" and "objective" states. Making such a distinction assumes imperfect fidelity of information transmission between systems. In Figure 6.1, the *intake* circle represents those phenomena that affect information transmission from the embedding system to the acting system. Such phenomena partially determine what information becomes available to the acting system. At the individual level of analysis, relevant intake phenomena would include common cognitive biases and errors of information processing (Kahneman and Tversky 1973). At the group level of analysis, relevant phenomena include "mind guards" (Janis 1975) and boundary spanners (Miles 1976). And, at the organization level of analysis, political action committees and formal environmental scanning activities would be relevant.

Second, the model acknowledges that once information is received, internal *processing* of the information occurs before observable outputs are produced. The complexities of this processing are not fully explicated by our framework. However, a few factors that the literature suggests may be particularly relevant to this processing phase are listed in Table 6.1 as "moderators of the uncertainty-reaction link."

Taken together, Table 6.1 and Figure 6.1 depict a complex view of stress and uncertainty in organizations. This view of stress helps identify a variety of issues that organizational psychologists should attend to when considering how to reduce or manage stress within an organization. In the remainder of this chapter, we will describe several implications of the uncertainty framework for understanding and managing organizational stress. These implications become clear in the context of a more detailed consideration of some of the elements of the uncertainty framework. Particularly important elements include the distinction between acting and embedding systems, the identification of information as the primary input for a system (and thus as the primary determinant of uncertainty and stress), and the sources of information relevant to various systems. Therefore, we have organized the remainder of our discussion around these aspects of the uncertainty framework. In our discussion, we include reviews of relevant literature and suggestions for new research directions.

Implications of Viewing Organizations as Comprising Acting and Embedding Systems That Experience Stress

Systems theory suggests a general rule for distinguishing acting from embedding systems, namely that the embedding system always is composed of multiple acting systems. Therefore, the embedding system typically represents a unit of analysis that is one level above (more abstract than) the acting system. When the acting system is an individual, the embedding system(s) will be one or more groups; when the acting system is a group, the embedding system is the larger organization within which the group exists. Finally, an organization can also be considered as an acting system, embedded within a larger political or economic system. For any acting system, the embedding system is the primary, most immediate source of uncertainty—stress.

The framework allows for the acting system to be embedded within multiple, and perhaps nonoverlapping, embedding systems. For example, when the individual is the acting system, each of his or her relevant role sets (such as co-workers, family, clients) can be viewed as embedding systems. The value of attending to a person's multiple role sets when studying stress responses is being recognized in research on the work-nonwork interface (see Greenhaus and Beutell 1985, for a review). Analogously, when an organization is the acting system, examples of embedding systems are the local community and the national political community. Of course, groups also can be embedded in multiple systems. When the acting system is a *work* group, the primary embedding system is likely to be the employing organization. For some work groups, a union might also be an important embedding system. An internal venture group is a somewhat unusual example of a work group because it is simultaneously embedded in a larger organization and the marketplace in which that organization competes. These multiple embedding systems can all be sources of uncertainty, and therefore of job stress. Thus, a primary implication of the uncertainty framework is: *To understand job stress it is necessary to identify all sources of uncertainty for organizational members.*

Following from the importance of identifying all sources of uncertainty is the need for job stress researchers to broaden their present scope when considering the sources of stress in individuals. Most research on job stress focuses exclusively on the immediate work setting as a source of stress. In particular, the individual's task and his or her supervisor's behaviors are the job stress antecedents most often examined. Occasionally, one's co-workers are also considered as potential contributors to job stress, as indicated by research on social support networks. The systems-theory perspective of the uncertainty framework suggests that this focus on the immediate work group is inappropriately microscopic, and thus inadequate for understanding an individual's job stress.

In addition to the immediate work group, we must also consider more macro units of analysis. For example, the relationship between a person's own work group and other work groups in the organization must be considered. Furthermore, individuals in an organization may be affected by the relationship between their employing organization and other organizations. Striking accounts of the importance of *inter*organizational events that create stress and uncertainty for employees within a particular organization appear almost daily in the news; yet they appear to be ignored by stress researchers. The banking industry provides an illustration. Government deregulation is reshaping the amount and nature of competition among banks. Whereas the banking industry was previously very stable and seldom saw new products being introduced, deregulation is speeding the development of a dizzying array of new financial instruments (products) that employees must be able to understand and sell. With increased competition has come a heightened awareness of the need to maximize employee productivity. To improve productivity, computerization is rapidly changing the tasks performed by employees, and personnel practices are being dramatically changed. Suddenly, employees who once accepted yearly raises and job security as facts of life are realizing they must either change and adapt to the revolution occurring in the banking industry or seek employment elsewhere.

This example is intended to illustrate the scope of analysis that would be necessary to develop an understanding of job stress for bank employees. Whereas a traditional study might assess the uncertainty and stress generated by supervisory styles of management (such as how much participation in decision-making is encouraged or how much initiating structure the supervisor exhibits), the uncertainty framework suggests that job stress levels could be better understood if one's analysis also included a consideration of: (a) how the reshaping of the banking industry affects the environmental sources of uncertainty for a particular bank as an organization; (b) the bank's response to the environment, including changes in the organizational structure, in technology, and in human resource management practices such as compensation and performance appraisal; and (c) the effects of these changes on the relationships among subgroups within the organization. Thus, the need to analyze stress as a phenomenon that occurs at multiple levels is a salient implication of our uncertainty framework.

A second implication of our framework is that *attempts to reduce stress and uncertainty at one level of analysis may create uncertainty at other levels.* As the banking example above suggests, we view uncertainty as originating primarily in the organization's external environment. It then flows through the organization, impacting on systems at all levels. This trans-level cascading is illustrated in more detail by Figure 6.2. The directional arrows begin with business objectives. Once these are established, the potential sources of uncertainty at the organizational level of analysis can be determined. The sources of uncertainty at this level are therefore the objectives themselves as well as other systems (such as government) in the environment; their impact then filters through the organization. Thus, the impact of the organization's environment is transferred indirectly to all levels. Most immediately, it is transferred to the group level of analysis. Depending on the group's response, environmental uncertainty may then be transferred to individuals. These cascading effects occur at each level in our analysis, emphasizing that addressing uncertainty at one level of analysis has implications for uncertainty at other levels.

Schuler and Jackson (1985) describe in detail how organizations can adjust their human resource management practices in order to reduce the uncertainties created for the organization by a changing competitive environment. For example, they argue that career ladders and training programs are practices that can be used by organizations to reduce the uncertainties generated by the future need for a labor pool with particular skills and abilities. These practices, designed in response to uncertainty created by the external business environment, affect the internal structure of the organization. For example, if an organization pursues a strategy that requires managers who have general knowledge across several areas of the

Figure 6.2   The flow of uncertainty throughout an organization

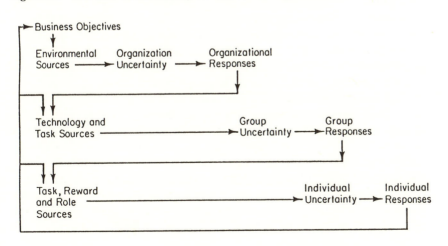

business, the organization must be structured to facilitate cross-functional training of potential managers. That is, the structure should help maximize interdepartmental communication and information sharing. Alternatively, an organization's strategy may require managers with high levels of expertise within narrowly defined fields of specialization. In this case, the organizational structure should facilitate intradepartmental communication. Both strategies can be described as attempts to increase information availability. It is worthwhile to note that each strategy will uniquely influence levels of uncertainty and stress. For example, highly specialized departmental functioning can reduce interdepartmental information sharing and increase interdepartmental competition for organizational resources to an extent that is detrimental to the achievement of overall business objectives.

Because of the cascading flow aspect of the uncertainty framework, such decisions about how to structure the organization will necessarily have implications for inter-group, intra-group, and individual functioning. Thus, we can continue to trace the effects of an organization's business strategy down to the level of an individual employee. Consider the employee in an organization structured to develop managers who are generalists. To the extent the organization maximizes an individual's simultaneous participation in multiple departments (as in a matrix organization), the organization will also maximize the individual's exposure to the conflicts that arise between departments. These conflicts, which are often described as "role conflicts" (Kahn et al. 1964), create uncertainty for the individual.

Organizational psychologists use the term *role conflict* to describe situations in which a person receives conflicting information about how he or she is expected to behave. In the uncertainty framework, the phrase "lack of consensus" is used instead of "conflict"; a role-conflict situation would therefore be described as one in which there is a lack of consensus in the information one has about how to behave. This lack of consensus creates feelings of uncertainty about the most appropriate actions. This example illustrates how the uncertainty framework can be used to evaluate in advance what types of effects an organizational change can be expected to have on groups and individuals in the organization. It also illustrates how solutions used to reduce uncertainty at one level of analysis (such as the organization) can result in increased uncertainty at another (for example, the individual) unless precautionary, counterbalancing changes are made.

In the above example, counterbalancing changes designed to minimize individual uncertainty might be taken by training group supervisors in the use of initiating structure, consideration, and participatory decision-making. These three supervisory behaviors appear to decrease role conflict (Jackson and Schuler 1985), apparently by providing useful information to subordinates. "Initiating structure" refers to direct and intentional efforts to make more information available to subordinates. Participatory decision-making may also affect information availability. While participation may not be used for the primary purpose of providing information to subordinates, the discussions that occur during decision-making sessions are likely to encourage information dissemination and conflict resolution (Jackson 1983). The access to information resulting from participation in decision-making may be one reason for the unexpected finding that managers experience less role strain than their subordinates (cf. Zalesnik, Kets de Vries, and Howard 1977). Upper-level managers are more likely to be involved in decision-making, and as a result of this participation, they know more about the informal workings of the organization (Davis 1953). In contrast to the relatively direct way in which initiating structure and participatory decision-making can translate into increased information availability, consideration behaviors, that is, showing concern for the socioemotional needs of individuals may provide information indirectly through a feedback process. That is, supervisors may use consideration as a positive reinforcer for a job well done, thereby clarifying the supervisor's expectations for the subordinate.

Implications of Assuming Information Is the Determinant of Stress and Uncertainty

There are numerous implications of adopting an information theory view of stress. Here we will discuss only three of these; the first two implications are particularly important for stress researchers, while the third, discussed below, is particularly important for personnel managers.

The first implication of the uncertainty framework's focus on information is that *to understand job stress, we must understand other organizational phenomena.* For stress researchers, one important implication of the framework we propose is that there are many pockets of research relevant to stress that are not typically integrated into research on job stress. One is research on organizational responses to environmental uncertainty. Another is research on personality differences. We drew heavily from the organizational literature to develop our list of information attributes shown in Table 6.1 (availability, ambiguity, rate of change, pattern of change). Below we present a brief overview of some of this often ignored literature to illustrate its relevance to viewing stress as uncertainty. In addition to the organizational literature, our framework also incorporates many concepts from the personality literature. The personality literature was particularly relevant to our formulation of possible responses to uncertainty and of important moderator variables. Therefore, a brief overview of relevant personality research follows our discussion of the organization studies. These two sections illustrate the diversity of phenomena that can be discussed using the uncertainty framework presented above.

Research on organizations. In the organization literature, "uncertainty" is often used to describe objective environmental conditions that constrain the actions of organizations. One school of theorists, those who adopt a resource dependence view of organizations, has defined uncertainty as the degree to which the future is unpredictable and as the extent to which this unpredictability causes difficulty in choosing a course of action (Hickson et al. 1971; Lorenzi 1980; Milburn and Billings 1976; Pfeffer and Salancik 1978). In these definitions, uncertainty is equated with unpredictability, and unpredictability is assumed to be caused, at least in part, by a lack of information.

Similar definitions of uncertainty are used by those who focus on the decision processes of organizations. For example, a decision theory perspective led Duncan (1973) to define uncertainty, in part, as lack of information about which environmental elements are relevant to a decision, lack of information about which outcomes are linked to decision choices, and lack of information about the state of the environment. As Table 6.1 shows, *unavailability* of information is one of several information attributes included in our framework.

While most organization theorists closely associate uncertainty with information availability, several also associate uncertainty with information *ambiguity* (Burns and Stalker 1961; Duncan 1972; Galbraith 1977; Lawrence and Lorsch 1969; Thompson 1967). The emphasis here is on the quality rather than the quantity of the information one has. In ambiguous situations, available information is vague, untrustworthy, or otherwise difficult to interpret (cf. Weick 1969). This makes problems difficult to define (McCaskey 1979) and consequently difficult to solve.

Although the organizational literature associates uncertainty most closely with information availability and ambiguity, several other information attributes shown in Table 6.1 also have been suggested by organization theorists. For example, an association between uncertainty and the *rate of change* in information is widely assumed, as is the association between uncertainty and irregularity and unpredictabiilty in the *pattern of change* (Emery 1967; Lawrence and Lorsch 1967; Miles, Snow, and Pfeffer 1974; Thompson 1967; Tosi, Aldag, and Storey 1973; Tung 1979). In the past, these distinct attributes of information have not been clearly distinguished, but we believe such distinctions must be made for a coherent picture of uncertainty to develop.

Given their interest in uncertainty, it should not be surprising that organization theorists have recognized the need to identify the sources of uncertainty. The fundamental tenet of the resource dependence view is that organizations must transact with environmental elements to acquire needed resources (Pfeffer and Salancik 1978). The relevant elements in the acting organization's environment are other organizations (Levine and White 1961). Of particular importance to business organizations are *suppliers, consumers, competitors, government agencies, unions,* and *creditors* (Evans 1966; Miles and Snow 1978). Economic, political, and sociocultural events and trends also cause environmental uncertainty, but they will typically be enacted through the agents presented in Table 6.1. In addition to recognizing other organizations as sources of uncertainty, researchers who focus on the organization as the acting system consider the *technology* used by an organization to be a major potential source of uncertainty (Perrow 1967; Hickson, Pugh, and Pheysey 1969; Slocum and Sims 1980). As shown in Table 6.1, both external environmental elements (such as other organizations) and technology are considered sources of uncertainty in the present framework.

Most discussions of the effects of uncertainty on organizations have focused on the relationship between technology-based uncertainty and organizational structure or design. Although the research designs employed to date do not permit causal statements, the common assumption underlying work on this topic seems to be that technological uncertainty determines, or should determine, structure. Some researchers have found that when technological uncertainty is high, organizations are more likely to be characterized as organic and/or decentralized (Leifer and Huber 1977; Hrebiniak and Snow 1980), but others have found uncertainty to be associated with more bureaucratic forms (Blau et al. 1976; Meyer 1968). Although the question of whether technological uncertainty has systematic and predictable effects on structure has not been answered, one dimension along which short-term reactions to uncertainty vary seems to be rule development and use.

As the preceding section shows, when organizational theorists discuss groups and uncertainty, they direct their attention outward from the acting group; they focus on aspects of the external, embedding environment and on information received by the group from that environment. In contrast to this, organizational psychologists who discuss groups tend to direct their attention inward; they focus more on group members as sources of information (as senders of role expectations). A noteworthy consequence of this difference in focus is that the organizational theory literature assumes that the locus of uncertainty is the group; whereas the organizational psychology literature assumes uncertainty is experienced by individuals in the group. This difference in the locus of uncertainty leads organization theorists to examine inter-group processes as outputs, whereas organizational psychologists examine intra-group processes and individual reactions as outputs.

When the group is the unit of analysis, the concept of uncertainty derives its importance partly from its effects on how information is gathered and distributed. When inter-group processes are the focus (Lawrence and Lorsch 1969; Galbraith 1973), uncertainty is assumed to increase the need for *information distribution*. Greater information demands, in turn, increase the difficulty associated with attaining high levels of inter-group performance. Task uncertainty also influences the appropriateness of different mechanisms for integrating efforts among the groups. Inappropriate mechanisms for coordination can encourage inter-group *conflict* and impair intergroup efficiency (Galbraith 1977). Even if appropriate coordinating mechanisms are used, increased uncertainty may be associated with increased inter-group conflict. Because some inter-group conflict is likely to be undesirable, *strategies* for resolving conflict must be devised and implemented.

In addition to examining the impact of task uncertainty on inter-group coordination and conflict, organizational theorists argue that a group's *power* in the organization is derived partly from its ability to deal with uncertainty. The more capable a unit is in controlling or absorbing uncertainty, the more it can control strategic contingencies and the more power it gains vis-à-vis other units in the organization (Hickson et al. 1971; March and Simon 1958). For example, Lawrence and Lorsch (1969) and Lawrence and Dyer (1983) found that units in an organization have more power to the extent they are successful in reducing uncertainty by tactics such as innovation and dealing with clients. Conversely, as units face less uncertainty, they become subject to more bureaucracy and more centralized control by the organization (Comstock and Scott 1977).

The brief overview of organizational theory and research presented above illustrates the relevance of one pocket of knowledge often ignored in research on job stress. Many other neglected areas of research exist as well. Although space limitations make it impossible to extensively review each of these, we note several areas of traditional psychology below to illustrate the diversity of research that can be interpreted within the uncertainty framework.

Research on individuals. Two research subjects that focus on the individual as an acting system were of particular importance in the development of the uncertainty framework: (1) the effects that personality characteristics have on task performance and emotional responses, and (2) the effects of predictability and control on the development of stress reactions. These research traditions were particularly important in the development of three sections of the taxonomy shown in Table 6.1: short-term reactions, long-term consequences, and moderators of the uncertainty-reaction link.

Personality traits that have been studied as determinants of how people respond to information in their environment include tolerance of ambiguity, dogmatism, field dependence, locus of control, cognitive complexity, and more recently, hardiness. Surprisingly, however, researchers of these topics seldom systematically analyze the dimensions along which information can vary, or the sources from which information is received. [Budner (1962), who was interested in tolerance of ambiguity, was an exception to this generalization.] Instead, the research on personality traits (in particular, tolerance of ambiguity) suggests a wide variety of reactions people *may* have to uncertainty, and subsequent long-term consequences. Personality traits are considered to be moderators that determine the particular form a person's reactions to uncertainty will take. Our assumption that this is true is shown by the inclusion of personality styles as a moderator in Table 6.1.

Tolerance-intolerance of ambiguity is the personality trait most frequently studied as a determinant of individual reactions to uncertainty due to ambiguity.* In her seminal article, Frenkel-Brunswick (1949) described five tendencies of people who are intolerant of ambiguity: (1) seeing solutions as black and white, (2) coming to premature closure on issues, (3) neglecting reality, (4) exaggerated concreteness, and (5) stereotyping. In our uncertainty framework, such reactions are classified as distorting information and ignoring or avoiding information. Presumably, these reactions are a direct means of reducing one's experienced uncertainty and the anxiety it produces.

Reactions such as these may account for the performance decrements associated with uncertain situations. In laboratory studies, where performance measures are likely to have good validity, there is impressive evidence of the detrimental effects of uncertainty on performance. Shalit (1977) analyzed 75 laboratory experiments in which subjects' performance had been evaluated by the experimenter along a success-failure dimension. These experimental situations were rated independently for the extent to which differing, equally plausible interpretations could be imposed on the situation in which the subject performed. High performance was found in situations having high information consensus. Shalit explained this relationship by pointing out that subjects confronted with easy-to-interpret situations are better able to devise effective strategies for action than are subjects confronted with situations they cannot easily appraise.

Although most individuals may respond negatively to uncertainty, others may thrive in the same situation. Thus Budner (1962) extended the meaning of ambiguity tolerance to imply a definite preference for ambiguous situations, suggesting that ambiguity can have positive as well as negative implications. MacDonald (1970) elaborated on this and hypothesized that some people may actually seek out ambiguity, enjoy it, and excel in the performance of ambiguous tasks. Some support for MacDonald's hypothesis is available. For example, Budner (1962) reported that medical students who were tolerant of ambiguity chose less structured fields like psychiatry, whereas intolerant students chose structured fields like surgery. Similarly, college art majors were found to be more tolerant of ambiguity than business majors. Furthermore, ambiguity tolerance distinguishes entrepreneurs from other managers (Schere 1981).

Personality research on how people react to uncertainty is driven by the assumption that personality is a critical moderator variable. When the trait

*Many of the possible reactions to uncertainty suggested by the literature on intolerance of ambiguity are also suggested in literature on related personality traits such as cognitive complexity, field independence, locus of control, and dogmatism. Space does not permit a detailed discussion of each here, but the interested reader is referred to Jackson et al. (1983).

of interest is ambiguity tolerance, the moderator is used to predict who will experience the greatest anxiety and who will attempt to reduce uncertainty by defensive means such as information distortion and shielding, rather than proactive means such as information seeking. Similarly, research evidence suggests that dogmatic individuals are relatively ineffective in novel situations perhaps because they are less creative, find it difficult to accept change, and view compromise as defeat (see Ehrlich and Lee 1969, for a review).

The degree of *control* one can exert is also a partial determinant of one's reactions to uncertainty. In personality research, measures of locus of control (Rotter 1966) assess the degree to which individuals feel controlled by the environment (external locus of control) or feel in control of the environment (internal locus of control). Compared to "internals," "externals" perceive less ambiguity in their environments (Organ and Greene 1974) and are more likely to attempt to reduce ambiguity by seeking information (Anderson 1977). These results suggest that being (or feeling) in control increases the probability that environmental uncertainties will be interpreted as challenging opportunities to be met by the development of new strategies, rather than as threats from which one should seek protection (cf. Lerner 1980; Schuler 1980).

Finally, research by cognitive psychologists suggests some important moderators that may determine people's reactions to uncertainty. This literature is particularly useful for specifying the conditions under which particular strategies are likely to be used. For example, an *important* issue typically leads to the use of more complex, analytic strategies. In contrast, nonanalytic strategies that simply require the rote application of rules may be preferred when making mundane, more routine decisions. Similarly, the complexity of the problem, defined as the number of alternative solutions to the problem and the number of attributes linked to each alternative, has been hypothesized to increase the likelihood that an analytic strategy will be selected. A nonanalytic strategy, however, is more likely to be used when an immediate deadline creates a *time pressure* or when the decision is reversible (Christenson-Szalanski 1980; Beach and Mitchell 1978).

As the two preceding overviews of research on organizations and research on individuals illustrate, the constructs that comprise our uncertainty framework can be used to interpret research conducted at different levels of analysis, as well as research on a variety of dissimilar phenomena. While this is the primary strength of the uncertainty framework, it also presents the major challenge to future researchers, as described next.

For job stress researchers, a critical implication of the uncertainty framework is that in the future, *stress research must find new ways to operationalize important variables*. With its emphasis on information as the determinant of uncertainty and stress, our framework presents a major challenge, namely to develop new measures for studying individuals, groups, and organizations. In order to develop a framework capable of describing diverse phenomena using a small set of constructs, a relatively high level of abstraction is necessary. In our framework, the abstract concept of "information" is the key element. Therefore, information must be measured. Furthermore, it must be measured on several dimensions (such as its availability, its rate and pattern of change, novelty, and so on), *and* it must be measured in terms of several sources (for example, co-workers, supervisors, formal policies, and so on). To our knowledge, appropriate operationalizations of "information" have yet to be developed and validated.

For practitioners, our framework suggests that *one way to minimize stress in an organization is by reducing uncertainty created by human resource management practices.* Whereas the first two implications discussed above are most relevant to researchers, this third implication is most relevant to personnel practitioners who are in a position to evaluate and change organizational practices. A perusal of the sources of uncertainty in Table 6.1 reveals many potential sources of stress over which the typical personnel practitioner has little or no control. For example, it would be difficult for an I/O psychologist to reduce stress levels in a bank by trying to change the rate at which deregulation of the banking industry occurs. Similarly, it might be difficult for a manager to have much influence over technological changes in the industry. Instead, the point at which an I/O psychologist or manager is most likely to impact on the system is when changes in the environment and technology create the need for new personnel practices.

For the individual employee, personnel practices are an important source of information. Ideally, they determine which tasks an employee is assigned to do (for example, through job analysis, selection, and placement), the way performance on those tasks is assessed (through performance appraisal), and consequences for task performance (through compensation systems and career planning). In other words, personnel practices are an organization's way of generating information about its human resources, and they provide a means by which the organization communicates information to its individual employees. By implication, personnel policies and practices can either create or reduce uncertainty for both the organization as a whole and for individual members.

In the past the personnel function has not typically been used to shape the business strategy and internal structuring of large organizations. Only recently has the strategic importance of human resource management been examined (Fombrun, Tichy, and Devanna 1984; Schuler and MacMillan 1984). For practitioners considering how alternative styles of human resource management are likely to impact on organizational processes and functioning, the uncertainty framework may provide a valuable tool for conducting "thought experiments" to assess the potential impact of implementing large-scale changes, such as a merger or a major reduction in the work force. For practitioners faced with a demoralized or unproductive work force, the uncertainty framework may provide a scheme for conducting a diagnosis of the problem to pinpoint sources of debilitating uncertainty and identify needed changes. Thus, the uncertainty framework should be useful to practicing personnel psychologists in general, not only to those concerned with stress management.

SUMMARY AND CONCLUSIONS

The primary objectives of this article have been (1) to illustrate the central role played by the concept of uncertainty across a variety of literature relevant to understanding stress in organizations, and (2) to suggest a framework for linking the literature together. Our framework of uncertainty, which consists of a taxonomy and a process model, was presented first. Several implications of this framework were then discussed. In this last section, we will summarize the major assertions that follow from the uncertainty framework and literature review.

Our conceptualization of uncertainty rests on the premise that uncertainty is experienced by a system in response to conditions in its environment. We assume that uncertainty in one system results in responses that change both the acting system and its embedding system. We have also argued that uncertainty originates in the environment and flows primarily in an external-to-internal direction, with effects transferred through organization, group, and individual levels. Uncertainty at one level results in responses at the next, which in turn cause additional, although perhaps qualitatively different, uncertainty. While uncertainty can flow in the opposite direction (from individual to group to organization levels), and while the sequence need not be transmitted directly from one level to the next contiguous one, our suggestion is that the primary flow of uncertainty in organizations occurs from higher to lower contiguous levels of analysis, as described below.

In the context of organizational objectives, organizations respond to environmental uncertainty from these sources through strategy and structure. Structuring occurs both between and within organizations. These responses are essentially efforts to limit information need or to facilitate action through greater predictability (Milliken 1984). These organizational-level responses, while serving to reduce uncertainty for the organization, may cause additional uncertainty, particularly of a technological and political nature.

In general, organizational responses are likely to influence group responses because they generate technical and political sources of uncertainty for the group. Responses to uncertainty at the group level include actions directed at the interaction of the members and/or at the task faced by the group

(Hackman 1968, 1976). Responses directed at member interaction would include establishment and clarification of the structure of the group by structural and task changes. Groups may also use affective coping strategies, such as increasing group cohesion and providing each other with social support (House 1981). Such social support may buffer the group from subsequent uncertainties. The group's leader can be critical in shaping the group's responses to uncertainty. For example, the leader can help the group clarify its structure, redefine its task, and build group cohesiveness. Alternatively, the leader may become a source of uncertainty for the individuals in the group.

As shown in Table 6.1, there are several sources of uncertainty for members of work groups: tasks, rewards, role expectations of supervisors, peers, subordinates, and others outside the work setting. It is likely that when the group's tasks are varied and unpredictable, individual uncertainty will be greater. Individuals may also experience reward-related uncertainty, especially if supervisors do not adequately convey reward contingencies, and/or if the personnel policies and practices of the organization are not sufficiently formulated. Finally, role-related uncertainty is likely to occur if, at the group level, the roles group members are to play are not clearly established, whether by the group or the supervisor.

Faced with one or more types of uncertainty, individuals can respond in several ways. Many of the individual responses to uncertainty are those typically associated with stress. Our assumption here is that uncertainty is not experienced by most individuals as a neutral condition. Psychological as well as some behavioral responses reflect an important aspect of uncertainty, namely that uncertainty can be associated with positive or negative outcomes. Thus, uncertainty may result in responses such as excitement and high performance (Schuler 1982), or it may lead to negative psychological and behavioral responses, such as anxiety and absenteeism. Finally, responses may vary as a function of time. That is, it is likely that some reactions occur immediately upon perception of the uncertainty while others only occur after a longer term of exposure to uncertainty.

Exactly how a system responds to uncertainty depends on many factors, but in general, systems can respond proactively or defensively. Proactive responses include direct attacks on the sources of uncertainty (for example, going to the supervisor to get role clarification and reduce uncertainty). Defensive responses include denial and avoidance, behaviors that essentially do not change the actual level of uncertainty. Although these two categories of responses are quite different, either or both may be appropriate. The appropriateness of responses to uncertainty will depend largely on the sources and nature of the uncertainty.

Which responses to uncertainty are chosen, and how quickly a response is made, are apt to be influenced by moderators. For example, a competitive strategy might be pursued by a group that has high control over resources, but a cooperative one would be required if the unit lacks control (and hence power). To the extent uncertainty is demanding of immediate resolution, the need for action will be particularly intense. A response that is immediately forthcoming may differ from responses that would have been enacted in the absence of time pressure. For individuals, personality may be a major determinant of reactions. Because moderating variables have the potential to exert significant impact on responses to uncertainty, they should be diagnosed along with the dimensions and sources of uncertainty.

The major implication of our framework is that many seemingly unique and unrelated variables that have been studied in the organizational sciences can be linked through a common association with uncertainty. Thus, we should be able to gain a greater understanding of organizational processes through retrospective analyses of previous studies using the lens of uncertainty. Of course, prospective studies designed around the construct of uncertainty are also called for. Using one or both of these approaches may provide important insights into our understanding and management of organizational stress at all levels in organizations. For both stress researchers and organizational practitioners, the uncertainty framework should be particularly valuable as a guide for the analysis of organizational conditions that are likely to create the "stress" of uncertainty. Such analyses are particularly important for those who wish to make changes in the work environment. Regardless of whether changes are being planned in order to alleviate existing uncertainty-related problems or for other reasons, the uncertainty framework should enable change planners to anticipate, and perhaps avoid, a variety of "unexpected" effects.

REFERENCES

Appley, M. H. and R. Trumbull. 1967. "On the Concept of Psychological Stress." In *Psychological Stress*, edited by M. H. Appley and R. Trumbull (New York: Appleton-Century-Crofts).

Anderson, C. 1977. "Locus of Control, Coping Behaviors, and Performance in a Stress Setting: A Longitudinal Study." *Journal of Applied Psychology* 62: 449-51.

Ball-Rokeach, J. 1973. "From Pervasive Ambiguity to a Definition of the Situation." *Sociometry* 36: 378-89.

Beach, L. R. and T. R. Mitchell. 1978. "A Contingency Model for the Selection of Decision Strategies." *Academy of Management Review* 3: 439-49.

Beehr, T. A. and R. S. Bhagat. 1985. *Human Stress and Cognition in Organizations: An Integrated Perspective* (New York: John Wiley and Sons).

Beehr, T. A., and J. E. Newman. 1978. "Job Stress, Employee Health, and Organizational Effectiveness." *Personnel Psychology*, 31: 665-698.

Blau, M., C. Falbe, W. McKinley, and P. Tracy. 1976. "Technology and Organization in Manufacturing." *Administrative Science Quarterly* 21: 20-40.

Budner, S. 1962. "Intolerance of Ambiguity as a Personality Variable." *Journal of Personality* 30: 29-50.

Burns, T. and G. M. Stalker. 1961. *The Management of Innovation* (London: Tavistock).

Christenson-Szalanski, J. J. 1980. "A Further Examination of the Selection of Problem-Solving Strategies: The Effects of Deadlines and Analytic Aptitudes." *Organizational Behavior and Human Performance* 25: 107-22.

Comstock, E. and W. R. Scott. 1977. "Technology and the Structure of Subunits: Distinguishing Individual and Workgroup Effects." *Administrative Science Quarterly* 22: 177-203.

Cooper, C. L. and J. Marshall. 1978. "Sources of Managerial and White Collar Stress." In *Stress at Work*, edited by C. L. Cooper and R. Payne (London: Wiley).

Davis, K. 1953. "Management Communication and the Grapevine." *Harvard Business Review* 31: 43-49.

Duncan, R. B. 1972. "Characteristics of Organizational Environments and Perceived Environmental Uncertainty." *Administrative Science Quarterly* 17: 313-27.

Ehrlich, H. J. and D. Lee 1969. "Dogmatism, Learning, and Resistance to Change: Review and a New Paradigm." *Psychological Bulletin* 71: 249-60.

Einhorn, J. and R. M. Hogarth. 1981. "Behavioral Decision Theory." *Annual Review of Psychology* 32: 53-88.

Emery, F. E. 1967. "The Next Thirty Years: Concepts, Methods and Anticipation." *Human Relations* 20: 199-237.

Evans, M. 1966. "The Organization Set: Towards a Theory of Interorganizational Relations." In *Approaches to Organizational Design*, edited by J. D. Thompson (Pittsburgh, PA: University of Pittsburgh Press), pp. 175-90.

Fishbein, M. 1980. "A Theory of Reasoned Action: Some Applications and Implications." In *Nebraska Symposium on Motivation, 1979*, edited by H. Howe and M. Page (Lincoln, Nebraska: University of Nebraska Press).

Fombrun, C., N. M. Tichy, and M. A. Devanna. 1984. *Strategic Human Resource Management* (New York: Wiley).

Ford, D. L., Jr. 1985. "Job-Related Stress of the Minority Professional: An Exploratory Analysis and Suggestions for Future Research." In *Human Stress and Cognition in Organizations: An Integrated Perspective*, edited by T. A. Beehr and R. S. Bhagat (New York: John Wiley and Sons), pp. 287-323.

Frenkel-Brunswick, E. 1949. "Intolerance of Ambiguity as an Emotional and Perceptual Personality Variable." *Journal of Personality* 18: 108-43.

Galbraith, J. R. 1973. *Designing Complex Organizations* (Reading, MA: Addison-Wesley).

_____. 1977. *Organization Design* (Reading, MA: Addison-Wesley).

Graen, G. 1976. "Role-Making Processes within Complex Organizations." In *Handbook of Industrial and Organizational Psychology*, edited by M. D. Dunnette (Chicago, IL: Rand McNally).

Greenhaus, J. H. and N. J. Beutell. 1985. "Sources of Conflict between Work and Family Roles." *Academy of Management Review* 10: 76-88.

Gupta, N. and G. D. Jenkins, Jr. 1985. "Dual Career Couples: Stress, Stressors, Strains, and Strategies." In *Human Stress and Cognition in Organization: An Integrated Perspective*, edited by T. A. Beehr and R. S. Bhagat (New York: John Wiley and Sons), pp. 141-75.

Hackman, J. R. 1968. "Effects of Task Characteristics on Group Products." *Journal of Experimental Social Psychology* 55: 162-87.

_____. 1976. "Group Influences on Individuals." In *Handbook of Industrial and Organizational Psychology*, edited by M. D. Dunnette (Chicago, IL: Rand McNally).

Hickson, D., A. S. Pugh and D. C. Pheysey. 1969. "Operations Technology and Organization Structure: An Empirical Reappraisal." *Administrative Science Quarterly* 14: 394-95.

Hickson, D. J., C. R. Hinings, C. A. Lee, R. E. Schneck, and J. M. Pennings. 1971. 1971. "A Strategic Contingencies Theory of Intraorganization Power." *Administrative Science Quarterly* 16: 216-29.

Hinings, C. R., D. J. Hickson, J. M. Pennings, and R. E. Schneck. 1974. "Structural Conditions of Intraorganizational Power." *Administrative Science Quarterly*.

Holmes, T. H. and R. H. Rahe. 1967. "The Social Readjustment Rating Scale." *Journal of Psychosomatic Research* 11: 213-318.

House, J. S. 1981. *Social Support and Stress* (Reading, MA: Addison-Wesley).

Howard, A. and R. A. Scott. 1965. "A Proposed Framework for the Analysis of Stress in the Human Organism." *Behavioral Science* 10: 141-60.

Hrebiniak, L. G. and C. C. Snow. 1980. "Industry Differences in Environmental Uncertainty and Organizational Characteristics Related to Uncertainty." *Academy of Management Journal* 23: 750-59.

Janis, I. L. 1975. *Victims of Groupthink* (Boston: Houghton Mifflin).

Jackson, S. E. 1983. "Participation in Decision-making as a Strategy for Reducing Job-related Strain." *Journal of Applied Psychology*, 68: 3-19.

Jackson, S. E. and R. S. Schuler. 1985. "A Meta-Analysis and Conceptual Critique of Research on Role Ambiguity and Role Conflict in Work Settings." *Organizational Behavior and Human Decision Processes* 30: 16-76.

Jackson, S. E., S. Zedeck, K. S. Lyness, and J. L. Moses. 1983. "Historical Overview and Critique of Research on Psychological and Organizational Ambiguity." Paper presented at the annual meeting of the American Psychological Association, Anaheim, California.

Jick, T. D. 1985. "As the Ax Falls: Budget Cuts and the Experience of Stress in Organizations." In *Human Stress and Cognition in Organizations: An Integrated Perspective*, edited by T. A. Beehr and R. S. Bhagat (New York: John Wiley and Sons), pp. 83-114.

Kahn, R. L., D. M. Wolfe, R. P. Quinn, J. D. Snoek, and R. A. Rosenthal. 1964. *Organizational Stress: Studies in Role Conflict and Ambiguity* (New York: Wiley).

Kahneman, D. and A. Tversky. 1973. "On the Psychology of Prediction." *Psychological Review* 80: 237-51.

Lawrence, P. R. and D. Dyer. 1983. *Renewing American Industry* (New York: Free Press).

Lawrence, P. R. and J. W. Lorsch. 1967. *Organization and Environment* (Homewood, IL: Irwin).

Lazarus, R. S. 1966. *Psychological Stress and the Coping Process* (New York: McGraw-Hill).

Leifer, R. and G. P. Huber. 1977. "Relations among Perceived Environmental

Uncertainty, Organization Structure, and Boundary-Spanning Behaviors.'' *Administrative Science Quarterly* 22: 235-47.

Lerner, A. 1980. "Orientation to Ambiguity." In *Uncertainty: Behavioral and Social Dimensions*, edited by S. Fiddle (New York: Praeger).

Levine, S. and P. E. White. 1961. "Exchange as a Conceptual Framework for the Study of Interorganizational Relationships." *Administrative Science Quarterly* 5: 583-601.

Lewin, K. 1951. *Field Theory in Social Science* (New York: Harper).

Lorenzi, P. 1980. "Applied Behavior under Uncertainty." In *Uncertainty: Behavioral and Social Dimensions*, edited by S. Fiddle (New York: Praeger).

MacDonald, A. P. 1970. "Revised Scale for Ambiguity Tolerance: Reliability and Validity." *Psychological Reports* 26: 791-98.

March, J. G. and H. A. Simon. 1958. *Organizations* (New York: John Wiley and Sons).

McCaskey, M. B. 1979. "The Management of Ambiguity." *Organizational Dynamics* 7: 31-48.

McGoldrick, A. E. and C. L. Cooper. 1985. "Stress at the Decline of One's Career: The Act of Retirement." In *Human Cognition and Stress in Organizations: An Integrated Perspective*, edited by T. A. Beehr and R. S. Bhagat (New York: John Wiley and Sons), pp. 177-201.

McGrath, J. E. 1970. *Social and Psychological Factors in Stress* (New York: Holt, Rinehart and Winston).

_____. 1976. "Stress and Behavior in Organizations." In *Handbook of Industrial and Organizational Psychology*, edited by M. D. Dunnette (Chicago, IL: Rand McNally College Publishing), pp. 1351-95.

McGuire, W. J. 1983. "A Contextualist Theory of Knowledge: Its Implications for Innovation and Reform in Psychological Research." In *Advances in Experimental Social Psychology*, vol. 16, edited by L. Berkowitz (New York: Academic Press).

Meyer, M. W. 1968. "Two Authority Structures of Bureaucratic Organization." *Administrative Science Quarterly* 13: 211-28.

Milburn, T. W. and R. S. Billings. 1976. "Decision Making Perspectives from Psychology: Dealing with Risk and Uncertainty." *American Behavioral Scientist* 20: 111-26.

Miles, R. H. 1976. "Role Requirements as Sources of Organizational Stress." *Journal of Applied Psychology* 61: 172-79.

Miles, R. and C. C. Snow. 1978. *Organizational Strategy, Structure and Process.* (New York: McGraw-Hill).

Miles, R. E., C. C. Snow, and J. Pfeffer. 1974. "Organization-Environment: Concepts and Issues." *Industrial Relations* 13: 244-64.

Milliken, F. J. 1984. "An Analysis of Organizational Responses to Environmental Uncertainty." Unpublished paper, Baruch College, City University of New York.

Organ, D. W. and C. N. Greene. 1974. "Role Ambiguity, Locus of Control, and Work Satisfaction." *Journal of Applied Psychology* 59: 101-2.

Perrow, C. 1967. "A Framework for the Comparative Analysis of Organizations." *American Sociological Review* 32: 194-208.

Pfeffer, J. and G. R. Salancik. 1978. *The External Control of Organizations: A Resource Dependence Perspective* (New York: Harper & Row).

Rizzo, J. R., R. J. House, and S. I. Lirtzman. 1970. "Role Conflict and Ambiguity in Complex Organizations." *Administrative Science Quarterly* 15: 150-63.

Rotter, J. B. 1966. "Generalized Expectancies for Internal versus External Control of Reinforcement." *Psychological Monographs* 80 (whole no. 1 609): 1-28.

Schere, J. L. 1982. "Tolerance of Ambiguity as a Discriminating Variable between Entrepreneurs and Managers." Doctoral dissertation, Wharton, University of Pennsylvania.

Schuler, R. S. 1980. "Definition and Conceptualization of Stress in Organizations." *Organizational Behavior and Human Performance* 23: 184-215.

———. 1982. "An Integrative Transactional Process Model of Stress in Organizations." *Journal of Occupational Behavior* 3: 5-13.

Schuler, R. S. and S. E. Jackson. 1986. "Managing Stress through PHRM Practices: An Uncertainty Interpretation." In *Research in Personnel and Human Resource Management*, vol. 4, edited by K. M. Rowland and G. R. Ferris (Greenwich, CT: JAI Press).

Schuler, R. S., S. E. Jackson, and D. J. Vredenburgh. 1984. *Conceptualizing Uncertainty in the Organization Sciences.* Unpublished manuscript, New York University.

Schuler, R. S. and I. C. MacMillan. 1984. "Gaining Competitive Advantage through Human Resource Management Practices." *Human Resource Management* 23: 241-56.

Shalit, B. 1977. "Structural Ambiguity and Limits to Coping." *Journal of Human Stress* 3: 32-45.

Slocum, J. W., and H. P. Sims. 1980. "A Topology for Integrating Technology, Organization, Job Design." *Human Relations* 33: 193-212.

Thompson, J. D. 1967. *Organizations in Action* (New York: McGraw-Hill).

Torrance, P. E. 1954. "The Behavior of Small Groups Under the Stress of Conditions of Survival." *American Sociological Review* 19: 751-55.

Tosi, H., R. Aldag, and R. Storey. 1973. "On the Measurement of the Environment: An Assessment of the Lawrence and Lorsch Environmental Uncertainty Subscale." *Administrative Science Quarterly* 18: 27-36.

Tung, R. L. 1979. "Dimensions of Organization Environments: An Exploratory Study of Their Impact on Organizational Structure." *Academy of Management Journal* 22: 672-93.

Van Harrison, R. 1985. "The Person-Environment Fit Model and the Study of Job Stress." In *Human Stress and Cognition in Organizations: An Integrated Perspective*, edited by T. A. Beehr and R. S. Bhagat (New York: Wiley and Sons).

Weick, K. E. 1969. *The Social Psychology of Organizing* (Reading, MA: Addison-Wesley).

———. 1974. "Middle Range Theories of Social Systems." *Behavioral Science* 19: 357-67.

Zalesnik, A., M. F. R. Kets de Vries, and J. Howard. 1977. "Stress Reactions in Organizations: Syndromes, Causes and Consequences." *Behavioral Science* 22: 151-62.

7

A SYSTEMS ASSESSMENT OF OCCUPATIONAL STRESS: EVALUATING A HOTEL DURING CONTRACT NEGOTIATIONS

MICHAEL S. NEALE,
JEFFERSON A. SINGER,
and GARY E. SCHWARTZ

Several years ago, at the request of the National Institute of Occupational Safety and Health, we initiated a survey of occupational stress management programs for nonmanagerial employees. We wanted to find out how U.S. corporations and labor unions defined stress at work and what they were doing to reduce it. As we have described in more detail elsewhere (Singer et al. 1986), our survey led us to a number of interesting conclusions. To summarize briefly the results of extensive contacts with labor and industry representatives, academicians, consultants, and health service providers, we found that stress and, therefore, stress management, were defined quite differently, depending on the role and orientation of the respondent. Most striking were the divergent perspectives of labor and management.

Union leaders tended to describe stress in terms of specific stressors that made the workplace aversive for their members. Identified stressors involved all aspects of work, but centered around extremes of demand (overload and underload) and lack of predictability or control. Labor officials winced at the very mention of "stress management." To them, such programs expected the individual to find solutions to organizational, environmental, and socioeconomic problems. Union representatives refused to blame their members for experiencing stress, choosing instead to formulate contractual and organizational solutions for particular stressors in the work environment.

Corporate respondents avoided characterizations of stress at work, preferring to emphasize the problems and lifestyles that people brought to the workplace. Occupational stress was implicitly seen as an inevitable aspect of the work situation to which individual workers must adapt. Personal strain was acknowledged by some to be a risk factor for disease and by others to reflect poor person-environment fit (French, Rodgers, and Cobb 1974). In any case, the responsibility for managing stress fell on the individual, who was encouraged to add relaxation and cognitive restructuring to a battery of lifestyle modification efforts that would improve his or her resistance and ability to cope with strain. Consonant with an emphasis on personal responsibility for managing stress and maintaining health, company-based stress management efforts were structured to help employees improve their health, habits, and adaptation to work. Virtually all of the corporate stress management programs that we reviewed were linked to larger efforts in health promotion, reflecting additional corporate priorities to reduce health-care costs and to improve productivity.

The results of our survey persuaded us that the definition of stress in the workplace involves a process that is inherently *political* and takes place within a larger socioeconomic context. Labor attributes stress to the task, the organization, and the work environment, while management locates stress in the experience and health of workers.

In our survey, we found groups from both camps who had begun to bridge this divide. Unions offered member assistance programs, safety and health committees, personal counseling, and health screenings. Corporations had introduced limited forms of worker participation and discussion (for example, quality circles and employee involvement), tacitly acknowledging that certain aspects of work might constitute stressors for their employees. Still, the vast majority of labor and corporate organizations tended to cling to their traditional perspectives, treating stress as *either* an organizational problem *or* an individual one.

Theoretical and empirical developments in assessing and reducing occupational stress depend on coming to terms with this discrepancy. What follows is a description of our initial efforts to integrate these divergent points of view by means of a systems-based assessment of occupational stress.

We reasoned that a systems perspective (Miller 1978) that portrayed the individual and the organization as interrelated would allow us to bridge the gap between labor and management views on stress. Thus, a stress assessment could take the individual worker or the organization as its starting point and then focus on their interrelationship. Stressors could emerge at any level in the interplay of the individual, organization, and larger social context. Systems theory suggested four overarching principles that would allow us to operationalize this integrative stress assessment: systems are *dynamic* in the interplay of their parts, they can be organized into a *hierarchy* of levels, they allow for *differentiated input and output*, and they are self-informing through *feedback* (Miller 1978).

These four principles dictated the content and the process of our stress assessment of a specific work site. We chose a time period for assessment where organizational change had created a new dynamic. In this case, it was our assumption that pending contract negotiations would constitute a stressor for the entire setting, heightening the adversarial nature of relations between labor and management, and in turn, *between hourly and salaried employees*. Second, we created an assessment that ordered the work site into hierarchical levels ranging from the individual's biology to the organization's socioeconomic context. Third, we created an assessment strategy that relied on extensive input from the organization before we distributed a stress survey as output back to the employees. Finally, feedback on rough drafts of the survey (the employees' feedback in the form of survey responses) and our feedback in a report to the union ensured that the work-site system was a self-informing process.

The remainder of this chapter is an effort first to clarify these four principles of systems theory, and then to demonstrate their operationalization through a stress assessment of a hotel during a period of labor negotiations.

OVERVIEW OF SYSTEMS THEORY

Our conceptual approach to occupational stress is based on a systems-ecological model (von Bertalanffy 1968; Bronfenbrenner 1977; Carroll and White 1982; Miller 1978; Schwartz 1982) in which individuals, organizations, and organizational subgroups are seen as open, living systems operating at different levels of complexity. Each comprises interacting parts and is embedded within multiple contexts or environments that provide the system with resources and feedback to maintain itself. Stress occurs when these reciprocal relationships create demands that exceed the resources available at any one level of the system. Demands exceeding resources constitute "stressors." An individual or organization's perception of deficient resources or excessive demands constitutes strain.

This definition of stress also emphasizes an ecological perspective. The essence of ecology, embodied in the work of Lewin (1935, 1936), Dubos (1965), and Carson (1962), is interrelatedness. Thus, a change in any part of a system is multidetermined and influences the entire system. Behavior at any level is a reflection of multiple contexts. Community psychologists (Barker 1968; Holahan and Spearly 1980; Moos 1976; Vincent and Trickett 1984) have abstracted fundamental principles of ecology and applied these concepts to a variety of environments and processes. Holahan and Spearly (1980), for example, have articulated several attributes of an ecological perspective that are relevant to stress and coping. These include the notions that behavior and systems are embedded in widening circles of relationships, that system-context (for example, person-environment) relationships are reciprocal, and that the perceptions of the individual provide useful data about person-environment interactions. Carroll and White (1982) have applied ecological theory to job burnout, noting its utility for balancing individual and environmental factors in the assessment or management of job stress.

The Dynamics of Work Stress

Both systems and ecological perspectives depict stress in dynamic terms. Alterations in the environment, individual, and/or the organization will lead to changes in the balance of demands and resources, increasing or decreasing stressors and perceived strain. This approach connects with our emphasis on stress as a *political* concept in the workplace. Labor and management will exploit the shifting dynamics of stress in an organization as a means of encouraging the employee to focus on aspects of stress friendly to their perspectives. Thus, employees' perceptions of stressors may actually swing from individual to organizational factors and back again. While the stress response can be measured in the laboratory or the field (Frankenhaeuser 1979), the definition of day-to-day stressors in the workplace is still a matter of debate.

As Karasek (1979) has argued, occupational stress may be defined as a characteristic of the job itself. As jobs increase in demand and diminish in control, they should become more stressful. However, an employee's perception of high demand or low control will be strongly influenced by the ongoing climate created by management and labor. Other researchers (Harrison 1978) suggest that there is a delicate fit of the person and the environment. The "person-environment" fit theory finds individual stress (experienced as negative emotion and physical symptoms) in the mismatch of a job's rewards and supplies with an individual's needs and preferences (cf. Chapter 5).

Conceiving of stress as a dynamic concept forces one to recognize that a poor fit between the individual and the environment is a function of shifting organizational and individual *realities* and *expectations*. Individuals and organizations progress and regress over time. These changes may promote poor person-environment fits, resulting in stress. At the same time, management and labor work to alter ideas about what the employee should *expect* or deserve. Their continual consciousness raising also redefines what is perceived as stress. The verdict is still out as to whether quality of work life and employee involvement interventions (such as those practiced by GM, Ford, Rolm, and Western Electric) achieve a consensual definition of work stress accepted by both labor and management. In the absence of this consensus, the perception of stress by employees remains open to persuasion and challenge (Tesh 1984).

The Hierarchical Organization of Work Stress

If we accept work stress as dynamically changing, we need to construct a model that varies in its levels of analysis. Just as the outcome of stress may be linked to a variety of negative feelings (frustration, boredom, anger, depression, isolation) and physical symptoms (sleep disturbance, muscle tension, stomach disorders, hypertension, headaches), the stressors themselves may be intermittently tied to an individual's sense of self-efficacy, lifestyle, family, co-workers, supervisors, and organization. Miller (1978) offers a second principle of systems theory that enables us to order the varying levels at which stressors might emerge, the *hierarchical organization* of systems. He posits a hierarchy of embedded wholes (systems), ranging from the cell to the supranational level, each composed of parts or subsystems in complex interaction.

Cummings and Cooper (1979) have applied aspects of Miller's systems model to occupational stress. Their description illustrates the utility of systems concepts for defining relationships between person and environment and between feedback and adjustment. Unfortunately, their paper failed to acknowledge the hierarchical nature of work environments. Person-environment interactions at work typically involve a person (organism), performing a task (behavior), within a setting (physical environment), as part of a work group (interpersonal environment), which represents one component or subsystem in a company or institution (organization). The organization, in turn, is subject to influence by local, national, and international market forces and by a host of social, political, and economic systems (Strand 1983).

Input–Output and Feedback

Systems theory, derived from cybernetics (von Bertalanffy 1950; Weiner 1948), emphasizes the role of information and feedback in maintaining equilibrium between a system and an environment. The fundamental characteristic of a living system is a transactional relationship with its environment by which some aspect of the environment (energy, matter, or information), is imported into the system, transformed, and exported back into the environment in a new form (von Bertalanffy 1950). This process provides the system with the resources and stability to withstand environmental variability and to pursue its own values. Absence or distortion of meaningful feedback for its behavior can promote a system's disregulation, leading to symptoms of strain or potential demise (Schwartz 1983).

Systems Principles Applied to the Assessment of Occupational Stress

In order to concretize our systems view of work stress, we sought out an assessment strategy that would recreate both a hierarchical model for content and a feedback orientation for process. First, we developed an assessment device that would order stressors from individual to organizational levels.

The patient evaluation grid (PEG), a diagnostic and treatment device used at the Yale Behavioral Medicine Clinic, provides a systems-based framework for analysis of direct and interactive contributions to mental and physical disorders. Formulated by Leigh and Reiser (1980), the PEG juxtaposes three contextual levels or systems (biological, psychological, and interpersonal-environmental) with three temporal dimensions (current, recent past, and long-term past). The result is a three-by-three matrix that organizes diagnostic and treatment information in a clear and accessible way. As a clinical instrument, the PEG provides an assessment structure for understanding behavior at multiple levels of the systems hierarchy (Schwartz 1981). Thus far, there have been no attempts beyond case study reports to utilize the PEG as an evaluative or research tool.

For our immediate purposes, we adapted the matrix structure of the PEG to include contributions to stress from seven sources. With regard to work, we identified the physical environment, task and interpersonal demands at the work setting, and the organization as sources of potential stress. With respect to the individual, we included biological and psychological aspects that might contribute to a poor fit with a given work situation. We also incorporated two non-work sources of stress in our matrix—socioeconomic factors and family responsibilities.

Since we were dealing with material from multiple settings and were primarily interested in cross-sectional comparisons, we transformed the time dimension into one that categorized the interventions into formal and informal responses to a stressor. By incorporating both formal (organizational) and informal (personal) responses into the grid, we acknowledged individual processes of adaptation evident in our clinical work. The distinction between relying on one's individual efforts to cope and exercising organizational structures on one's behalf seemed useful in understanding employee responses to stressors.

The resulting seven-by-three matrix, which we called the occupational stress evaluation grid (OSEG), proved to be a useful device for organizing our inquiries and describing our findings in the assessment of occupational stress (Table 7.1).

Developing a Research Process for Systems Assessment

With a hierarchical model of stress in place, we devised a research method that would mimic the input-output and feedback mechanisms of cybernetic theory. Our assessment procedure included a series of steps that called for built-in checks by representative employees on our emerging picture of the work site. This sequence alternated between taking in information and giving back our findings through meetings and rough drafts of our survey and eventual report. Throughout, we obtained information from individuals at different levels in the system's hierarchy (union officials and rank-

and-file members). Similarly, idiographic and nomothetic methods provided a sense of both individual and organizational attitudes about stressors.

This research strategy, roughly similar to that used in organizational diagnosis or survey feedback research (Alderfer 1980; Nadler 1977), engaged the organizational structure of the setting and the larger political context of the management-labor relations. In other words, we interacted with union members around problem definition, data collection, and analysis of results in such a way as to become part of the political context of the setting (in this case, contract negotiations). The process of the assessment enabled us to experience the disharmony between the union and management. We were also able to feed this information back to the union and management. Finally, we observed the result for the system of our assessment and feedback.

The following case study exemplifies the mechanics and process of our assessment. This detail provides a useful illustration of the advantages and difficulties of research collaborations with labor (for a more extensive account of the "nuts and bolts" of this stress assessment, see Singer, Neale, and Schwartz, 1987, or for another type of collaboration with labor, see Lewicki and Alderfer 1973). It also highlights how entry into and communication within the system are diagnostic tools of equal importance to the survey data gathered later on.

A SYSTEMS ASSESSMENT OF OCCUPATIONAL STRESS: A CASE STUDY

In the previous section, we emphasized four components of a systems perspective on occupational stress: (1) stress as a dynamic concept, (2) hierarchical organization, (3) differentiation of input and output, and (4) feedback. We proposed a dual strategy for applying these principles. First, we organized stress into a hierarchical grid, the OSEG. Second, we insisted that the process of assessment itself must be shaped around input-output and feedback mechanisms. The next section describes an assessment of unionized employees in a hotel during contract negotiations. It should serve as an instructive example of the utility and complexity of our dual assessment strategy.

Rationale for Choosing a Hotel

To put our research strategy and the OSEG into action, we looked for a relatively self-contained workplace that managed to offer a variety of organizational levels. Additionally, we wanted a work site that might afford us the possibility of union-management collaboration. A hotel, with its unionized work force divided into discrete but interdependent departments, provided the size, complexity, and variety we desired. The employees of a

Table 7.1 Occupational Stress Evaluation Grid

Levels	Stressors	Interventions	
		Formal	Informal
Sociocultural	Racism Ecological shifts Economic downturns Political changes Military crises Sexism	Elections Lobbying/political action Public education Trade associations	Grass-roots organizing Petitions Demonstrations Migration Spouse employment
Organizational	Hiring policies Potential plant closings, layoffs, relocation, automation, market shifts, retraining Organizational priorities	Corporate decision Reorganization New management model Management consultant in-service/retraining	Social activities Contests Incentives Manager involvement and ties with workers Continuing education Moonlighting
Work setting	Task (time, speed, autonomy, creativity) Supervision Co-workers Ergonomics Participation in decision- making	Supervisor meetings Health/safety meetings Union grievance negotiations Employee involvement Quality circles Company-initiated redesign In-service training	Slow-downs/speed-up Redefine tasks Support of other workers Sabotage, theft Quit, change jobs
Interpersonal	Spouse (divorce, separation, marital discord) Death Child problems	Legal services Time off Counseling, psychotherapy Insurance plans	Seek social support and advice Seek legal or financial assistance Self-help groups Vacations/leave of absence

	Friends Parents In-laws	Family treatment Loans/credit unions	Child care
Psychological	Personality, coping behavior (e.g., Type A, repression) Emotion/mood/"stress" expectations, beliefs, goals Self-inefficacy Mental illness	Employee assistance (referral/in-house) Counseling, therapy cognitive, behavioral, biobehavioral Medication Supervisory training	Social support (friends, family, co-workers, church) Self-help groups/books Self-medication Recreation, leisure, sexual activity "Sick" days
Biological	Circadian rhythm Nutrition, sleep, exercise, weight, age, sex, race (genetic) Current illness impairment/disabilities Drugs Pregnancy	Rescheduling Placement and screening Health education Counseling Substance abuse treat. Biobehavioral treat. Maternity leave Health promotion	Change sleep/wake habits Sleep on job Bag lunch Drugs Cosmetics Diets, exercise Medication Self-care Dietary change
Physical/environmental	Climate Poor air Noise Toxic chemicals Pollutants Poor lighting Architecture Radiation	Clothing and equipment Climate control Ventilation Chemical control Interior decoration Muzak Protection Medical office	Own equipment, decoration Walkman Soap operas Music Personal physician

Source: Compiled by the authors.

hotel traditionally present a mixture of ethnic groups, educational training, age, sex, and income levels. Such diversity would allow a test of the thesis that stress could not be considered a generic malady, easily treated with the same programs across work groups and types of workers. Equally important, the range of work required from union members in a hotel extends from laundry and custodial tasks to electrical engineering to preparation and service of expensive cuisine. Such qualitatively distinct work should produce corresponding differences in employee-perceived stressors.

Finding the Hotel

It was apparent to us that unionized employees' definitions of stress diverged more from those of management than from non-unionized employees, so we sought out a unionized work force. This made an attempted integration of perspectives more challenging and potentially useful. We first met with a local representative of a large hotel employees union. Offering an overview of our NIOSH findings on the different labor and management perspectives on stress, we indicated our interest in trying to perform a collaborative assessment of stress in a hotel. We explained the OSEG framework and suggested that it could best be tested if labor and management worked together with us.

The representative, while unwilling to overextend the limited resources of the union, agreed to aid us in an assessment. He proposed we assess a particular hotel whose approximately 200 union members had been undergoing a great deal of stress since its recent takeover by a multinational corporation. He emphasized that the union's difficulties were neither money (the pay was good) nor working conditions (the hotel was the nicest in the city). Rather, the work force had been receiving increased demands from the new management, while at the same time perceiving that management was unsympathetic to its scheduling, equipment, and personal needs. In addition, since the union was organizing for contract proposals and negotiations, he felt a stress assessment would help union members clarify and communicate their demands to each other and to management.

From a tactical point of view, the union was clearly in favor of our concern with making this project a collaboration with management. If management agreed to participate, the stress assessment would be sure to reach more members and generate more open discussion among hotel personnel about existing stressors. Even though a stress assessment might improve management's image as a caring employer, it would also create pressure for management to follow through with contractual changes. Based on feedback from the membership, the union was secure that our assessment would indeed identify stressors; there was little chance we would do the assessment and give the hotel a clean bill of health. On the other hand, if management refused to sponsor our assessment (the more likely alternative from the union's perspective), the union would have another useful organizing opportunity to demonstrate the unresponsiveness of the hotel to its employees.

Aware of our position in the union's strategy, we decided to pursue the assessment, regardless of management's decision whether or not to collaborate. Prior contacts with representatives from a variety of national and international unions had revealed a rather shaky relationship between labor and psychology (Singer et al. 1986). This uneasiness was based primarily on a long history of management-financed consultation efforts, with an emphasis on productivity rather than improvement of working conditions (Huszczo, Wiggins, and Currie 1984). Labor skepticism about psychology and the newer concept of "work stress" persists, due in part to the individualistic orientation of most stress management consultants and their focus on managerial or executive-level personnel rather than hourly employees. In light of this, part of our agenda in this assessment was to test the possibility of collaboration with a union in a stress reduction intervention. We hoped to improve psychology-labor relations by following through on the stress assessment, even if management declined involvement. Further, since there had been little psychological research on the stress of contract negotiations, we were also eager to use this opportunity to examine this process. Still, the integrative framework of the OSEG dictated that we make every effort to include management equally at each step of the assessment.

Accordingly, we mailed the same detailed letter to both the general manager of the hotel in question and the paid staff of its local union. The letter described our proposed stress assessment of unionized employees. It outlined in general terms a procedure involving interviews of representative employees and a hotel-wide survey. We emphasized that ours was a nonpartisan approach, sponsored by a NIOSH research contract, and that our goal was to demonstrate the utility of a comprehensive assessment of stress. The letter concluded with a request for a meeting or telephone call to discuss the proposed assessment. After two weeks without a reply from the general manager, we followed up the letter with several phone messages. Finally, we received a one-paragraph letter from the general manager declining any participation in the assessment. His note indicated that in light of recent shifts in management, renovation of one of the hotel's restaurants, and upcoming labor negotiations, an assessment of stress at this time would not be possible. Independent efforts to generate support for the assessment at the level of the parent corporation also proved unsuccessful. At this point, we went ahead with the project in conjunction with the paid staff of the hotel's union.

BEGINNING THE ASSESSMENT OF STRESSORS

Drawing on our four-component system, we applied our "content-process" strategy to the assessment of stressors faced by unionized employees at the hotel.

Stress as a Dynamic Concept

In the context of contract negotiations, we hoped to show that perceived stressors affecting the employees would be a particular function of the organizing drive of the union, the effects of a new and unpopular management, and the enduring characteristics of the work.

Our goal was to determine whether certain perceived stressors would gain prominence due to the "climate" of the workplace at a specific moment in the organization's history. A second assessment, after settlement of the contract, might turn up a different emphasis on stressors. Using the OSEG as our guide, our prediction for the hotel at this juncture was that stressors at the *organizational level* would relate to the self-report of the greatest emotional and physical distress. In other words, *management policies, management practices, job security, and cost-cutting* would be targeted as the greatest stressors by a work force on the eve of a contract expiration. The ascendancy of these stressors at this particular time in the hotel's history would provide support for a dynamic definition of stress if they proved to be substantially different from outcomes of a later assessment.

A Hierarchical Organization of Stress

In order to detect the emergence of different levels of stressors for employees at the hotel at different moments in the organization, we needed to separate these stressors into discrete, quantifiable units. To accomplish this purpose, we set out to divide the hotel into the levels depicted in the OSEG. Thus, in our initial interviews with employees and in the later questionnaire, we attempted to cluster our questions into the OSEG categories. Table 7.2 (columns 1 and 2) catalogs the refitting of the OSEG grid to the specific characteristics of the hotel. The preliminary division of the hotel into the levels of the OSEG allowed us to generate lists of potential stressors within each level.

Table 7.2 An OSEG Assessment of an Urban Hotel

OSEG levels	Sample stressors*	Subscale labels
Sociocultural	Gender- or race-based discrimination Economic downturn/recession Seasonal business cycle National labor relations climate	

Organizational	Corporate ownership/structure
	Labor negotiations
	Staffing and hiring policies
	Layoff/reclassification
	Management ethos
	Cost-cutting
		Job security
		Satisfaction with
		   management policy
		Satisfaction with
		   management practice

Table 7.2 (continued)

Work setting: interpersonal	Multiple supervision Management style/competence Work-group structure/norms "Outsiders"	Upper management positive Upper management negative Lower management Co-worker relations
Job characteristics	Unpredictable scheduling Conflicting demands Time pressure High demands/additional duties Low decision latitude Inadequate supplies/equipment Heavy lifting and pushing	Scheduling Job overload Autonomy External control
Physical environment	Climate extremes Poor ventilation Hazardous situations Poor recreational facilities Poor quality food Uncomfortable positions	Physical demands
Family/social	Schedule interference Child-care responsibilities Financial difficulties Dual-career or blended families	
Individual: psychological	Emotional experience of work Mood/memory changes Career/job expectations Lack of control/helplessness Motivation	Positive Emotion Negative emotion
Biological	Substance use/abuse Tension/pain Sleep difficulties Digestive problems Hypertension	Muscle tension and pain Sleep disturbance

Source: Compiled by the authors.

*Sample stressors reflect questionnaire items/sets of items derived from original OSEG and 36 hours of interviews with 12 representatives from different jobs/areas of the hotel.

Additionally, we were able to clarify which levels of the grid that we would be unable to assess. The highest level, sociocultural factors, were impractical for us to evaluate. We had no real expertise or method for determining how national or statewide economic trends in the hotel industry might be affecting the particular hotel in question. Similarly, we had little information, other than observation and anecdote, about long-standing issues of gender or racial discrimination in hotels. Five levels down, the family-social factors also presented a difficult task. We felt uncomfortable asking too many questions about employees' personal and home lives on a questionnaire designed to examine stressors at work. Faced with the inevitable tradeoffs of community research, we decided not to risk alienating potential respondents with questions considered too intimate or prying.

The Research Process

Having defined stress dynamically and hierarchically, we applied the last two of our systems principles, *the differentiation of input and output in the system* and *feedback* from the employees to us and from us to the employees. We solicited employee input at the initial stage of the assessment in the following manner. Table 7.3 presents a draft of the research strategy we created to work with the union. Step 1 is described above; step 2 involved input from the two paid union staff representatives.

Table 7.3   Overall Assessment and Research Strategy

1. Contact labor and management representatives for potential collaboration.
2. Define work units and organizational structure (demographics).
3. Identify representatives within work units for interview.
4. Develop work history format; select relevant questionnaire items.
5. Interview work unit representatives (10-12) about work experiences. Feed back results to work-unit representatives for verification.
6. Devise a stressor survey based on interview information.
7. Survey organization about work-related stressors. Feed back results to the entire organization.
8. Devise a stress response survey (with scenarios?) specific to work units and to identified stressors.
9. Survey work units about responses to work-related stressors. Feed back results to work units.
10. Compile stressor–response results and formulate profile of organization.
11. Identify stressful event for organization, using management and labor assistance.
12. Survey work units about stressors and responses related to stressful event, again using instruments specific to work units and identified stressors. Feed back results to work units and organization.

Table 7.3 (continued)

13. Devise interventions at work-group level to deal with stressful events, based on survey responses.

14. Identify another stressful event for organization, this time implementing intervention strategy.

15. Survey work units about response to stressful event and effectiveness of intervention strategy. Feed back results to work units and organization.

16. Compare stressors and responses for both stressful events.

17. Attempt to establish this research-intervention strategy as an ongoing organizational process, with individuals trained to implement it.

Source: Compiled by the authors.

The hotel was divided into essentially discrete departments: front desk (bellmen, clerks, telephone operators); food and beverage (bartenders, waiters, waitresses, hostesses, cooks, bus staff, pantry workers, dishwashers); housekeeping (maids, housemen, laundry, linen workers); banquet (waitresses, waiters, housemen); and engineering (utility electricians and plumbers, maintenance). We then met with shop stewards representing each department. The shop stewards reaffirmed the basic complaints of the paid staff about the hotel. Additionally, they provided us with a list of 12 employees distributed across the different departments of the hotel (step 3). These representatives were chosen for their length of service and their knowledge of health and safety issues at the hotel.

Our goal here was to perform a diagnostic occupational history, using these employees as spokespeople for the general conditions of their particular departments (step 5a). The interview with each employee was divided into two parts. In the first segment, we took a history of previous work experience and of the various duties they had performed at the hotel. We then asked each representative to describe both a typical day and a stressful day in his or her department. Their descriptions were extremely detailed, covering the simultaneous phone-answering, computer-scanning, and registration of guests by the front desk clerk to the dough-rolling and jam-spreading for 1,000 daily turnovers of the pastry chef's assistant. While stressors differed for each department, the initial concern with poor labor-management relations was borne out across all departments.

We followed these histories by orally administering a pilot version of our stress questionnaire, divided into the OSEG levels indicated previously. In addition to items we had created, we drew questions from the *Quality of Employment Survey* (Survey Research Center 1977), *Office Workers: Health and Well-Being Survey* (Gordon, Stellman, and Snow 1982), and the

CWA Local 1180 Stress Questionnaire (Love 1983). The list of items extended from air quality in the laundry to the state of the hotel business in the city.

We met with each representative at the union hall in interviews that lasted from 2 to 3 hours. The difficulty in arranging these meetings foreshadowed our later complications with survey returns. The interviewees were paid $10 for their participation, but even with this mild incentive they were hard to pin down to meeting times. Part of the problem was the nature of hotel work itself, with its odd shifts and frequent changes in schedules. Difficulties in arranging interviews presented us with an early sign that scheduling at the hotel might be a significant stressor at the level of both job characteristics and organizational policy. Participation problems also informed us about the nature of relations between the employees and the staff of the union.

With notes from each interview spanning 15-20 pages, we quickly realized that the amount of information generated by a comprehensive systems analysis was too overwhelming for our limited resources. For this reason, we decided to restrict our initial efforts to the study of stressors and not employee responses to the stressors. It was clear that an assessment of responses would be at least as intricate and detailed as our assessment of the stressors. Faced with the deadline of the contract expiration date, we decided it would be more useful and manageable to focus specifically on the pattern of stressors we could identify (steps 1-7). We might then propose an assessment of stress responses in a follow-up investigation.

The Stress Survey—Output to the System

Based on the 12 interviews, we created our stress survey. It expressed our first *output* to the system of the hotel. We distributed the survey to each of the shop stewards and asked them to fill it out (step 5b). Their reactions and suggestions to us (before we distributed the survey hotel-wide) exemplified the last systems principle of a *feedback loop*. Using their reactions, we clarified the wording of items and generally shortened the questionnaire (step 6).

The final questionnaire covered the organizational, work-setting (interpersonal, job characteristics, and physical environment), and individual (psychological and biological) levels of the OSEG. At the organizational level, we included items that focused on job security and treatment by the "hotel." Questions regarding management of the work setting distinguished between upper-level managers (such as the hotel's general manager or the food and beverages manager) and lower-level managers, such as one's immediate supervisor. Also included at the level of the work setting were questions about scheduling, co-workers, and the physical environment. Among these work-setting items, we embedded 20 of Karasek's (1979) questions concerning the level of demands and control attached to a particular job. Karasek et al. (1981) had previously demonstrated the connection of high-demand—low-control jobs to employees' proneness to coronary heart disease. For our psychological and physical items, we provided a list of emotions in a typical day at work and a list of physical symptoms from the *Symptom Checklist 90* (Derogatis 1975).

Our conversations with department representatives also allowed us to add an additional page to each questionnaire (color coded by department) that asked questions about stressors specific to each department of the hotel. These questions were included to allow us to discriminate patterns of stressors unique to work groups across the hotel.

Distribution of the Stress Survey

Another area in which we depended on paid staff and shop stewards of the union involved distribution of the final version of the survey. Their past experience had indicated that a mailing would not produce an adequate return rate. The union staff suggested that contract proposal meetings would be the best opportunity for reaching the largest number of members. The meetings were to be held in three large assemblies in order to include the different shifts of employees. Shop stewards would then be responsible for distribution of the remaining questionnaires to employees who missed the meetings.

One of our investigators was allowed to attend the proposal meetings and make a short request to employees to fill out and return the survey. Additionally, a paid staff member and a shop steward spoke in support of the survey. Each survey came with a cover letter and a stamped envelope addressed to the union's office. Each department's set of questionnaires, coded by color, were distributed in separate stacks around the assembly hall. In all, 100 surveys were handed out at the meetings. Shop stewards and our research team distributed an additional 150 surveys to employees who did not attend the meetings or who had misplaced or lost their first survey.

Data Collection

In many ways, the process of collecting completed questionnaires revealed as much about the organization of the hotel (and the union) as did the results. Shop stewards varied greatly in their commitment to distributing and collecting questionnaires. Similarly, whole departments varied in their response rates, reflecting both the steward's involvement and the nature of the department itself. Educational background, language differences, amount of satisfaction in a department, and relationships with superiors all played a role in determining the level of response in a given department. Table 7.4 gives the various departmental response rates, as well as the

Table 7.4   Demographics of Sample

Unionized employees in the hotel: 196

Participants in the survey: 82/196 (42%) unionized employees

Response rate by department:
   Banquet: 12/25 (48%)
   Engineering: 2/7 (29%)
   Food and beverage: 33/82 (40%)
   Front desk: 14/32 (44%)
   Housekeeping: 21/57 (37%)

Mean age ($n = 69$): 37.7 years (SD = 13.45)

Sex ($n = 74$):
   Male: 32 (43%)
   Female: 42 (57%)

Education ($n = 61$):
   12 years (SD = 3.40)

Race ($n = 73$):
   White: 48 (68%)
   Black: 15 (21%)
   Hispanic: 7 (10%)
   Asian: 1 (1%)

Marital status $n = 70$):
   Married: 30 (43%)
   Single: 26 (37%)
   Divorced/separated: 13 (19%)
   Widowed: 1 (1%)

Number of children ($n = 70$):
   None: 29 (41%)
   One: 6 (9%)
   Two: 16 (23%)
   Three or more: 19 (27%)

Length of employment in present job title ($n = 72$):
   5.8 years (SD = 4.80)

Years at hotel ($n = 72$):
   5.78 years (SD = 3.43)

Source: Compiled by the authors.

overall rate of response. The responses are also broken down on other demographic variables, including sex, age, education level, and years of service at the hotel.

We can offer some observations that suggest potential hypotheses for differing return rates. The front desk responded most enthusiastically, due most likely to their higher educational level and to active involvement of their steward in the union. The completed surveys from the front desk employees indicated they were highly stressed due to difficulties with high demands, understaffing, and lack of supervision. The food and beverage department, although experiencing an equivalent sense of stress, appeared less organized, relying on a newly appointed steward. There was also much less representation in survey returns from the "back of the house" members of the department (dishwashers, bus staff, pantry workers). With this group, language difficulties with the survey may have been a problem. Still, the steward who handled the cooks and cooks' assistants put in a good effort to solicit returns.

Similarly, the housekeeping department suffered from a less-than-effective organization and from language differences. We had originally suggested producing a Spanish-language version of the questionnaire, but the union staff assured us this would only be necessary for about 12 employees. Our own observations led us to believe there were additional employees who would have benefitted from a translated survey.

Of the remaining two departments, we put little emphasis on engineering, since it comprised only seven employees. Efforts with the banquet staff started poorly due to the steward's absences, but a rank-and-file member (taking courses part-time in psychology) became interested and proved to be helpful in obtaining completed questionnaires.

This description of the slightly chaotic conditions concerning questionnaire retrieval should indicate the extreme difficulty one faces in pursuing a survey with only union cooperation and no management sponsorship. We were dependent on the organizational structure of the union to do our leg work for us. This proved very variable and slow. It also illustrated to us the gap that may exist between paid staff, stewards, and rank-and-file. Rank-and-file members, presented with the survey, would sometimes ask if this paper came from the "union." Their question clearly implied they saw themselves and the "union" as separate entities, even though the entire bargaining unit was composed of members. On the other hand, the eventual survey returns showed a strong belief that the union was doing much more than management to improve their work life.

The paid staff of the union local was so overworked that its ability to mobilize stewards to aid us was severely limited. The national union was still in the midst of a large strike in Las Vegas during much of the planning stage of the survey and at the same time as the initial work. Accordingly, the paid staff for the local was covering not only their region, but a neighboring region as well. In addition, two other hotels in the city (both belonging to the same local) had contracts expiring on the same date as our hotel.

All this pressure on the union and its resources resulted in our research team taking a much more active role in the data collection. We positioned researchers in the employee cafeteria during shift changes, lunch hours, and coffee breaks. The researchers would pass out questionnaires, collect them as they were finished, and generally talk up the usefulness of filling out the survey. Spanish-speaking employees and stewards were recruited to encourage the Hispanic housekeeping staff to participate in filling it out. Often these members would bring it home and have their sons or daughters help to translate the questions.

Persisting through some frustrating weeks, we achieved a respectable return rate (42 percent), with some time left to analyze the data before contract negotiations started. Our goal was to give the union feedback on specific stressors within departments and across the hotel in time for their use in negotiations. In this way, they could seek actual contract language or concessions to deal directly with the stressors.

Results of the Survey

To analyze the questionnaire data, we grouped items into a priori subscales. These subscales were submitted to separate factor analyses. Items on factors with eigenvalues equal to and greater than 1 were examined for their loadings. Items that loaded above .40 on one and only one factor were combined with the other high-loading items on their factor and were averaged to form new scales. These new scales were intercorrelated and then submitted to multiple regressions predicting perceived physical and emotional well-being.

The major question we examined through the survey was whether stressors at different levels of the OSEG would be correlated in different and systematic ways with the employees' perceived well-being. More specifically, could we show that during a time of new management and contract negotiations, stress would become focused at the organizational and not the job characteristic level? We hypothesized that employees would link negative emotions at work and reported physical symptoms to a feeling that management policies and practices were unfair or arbitrary. After all, this was the main focus of the union's organizing efforts. Concern with the control or demands of their particular work would not be connected to perceived stress at work nearly as much as these organizational issues.

Factor Analyses of the Stress Survey Items

In order to create stable factors from the survey items, we divided items into a priori subscales based on levels of the OSEG. Factor analyses would allow us to test if our rationally defined subscales held together based on the actual replies of the employees. They would also tell us which items were tapping into the same dimension and which had failed to tap any useful dimension. Items on the same dimension could be averaged to form approximate factor scores. To examine these questions, we performed eight separate principal axis-varimax rotated factor analyses (for details, see Singer, Neale, and Schwartz 1985a).

Table 7.5 presents 16 new subscales created from approximate factor scores. The titles indicate the new subscales with their items benath them. The titles in parentheses refer to original a priori groupings of items on which factor analyses were performed. Titles that are the same as the a priori grouping in parentheses emerged from the same factor analysis. Returning to the last column of Table 7.2, we can see how well the factor-analyzed subscales of our survey fit with the levels of the OSEG. It should be noted that all the scales registered Cronbach alphas (a test for the strength of relationship of items within a scale) of .6 and above, except for the "physical demands" subscale. One reason for this scale's poor inter-reliability might be the large variation in physical demands faced by workers in the hotel. A bellman and a laundry worker handle very different physical tasks and environmental hazards. Due to the physical demands scale's lack of reliability, we removed it from all subsequent correlation and regression analyses.

Table 7.5   Subscales Based on Factor Analyses of OSEG-derived Items

---

Organizational

Job security (Karasek, control and demand)

1. During the past year, how often were you in a situation where you faced job loss or layoff? (.70)
2. How likely is it that during the next couple of years you will lose your present job with the hotel? (.69)

Satisfaction with management policy (organizational policies and practices)

1. How helpful is the hotel in training you to do your job? (.60)
2. How often does the hotel treat you like an expert at your job? (.73)
3. How much are you treated like an adult by the hotel? (.64)
4. How helpful has the hotel management been in improving your work life? (.72)
5. How often do you have the equipment to do your job properly? (.50)

Dissatisfaction with management practice (organizational policies and practices)

1. How likely is it that you will find a new job in the next year? (.49)
2. How fair is the hotel in paying you what you deserve? (−.61)
3. Do you feel you are doing more work than you used to for basically the same pay? (.58)
4. Is the hotel making you do work that used to be done by other employees in the hotel? (.51)
5. How likely is it that in the next couple of years you will be given different duties without being promoted? (.52)

Table 7.5 (continued)

Work Setting—Interpersonal

Supervisory relations (upper and lower management)

Upper management—positive

1. My supervisor is helpful to me in getting my job done. (.79)
2. My supervisor is concerned about the welfare of those under him/her. (.82)
3. My supervisor pays attention to what I am saying. (.59)
4. My supervisor succeeds at getting people to work together. (.83)

Upper management—negative

1. My supervisor interferes with or makes it hard for me to do my work. (.66)
2. I get mixed messages about what to do from my supervisor. (.63)
3. I am exposed to hostility or conflict from my supervisor. (.54)

Lower management

(All of the above positive and negative items loaded according to their valence on the lower management factor (.47-.72) in addition to the item below.)
1. My supervisor knows his/her job and does it well. (.70)

Co-worker relations (co-worker)

1. People I work with take a personal interest in me. (.45)
2. People I work with are friendly. (73)
3. People I work with are helpful in getting the job done. (.79)
4. People I work with help me get through the day. (.78)

Work Setting—Job Characteristics

Scheduling (Scheduling policies and practices)

1. How often is your schedule posted for the coming week? (.53)
2. How often are you given enough notice about changes in your work hours? (.51)
3. How much are you able to predict your work schedule for the next week? (.73)
4. How likely is it that your schedule will be changed at the last minute? (−.61)

Job overload (Karasek, control and demand)

1. How often do you fall behind? (.60)
2. How often do you leave your job without finishing what you should have done? (.58)
3. Does your job require you to do things over and over again? (.41)
4. Do you have time to finish your work? (−.61)
5. Are your tasks often interrupted before they can be completed, requiring attention at a later time? (.42)

Autonomy (Karasek, control and demand)

1. Does your job allow you freedom as to how you do your work? (.53)
2. Does your job require you to keep learning new things? (.59)

Table 7.5 (continued)

3. Do you have a lot of say about what happens on your job? (.57)
4. Does your job allow you to use schooling or work experience you had before starting your present job? (.53)

External control (Karasek, control and demand)

1. Does your job require you to make decisions on your own? (.59)
2. Does waiting on work from other people or other departments often slow you down on the job? (.44)
3. How often do you skip your break? (.54)
4. Does your job require you to work without sitting for long periods of time? (.43)

Work Setting—Physical Environment

Physical demands (physical environment)

1. Is your workplace too cold? ($-.43$)
2. Do you work with hazardous materials? (.53)
3. Does your job require you to lift or push heavy objects? (.61)
4. Does your job require you to work in uncomfortable positions or use awkward motions? (.52)

Individual

Psychological (Emotional experience at work)

Positive emotion

1. Part of a team (.53)
2. Proud (.73)
3. Enthusiastic (.87)
4. Appreciated (.75)
5. Happy (.53)

Negative emotion

1. Stretched to the limits of your energy and capacity (.59)
2. Isolated (.60)
3. Powerless (.71)
4. Frustrated (.55)
5. Depressed (.64)
6. Bored (.48)

Biological (Physical symptoms)

Muscle tension and pain

1. Neck Pains (.70)
2. Back Pain (.65)
3. Muscle aches and pains (.54)
4. Neck tension (.82)

Table 7.5 (continued)

5. Back tension (.69)
6. Shoulder tension (.82)

Sleep disturbance

1. Fatigue (.51)
2. Difficulty falling asleep (.76)
3. Early morning awakening (.62)
4. Restless or disturbed sleep (.65)

Source: Compiled by the authors.

Each item used a 1-5 Likert scale. Factor Analyses based on a priori subscales derived from the OSEG are listed in parentheses. Factor-analyzed subscales are listed in capitals. Items included if they loaded above .40 on one and only one factor.

If our assessment was accurate, the subscales "satisfaction with management policy" and "dissatisfaction with management practice" should have correlated most highly with subjective reports of negative emotion and physical symptoms. Additionally, one might still have expected to see dissatisfaction with management policies and practices filtering down to the level of "job overload" and "autonomy."

Correlations of Organization, Work Setting, and Subjective Well-Being Subscales

Tables 7.6, 7.7, and 7.8 present the intercorrelations and the correlations of the organization, work setting, and subjective well-being subscales. In Table 7.6, the significant intercorrelations of the "policy" and "practice" subscales with "upper management" (executives and department heads), "lower management" (immediate supervisors), "job security," "overload," "autonomy," and "external control" subscales range from $-.25$ to .59. These findings suggest a consistent picture in the perception of the employees. The more positively they felt about policies and practices of the hotel, the more positively they felt about both upper management and their immediate supervisors; the more secure they felt about keeping their jobs, the less overload and the greater autonomy they reported experiencing at work. Further examination of the relationship of "autonomy" to "upper management" reveals that the better employees felt about upper management, the more autonomous they felt at work. Similarly, the more "overload" they felt at work, the less positively they felt toward "lower management." It should be noted as a caution that all of these correlations say nothing about the direction or causality of the relationships. Even the regressions to be presented later on will not inform us about the causal order of these workplace factors.

Table 7.7 provides the correlations of the four subjective well-being subscales with the 11 organization and work setting subscales. As hypothesized, the organizational and management subscales were most strongly correlated with the four subjective well-being subscales. Of particular note is the strong inverse relationship (− .47) of "negative emotion" at work with "satisfaction with management's policies." There emerged an even more powerful relationship (.53) between "negative emotion" at work and "dissatisfaction with management's practices." On the other hand, "positive emotion" at work was related strongly (.49) to "satisfaction with management's policies" and to positive views of "upper management" (.41). Even perceived "muscle tension" and "sleep disturbance" increased as "satisfaction with management policies" decreased (− .30 and − .29, respectively). Interestingly, "muscle tension" and "sleep disturbance" appear to have been related to (− .31 and − .36) perceptions of "lower management" as well.

In examining the more traditional job characteristics of work load, autonomy, and external control (Karasek 1979), one notes that "autonomy" was positively related to "positive emotion" at work (.28), and "external control" was positively related to "negative emotion" (.39).

Regressing the Well-Being Subscales on the 11 Organization and Work Setting Subscales

Our original hypothesis was that the influence of contract negotiations and the union's organizing drive would direct employees' attention to management policies and practices. Their dissatisfaction with these two organizational elements would show the strongest link to their perception of emotions at work and physical symptoms. To a lesser extent, the more traditinal job characteristic stressors of controllability and demand would also show a relationship to subjective well-being.

Table 7.9 presents multiple regressions, predicting positive and negative emotion muscle tension and sleep disturbance from the 11 organization and work setting subscales. Regressions for the two "emotion at work" subscales are highly significant and show interesting differential relationships of organizational variables to positive and negative emotion.

Positive Emotion at Work

"Positive emotion" is strongly and directly related to "satisfaction with management policies." Thus, employees' perceptions of being treated like an adult and expert, of receiving proper training and equipment, and of having their work life improved, all strongly predicted how enthusiastic, appreciated, happy, and proud, and how much a part of a team they felt. Many other subscales one might have expected to predict satisfaction at work did not ("co-worker relations," "autonomy," "job security"). Inter-

Table 7.6 Correlations of 11 Organization and Work Setting Subscales

	JSEC	PLCY	PRAT	UM+	UM–	LM	CWK	SCHD	LOAD	AUTO	ECO
Job Sec	1.00 80	-.41[a] 77	.45[a] 78	-.26[b] 76	.30[c] 76	-.32[c] 77	.16 79	-.24[b] 80	.28[b] 78	-.11 78	.18 80
Policy		1.00 78	-.32[c] 75	.59[a] 73	-.37[c] 73	.37[c] 75	-.12 77	.25[b] 78	-.28[b] 76	.36[c] 76	-.25[b] 78
Practice			1.00 78	-.25[b] 74	-.26[b] 74	-.44[a] 75	.24[b] 77	-.20 78	.27[b] 76	-.01 76	.36[c] 78
UManage +				1.00 77	-.52[a] 76	.36[c] 76	-.03 77	.15 77	-.11 76	.38[a] 76	-.24[b] 76
UManage –					1.00 77	-.37[c] 75	.14 77	-.23[b] 77	.05 77	-.08 76	.20 76
LManage						1.00 79	-.10 79	.15 79	-.34[c] 78	.31[c] 78	-.19 78

192

	Co-Workr	Schedule	Overload	Autonomy	ExContrl
Co-Workr	1.00 81	.07 81	-.02 80	-.02 80	.03 80
Schedule		1.00 82	-.25[b] 80	-.02 80	-.17 81
Overload			1.00 80	-.18 79	.23[b] 79
Autonomy				1.00 80	.17 79
ExContrl					1.00 81

[a] $P < .001$.
[b] $P < .05$.
[c] $P < .01$.

Note: See Table 7.5 for full subscale titles.
Source: Compiled by the authors.

Table 7.7 Correlations of Four Well-Being Subscales with 11 Organization and Work Setting Subscales

	JSEC	PLCY	PRAT	UM+	UM−	LM	CWK	SCHD	LOAD	AUTO	ECO
+Emotion	−.14	.49[a]	−.25[b]	.41[a]	−.22	.37[a]	.06	.12	−.12	.28[b]	−.02
	75	73	73	74	73	76	77	77	76	76	76
−Emotion	.35[c]	−.47[a]	.53[a]	−.42[a]	.26[b]	−.32[c]	.07	−.02	.21	−.19	.39[a]
	76	74	74	74	75	76	78	78	78	77	77
MusTen	.24[b]	−.30[c]	.20	−.32[c]	.18	−.31[c]	−.01	.03	.24[b]	−.29[b]	.12
	73	72	71	72	72	72	74	74	73	73	73
SleepD	.19	−.29[b]	.17	−.31[c]	.09	−.36[c]	−.03	.01	.19	−.28[b]	.15
	71	70	69	70	70	70	72	72	71	71	71

[a]$P < .001$.

[b]$P < .05$.

[c]$P < .01$.

Note: See Table 7.5 for full subscale titles.

Source: Compiled by the authors.

Table 7.8 Intercorrelations of Well-Being Subscales

	+ Emot	− Emot	MusTen	SleepD
+ Emotion	1.00	− .20	− .26[a]	− .18
	77	75	70	68
− Emotion		1.00	.38[b]	.39[b]
		78	71	69
Muscle tension			1.00	.61[b]
			74	72
Sleep disturbance				1.00
				72

[a]$P < .05$.
[b]$P < .001$.
Source: Compiled by the authors.

estingly, "dissatisfaction with management practice" was not inversely related to "positive emotion" at work. This finding suggests that for this work force, being paid what one deserves, not being given more than one used to do, and not being given different duties without being promoted will not automatically predict an employee's increased positive experience of work.

Negative Emotion

Results for the "negative emotion" regression are highly significant and quite consistent with our prediction (see Table 7.9). The R-squared (or the amount of the relationship accounted for by the regression) is a respectable .44 [$F(12, 61) = 3.77$; $p < .0005$] and the two powerful predictors are "satisfaction with management policy" and "dissatisfaction with management practice." "Management policy" is inversely related to "negative emotion." The better global treatment by management in areas of training, equipment, and respect, the less negative emotion employees experienced at work (that is, the less powerless, depressed, frustrated, and bored they feel). On the other hand, "dissatisfaction with management practice" is positively related (beta = .29) to "negative emotion at work." This raises an interesting distinction about how employees react to the practices of management. A look at the items in the "management practice" subscale shows that all but one ("looking for job in the next year") are related to a perception of fairness on the part of management. Thus, it would seem that management's fair practices did not influence positive emotion in employees, but their lack of fairness did promote negative emotion in employees. It

Table 7.9 Regressing the Well-Being Subscales on 11 Organization and
Work Setting Subscales

	Parameter estimate	T value	P	Beta
Positive Emotion				
$F(11, 63) = 2.71; P < .008$				
R-squared: .36				
Adjusted R-squared: .23				
Intercept	−1.79	−1.33	.19	.00
Job security	.00	−.01	.99	.00
Policy	.49	2.82	.007	.46
Practice	−.02	−.14	.89	−.06
UManagement +	.13	1.09	.28	.17
UManagement −	.08	.66	.52	.09
Lower management	.19	1.33	.19	.19
Co-worker	.07	.55	.58	.07
Schedule	.12	.96	.34	.12
Overload	.22	1.33	.19	.17
Autonomy	−.06	−.40	.69	−.05
External control	.26	1.63	.11	.22
Negative emotion				
$F(11.64) = 3.77; P < .0005$				
R-squared: .44				
Adjusted R-squared: .32				
Intercept	2.15	1.79	.08	.00
Job security	−.01	−.06	.95	−.01
Policy	−.39	−2.46	.02	−.38
Practice	−.29	2.06	.04	.29
UManagement +	−.03	−.26	.80	−.04
UManagement −	.00	.05	.96	.01
Lower management	−.01	−.06	.95	−.01
Co-worker	.00	.02	.98	.00
Schedule	.15	1.39	.17	.16
Overload	−.10	−.69	.49	−.08
Autonomy	−.04	−.29	.77	−.04
External control	.25	1.76	.08	.22
Muscle tension and pain				
$F(11, 63) = 1.20; P < .31$				
R-squared: .20				
Adjusted R-squared: .03				
Intercept	3.63	2.33	.02	.00
Job security	.05	.29	.77	.05
Policy	−.11	−.56	.58	−.10
Practice	−.05	.26	.80	.05
UManagement +	−.08	−.53	.60	−.10
UManagement −	.03	.17	.87	.03

Table 7.9 (continued)

	Parameter estimate	T value	P	Beta
Lower management	−.16	−.90	.37	−.15
Co-worker	−.08	−.58	.56	−.08
Schedule	.12	.76	.45	.11
Overload	.11	.56	.58	.08
Autonomy	−.22	−1.19	.24	−.19
External control	.02	.10	.92	.01

Sleep disturbance
$F(11, 61) = 1.56$; $P < .14$
R-squared: .26
Adjusted R-squared: .09

	Parameter estimate	T value	P	Beta
Intercept	5.14	3.32	.002	.00
Job security	.04	.24	.81	−.04
Policy	−.15	−.72	.47	−.13
Practice	.03	−.16	.87	.03
UManagement +	−.18	−1.14	.26	−.22
UManagement −	−.19	−1.17	.25	−.21
Lower management	−.32	−1.85	.07	−.31
Co-worker	−.08	−.54	.59	−.07
Schedule	.11	.69	.49	.10
Overload	−.11	−.56	.58	−.08
Autonomy	−.13	.67	.51	−.11
External control	.05	.25	.80	.04

Source: Compiled by the authors.

might be argued that the employee expects or believes he or she deserves fair treatment. When the employee receives fair treatment, he or she will not be overly happy, since such action is perceived as the employer's responsibility. On the other hand, not to receive fair treatment from management is to be deprived of what one "rightfully" deserves and, accordingly, to experience negative emotion.

The finding that management policy is related differentially to positive and negative emotion at work also fits with the above interpretation. Specifically, the offering of fair treatment, quality equipment, and training may not be considered "givens" by employees. They are clearly missed if not provided, as their inverse relationship to negative emotion suggests. However, employees appeared not to take them for granted if they were provided, as evidenced by employees' greater positive emotion with their increased presence.

Surprisingly, only the management "policy" and "practice" subscales predicted negative emotion. Thus, these employees' negative emotion at work during this time was not a function of workplace conditions, overload, autonomy, demand, or any other work setting variables that are traditionally linked to the self-report of stress. Given extensive evidence from other research that job characteristics, job demands, and interpersonal relations constitute real stressors for employees at work (Karasek et al. 1981), hotel employees' perception of workplace stressors as organizationally focused may have been quite specific to the *context* of our survey and to the particular time period of contract negotiations.

It is quite possible that the organizing campaign and general atmosphere at the hotel created a polarized attitude in the employees along the lines of "With this new management, everything has gone downhill." This view of the hotel would cause a kind of global good-bad judgment that would reduce discrimination of stressors within specific levels of the OSEG. The overall effect would be for the employee to see most aspects of work in a similar negative light and to put the blame on management policies and practices. If this were the case, it would explain why relationships of measures other than "management policies" and "practices" to the emotion subscales no longer held in the multiple-regression analyses. A follow-up survey in a period between contract negotiations might find more subtle variation in union members' ratings of perceived stress produced by job characteristics, co-workers, supervisors, and levels of controllability.

Perceived Physical Symptoms

Neither the muscle tension and pain nor the sleep disturbance regressions proved to be significant (Table 7.9). The sleep disturbance multiple regression showed a slight trend for relations with lower management to be inversely related to sleep disturbance (beta $= -.34; p < .07$). This relationship, although not statistically significant, suggests that the better one worked with one's immediate supervisor, the less likely one was to suffer sleep disturbances. This makes some intuitive sense to anyone who has ever been under the minute scrutiny of an unpleasant supervisor. It is certainly not the kind of relationship that is conducive to peaceful dreams.

DISCUSSION

The assessment described above represents a beginning in the application of systems theory principles to the investigation of occupational stress. It is necessarily a selective adaptation of Miller's (1978) comprehensive theory. Other systems principles, such as emergence, redundancy, and type of feedback, might have been operationalized and tested (see Katz and Kahn 1978, for an extensive application of systems theory to organizations). Our interest in organizational-individual interactions led us to find the dynamic and hierarchical aspects of a system most useful and intriguing. These ideas applied to stress also fit quite closely with the point of view espoused by recent reviews of occupational stress literature. Shirom (1982) and Beehr and Newman (1978) have all emphasized the need for longitudinal, multivariate, and individual-organizational studies of occupational stress.

The results of this assessment of stressors in a single hotel demonstrate an apparent sensitivity in employees to the atmosphere of contract negotiations that argues for longitudinal versus cross-sectional investigations of work stress. Is the strain between management and employees at the hotel a temporary rift brought on by the change in ownership and the union's organizing drive? Only additional assessments will allow us to uncover the actual pattern of employees' perceptions of stress at different stages in the organization.

Similarly, generalization of the findings over settings, as well as over time, would be quite instructive. Would the two other hotels in the city reflect the same profile if assessed during their own contract negotiations? Would repeated assessments at all three hotels eventually uncover similar patterns of work stress across the three settings? These questions address the complicated problem of how much variance in the report of stress is accounted for by the particular organization of one hotel or by hotel work in general, regardless of setting.

In focusing on these issues, we have chosen to emphasize the relationship between the individual and the organization. This means that we necessarily underplay some of the extra-organizational factors (Strand 1983) that are implicated in stress. For this reason, we would foresee the OSEG and the systems assessment used in conjunction with more life-style and personality measures (Holmes and Rahe 1967; Jenkins, Zyzanski, and Rosenman 1971) as well as with stress measures focused on role conflict and ambiguity at work (Kahn, Wolfe, Quinn, and Snoek 1964). As Parker and DeCotiis (1983) have noted, researchers will ultimately have to settle for partial tests of complex models. No one instrument or research approach could possibly capture every source of variance in the identification of stressors. If one adds to this an examination of coping responses to stress (which we chose not to include in this assessment), the complexity becomes a bit overwhelming.

An additional constraint on our assessment, although not a self-imposed one, was the lack of management collaboration. An important consequence of management's noninvolvement was the increased logistical difficulty of reaching a fully representative picture of the hotel. With management's assistance, we might have had a room or office in the hotel as a base for our work. This presence would have meant access to employees during work time and a generally higher profile in the organization. Such exposure would certainly have increased our response rate and expedited the general assessment process.

From a political point of view management's noninvolvement made us advocates of the union's perspective on stress. Thus, our interviews and our survey helped the union to raise consciousness in the hotel about management practices. The assessment did this, not by advocating a certain type of response to our questions, but rather by simply raising these issues through questions. The survey not only took in information, but through its inquiries, encouraged employees to think about organizational stressors that they might not have considered previously. In performing this role for the union we were, in effect, the equivalent of the more familiar stress consultant, who, by training employees in relaxation techniques and health habits, raises the consciousness of employees about their individual responsibility for stress.

The final point we would like to advance is that our assessment allowed us to enter and become part of the hotel's system and its response to stressors. We had designed our assessment to follow a research strategy of feedback and differentiation of input-output. At different times in our interactions with the union and with employees, we received or provided information. By feeding back to shop stewards the results of the interviews we had performed with representatives they had selected, we were asking for their check on our understanding of the hotel up to that point. In the same vein, our presence at the contract proposal meetings allowed us to match complaints raised there with the ones we were inquiring about in the survey.

We also attempted to make the assessment process an empowering one by involving employees in the planning, data collection, and discussion of results. This point of view could be contrasted with a "hit and run" strategy where researchers simply hand out and collect a previously designed survey. While the body of this chapter rests on the survey results, the information-rich nature of the qualitative interviews should not be underestimated. The interviews, almost all with rank-and-file members (as opposed to stewards), brought members to the union hall and gave them an experience of union activism and involvement. In this sense, the assessment played a role in the organization beyond the survey findings.

An idealistic goal for future assessments would be to involve employees (managers, union officials, rank-and-file) even further in the process, so that they could learn to do self-assessments of their own organizations. In systems terms, this capacity for organizational self-assessment would build a continual feedback loop into the setting that would allow it to regulate and minimize stress without the intervention of "outside experts" (Tesh 1984).

To finish on a practical and positive note, the assessment ended by proving quite useful to the employees in their actual contract negotiations. At the bargaining table, the union raised the fact that they had some strong survey results about management practices and stress. Management showed some surprise that the survey had been completed after their initial refusal to participate. This conversation came in the context of a union demand for monthly employee participation meetings between shop stewards and the upper management of the hotel. The union ultimately won this concession in the signed contract, and management has since expressed interest in the results of the survey and in initiating a collaborative follow-up. Thus, the assessment procedure, by entering into the process of the system, actually played a role in generating a response to an organizational stressor it had identified. This development is an encouraging sign that systems theory may provide the type of integrative approach that will narrow labor and management differences on the sources and treatment of occupational stress.

Acknowledgments—This research was supported by NIOSH contract number 84-2435. We would also like to acknowledge the invaluable assistance of the hotel employees' union, its staff, and its members, without whom this project would have been impossible.

REFERENCES

Alderfer, C. P. 1980. "The Methodology of Organizational Diagnosis." *Professional Psychology* 11: 459-68.

Barker, R. G. 1968. *Ecological Psychology: Concepts and Methods for Studying the Environment of Human Behavior* (Stanford, CA: Stanford University Press).

Beehr, T. A. and J. E. Newman. 1978. "Job Stress, Employee Health, and Organizational Effectiveness: A Facet Analysis, Model, and Literature Review." *Personnel Psychology* 31: 665-99.

Bronfenbrenner, U. 1977. "Toward an Experimental Ecology of Human Development." *American Psychologist* 32: 513-31.

Carroll, J. F. X. and W. L. White. 1982. "Theory Building: Integrating Individual and Environmental Factors within an Ecological Framework." In *Job Stress and Burnout*, edited by W. S. Paine (Beverly Hills, CA: Sage), pp. 41-60.

Carson, R. 1962. *Silent Spring* (Boston: Houghton Mifflin).

Cummings, T. G. and C. L. Cooper. 1979. "A Cybernetic Framework for Studying Occupational Stress." *Human Relations* 32: 395-418.

Derogatis, L. R. 1975. *The SCL-90-R* (Baltimore, MD: Clinical Psychometric Research).

Dubos, R. 1965. *Man Adapting* (New Haven, CT: Yale University Press).

Frankenhaeuser, M. 1979. "Psychoneuroendocrine Approaches to the Study of Emotion as Related to Stress and Coping." In *Nebraska Symposium on Motivation 1978*, edited by H. E. Howe and R. A. Dienstbier (Lincoln, NE: University of Nebraska Press.

French, J. R. P., W. Rodgers, and S. Cobb. 1974. "Adjustment as Person-Environment Fit." In *Coping and Adaptation*, edited by G. V. Coelho, D. A. Hamburg, and J. E. Adams (New York: Basic Books), pp. 316-33.

Gordon, G. C., J. M. Stellman, and B. R. Snow. 1982. *Office Workers: Health and Well-Being Survey* (New York: Columbia University School of Public Health.

Harrison, R. V. 1978. "Person-Environment Fit and Job Stress." In *Stress at Work*, edited by C. L. Cooper and R. Payne (London: Wiley).

Holahan, C. J. and J. L. Spearly. 1980. "Coping and Ecology: An Integrative Model for Community Psychology." *American Journal of Community Psychology* 8: 671-85.

Holmes, T. H. and R. H. Rahe. 1967. "Social Readjustment Rating Scale." *Journal of Psychosomatic Research* 11: 213.

Huszczo, G. E., J. G. Wiggins, and J. S. Currie. 1984. "The Relationship between Psychology and Organized Labor: Past, Present, and Future." *American Psychologist* 39: 7-15.

Jenkins, C. D., S. J. Zyzanski, and R. H. Rosenman. 1971. "Progress toward Validation of a Computer-Scored Test for the Type-A Coronary-Prone Behavior Pattern." *Psychosomatic Medicine* 33: 193-202.

Kahn, R. L., D. M. Wolfe, R. P. Quinn, and J. D. Snoek. 1964. *Organizational Stress: Studies in Role Conflict and Ambiguity* (New York: Wiley).

Karasek, R. A. 1979. "Job Demands, Job Decision Latitude, and Mental Strain: Implications for Job Redesign." *Administrative Science Quarterly* 24: 285-307.

Karasek, R., D. Baker, F. Marxer, A. Ahlbom, and T. Theorell. 1981. "Job Latitude, Job Demands, and Cardiovascular Disease: A Prospective Study of Swedish Men." *American Journal of Public Health* 71: 694-705.

Katz, D. and R. L. Kahn. 1978. *The Social Psychology of Organizations*, 2d ed. (New York: Wiley).

Leigh, H. and M. F. Reiser. 1980. *The Patient: Biological, Psychological, and Social Dimensions of Medical Practice* (New York: Plenum).

Lewicki, R. J. and C. P. Alderfer. 1973. "The Tensions between Research and Intervention in Intergroup Conflict." *Journal of Applied Behavioral Science* 9: 424-49.

Lewin, K. 1935. *A Dynamic Theory of Personality* (New York: McGraw-Hill).

_____. 1936. *Principles of Topological Psychology* (New York: McGraw-Hill).

Love, M. 1983. *Communications Workers of America Local 1180 Stress Questionnaire* (New York: CWA Local 1180, 225 Broadway).

Miller, J. G. 1978. *Living Systems* (New York: McGraw-Hill).

Moos, R. H. 1976. *The Human Context* (New York: Wiley).

Nadler, D. A. 1977. *Feedback and Organization Development* (Reading, MA: Addison-Wesley).

Parker, D. F. and T. A. De Cotiis. 1983. "Organizational Determinants of Job Stress." *Organizational Behavior and Human Performance* 32: 160-77.

Schwartz, G. E. 1981. "A Systems Analysis of Psychobiology and Behavior Therapy: Implications for Behavioral Medicine." *Psychotherapy and Psychosomatics* 36: 159-84.

_____. 1982. "Testing the Biopsychosocial Model: The Ultimate Challenge Facing Behavioral Medicine?" *Journal of Consulting and Clinical Psychology* 50: 1040-53.

_____. 1983. "Disregulation Theory and Disease: Applications to the Repression/ Cerebral Disconnection/Cardiovascular Disorder Hypothesis." *International Review of Applied Psychology* 32: 95-118.

Shirom, A. 1982. "What is Organizational Stress? A Facet Analytic Conceptualization." *Journal of Occupational Behaviour* 3: 21-38.

Singer, J. A., M. S. Neale, and G. E. Schwartz. 1985. "An Application of Systems Theory to Occupational Stress: Assessing Hotel Employees during Contract

Negotiations." Paper presented at American Psychological Association, Los Angeles.

_____. 1987. "The Nuts and Bolts of Assessing Occupational Stress: A Collaborative Effort with Labor." In *NIOSH Manual on Stress Reduction*, edited by Lawrence Murphy (Cincinnati, Ohio: NIOSH P.O.).

Singer, J. A., M. S. Neale, G. E. Schwartz, and J. Schwartz. 1986. "Conflicting Perspectives on Labor and Management Definitions of Stress: A Systems Approach to Their Resolution." In *Health and Industry: A Behavioral Medicine Perspective,* edited by M. Cataldo and T. Coates (New York: Wiley).

Strand, R. 1983. "A Systems Paradigm of Organizational Adaptations to the Social Environment." *Academy of Management Review* 8: 91-97.

Survey Research Center. 1977. *Quality of Employment Survey* (Ann Arbor, MI).

Tesh, S. N. 1984. "The Politics of Stress: The Case of Air Traffic Control." *International Journal of Health Services* 14, no. 3.

Vincent, T. A. and E. J. Trickett. 1984. "Preventive Interventions and the Human Context: Ecological Approaches to Environment Assessment and Change." In *Prevention Psychology: Theory, Research, and Practice in Community Intervention*, edited by R. D. Felner, L. A. Jason, J. Morisugu, and S. S. Farber (New York: Pergamon).

von Bertalanffy, L. 1950. "The Theory of Open Systems in Physics and Biology." *Science* 111: 23-29.

_____. 1968. *General Systems Theory* (New York: Braziller).

Weiner, N. 1948. *Cybernetics or Control and Communication in Animal and Machine* (Cambridge, MA: MIT Press).

8

EMPLOYEE ASSISTANCE PROGRAMS: MANAGING ORGANIZATIONAL STRESS AND STRAIN

STEVEN C. NAHRWOLD

All jobs are stressful. What makes a job stressful, however, can differ, depending on the person and situation. Some sources of stress exist in an employee's personal life and others originate at work. People who are affected by stress in their lives are not always the most reliable guides in making the distinction between the two sources. Often the stress of one influences and intermingles with the other. Some situations at work are stressful to an individual because of unique characteristics in their personality make-up. The same situations cause other people to flourish.

Managers concerned with stress and health professionals who work in business environments realize the enormous complexity of occupational stress. It is a broad and ambiguous issue. Despite the ubiquity and necessity of stress, most would agree that there are work environments that are excessively stressful to a wide variety of people. Such places might place conflicting demands on employees or be confusing, chaotic, or even hostile and unrewarding.

Businesses are realizing that they can no longer ignore the issues of stress on the job, and not only because of media attention to the issue. A recent article in the *Harvard Business Review* states, "Managers can no longer choose whether to recognize and deal with the symptoms of stress on the job—it has become a legal obligation" (Ivancevich, Matteson, and Richards 1985: 60). The authors cite three trends that have contributed to a rise in employee compensation suits for stress-related illnesses. The first is workmen's compensation laws in some states that include injuries that result from prolonged stress on the job. The second is the growing medical research connecting workplace stress and certain illnesses; and the third is employees' own belief that there is a link between job stress and illness (Ivancevich, Matteson, and Richards 1985).

Another major reason why companies are addressing the issue of organizational stress and employee health is the skyrocketing costs of medical benefit plans. Since research has demonstrated a strong relationship between stress and illness, they are tackling organizational stress in an attempt to improve employee health and reduce medical costs. Another outcome of that concern is the "employee wellness" concept. It means that companies are sponsoring programs to promote health and prevent disease.

As more and more companies are taking seriously the detrimental effects of occupational stress, they are developing internal or external resources to help reduce job stress. Medical departments are more frequently asked to offer seminars on stress management to employees. They have also become more sensitive to symptoms of stress in employees seeking help. In larger companies, employee "wellness" programs are usually conducted by the medical department. Human resource or employee relations departments are also starting to monitor and intervene in the issue of organizational stress. One technique is to have key personnel people meet regularly to discuss high-stress areas in their organization. They involve employees in areas of personnel who regularly handle medical, discipline, transfer, termination, attendance, benefits, legal, and safety issues. The presumption is that high-stress areas within an organization will have higher activity in several of these areas. As data or antedotal information is compared, high-stress areas within an organization can be located and remedial interventions can be made.

Some companies have tapped their employee assistance program (EAP) to help ameliorate corporate stress. The EAP has been asked to expand its mandate from a reactive counseling service to include proactive programs for prevention and organizational intervention. This is a new development in the history of the employee assistance movement. Whether EAPs can and should move in that direction is the subject of a lively debate.

TYPES OF EMPLOYEE ASSISTANCE PROGRAMS

Right now, the EAP concept covers a broad range of programs. In some companies, the "program" is simply a set of policies and procedures for personnel people to follow when dealing with substance abuse or psychiatric disturbances in employees. Most others have special staff to administer the program, but the structures are very diverse. The EAP may be established within the company (in-house), or contracted with an outside provider; or the union might sponsor a program such as that described in chapter 9. When located in-house, an EAP may be part of the medical department or located within the human resources, the employee relations, or even the training and development offices. Counseling offices can be located on-site or off-site. Some programs are concerned only with substance abuse, while others are "broad brush" and assist with any personal concern. Staff qualifications range from recovering alcoholics without formal training in behavioral science, to psychiatrists or Ph.D.-level psychologists. There is also a wide spectrum of counseling services offered. They range from a telephone hotline offering referrals to personal contact providing evaluation, short-term counseling, referral, and follow-up visits. One major employer's program even provides longer-term psychotherapy for less serious emotional disorders.

BRIEF HISTORY OF THE EAP MOVEMENT

This variety of EAP models reflects the history of this movement over the past 50 years. Most authors trace the origin of employee assistance to the founding of Alcoholics Anonymous in 1935. The AA movement fostered the disease concept of alcoholism and promoted a long-term treatment for recovery. By the 1940s, several influential medical directors of major corporations were actively promoting informal helping relationships between alcoholic employees and AA members (Trice and Sonnenstuhl 1985). While the "program" at this time was basically a set of policies for dealing with alcoholism, it was an important start. Later in the 1940s and 1950s, supervisors were trained to detect alcoholism in the workplace. Unfortunately, they generally only referred when the symptoms were severe and thus in the late stages of the disease. Hence, recovery was often less successful (Sherman 1983).

During the 1960s and 1970s the scope of EAPs began to expand to include other employee problems besides alcoholism. There were numerous reasons for this. One was the shift in criteria for management referral. No longer did supervisors have to detect a disease (alcoholism) prior to referral. They were trained to refer on the basis of deteriorating job performance and were to leave the diagnosis to program staff. Since other problems can also cause performance decline, staff began to receive referrals who were not alcoholic. If the new program philosophy became "helping people keep their job," then the staff could not turn away employees with emotional or family problems. During those decades, employers were also compelled to hire more disadvantaged minority and handicapped people who needed more psychosocial supports in order to successfully remain employed. Programs thus became part of a company's efforts to take affirmative action in employing the socially disadvantaged. Also, during the 1960s and especially the 1970s, there were many changes in labor law and public consciousness concerning employee rights, due process before termination, concern for employee welfare, and quality of work life.

Labor and government have, over the past two decades, increasingly stressed the psychological impact of working conditions. Court decisions, workmen's compensation cases, and other forces began to place increased responsibility for employee mental health on business. It became progressively more difficult to use potentially discriminatory testing to screen employees and, once hired, more difficult also to terminate them. There has also been a growing consensus that business has a responsibility to attempt to rehabilitate employees with behavioral problems.

These social and legal pressures, along with an awareness of the huge cost of alcoholism and mental illness, have contributed to the widespread acceptance of employee assistance programs. EAPs are now not only part of enlightened and humane employee relations, but also make good financial business sense.

Now in the 1980s, business has focused its concern on additional issues involving environmental stress, corporate culture, managing rapid technological change, employee benefit costs, health promotion, and others. Competing successfully in a global economy, with its attendant concerns about quality and productivity, has made many U.S. industries reexamine all aspects of their corporate environment and management philosophy. The enormous popularity of books like *In Search of Excellence* (Peters and Waterman 1983) illustrates today's reexamination of the intangible yet essential psychological environment at the workplace.

EMPLOYEE ASSISTANCE PROGRAMS AND ORGANIZATIONAL STRESS

Some well-established employee assistance programs have discovered that they can help business address the above concerns. They are expanding their mandate beyond counseling individuals and are making an impact on several aspects of corporate life. For example, they are providing programs on stress management to groups of employees; advising management on ways to introduce change; offering group counseling, advice, and support to employees facing job loss due to layoffs; consulting with corporate training departments on "people" skill training for management; and conducting important research. These EAP staff do not consider themselves a substitute for traditional business consultants with expertise in management, organizational dynamics, or industrial psychology; yet there are many areas in which they can make a contribution.

Prerequisites of a Proactive Program

Not every EAP is in a position to expand its influence. Certain criteria are generally prerequisites for programs to become proactive in terms of prevention or organizational intervention.

First of all, a program and its staff should be well established in a company for many years before they expand. This allows staff to be thoroughly knowledgeable about an organization, and allows the organization to develop trust in the staff's abilities. It is also presumed that a program will have a sizable case load, like most successful programs. The usual annual usage rate for mature programs is about 10 percent of the employee population. Another prerequisite is that program staff have access to senior management. In nearly all organizations, this level makes most of the key decisions and is most responsible for the corporate environment. Hence, access is necessary for impacting on corporate policy. Of course, if an EAP wishes to expand its influence in a company, the program staff should have the professional credentials and experience necessary to handle the expanded duties.

There are other conditions that are necessary for any EAP to become successful and grow in influence. First, a program must have a supportive environment in order to succeed. Unfortunately, there are some that do not have that benefit. They must wage a constant struggle to survive.

Second, most programs survive and, more importantly, flourish on the basis of staff quality. While nearly all programs have policies and facilities that have a life of their own, it is unavoidable that programs are identified with the people who staff them. The responsiveness, competence, and credibility of the staff are inseparable from program image and success. At the most basic level, this means that the staff must provide competent, ethical service delivery. Inappropriate referrals, breaches of confidence, overpromising of results, and excessive red tape damage both staff and program credibility.

Program staff also must fit in in terms of their dress, demeanor, and attitudes. Since staff are subject to the same criteria for acceptance as employees in other parts of an organization, fitting in should not be confused with political gamesmanship. It means that staff must not only be competent, sincere, and hard-working, but they must also adhere to most of the informal rules of the culture in which they work.

Third, the program should have comfortable facilities in an accessible location. Cramped, uncomfortable, or unattractive offices send a negative message about the program's image and importance. In addition, offices should be in a quiet, out-of-the-way place where the employee's anonymity is preserved as much as possible.

Fourth, the staff must be open to opportunity and willing to experiment with ways to expand their influence. As previously mentioned, a crucial ingredient in this effort is staff continuity. It takes time to be accepted and trusted. Many opportunities to grow come automatically when a program and the people who run it have been around for a while.

Last, program success depends on luck. Major changes in the culture, top management, or the financial fortunes of the company can dramatically affect a program. Even though companies in crisis probably need a program more than ever, it is not uncommon for the so-called "softer" human development and human relations functions to be curtailed or eliminated during such periods. This is unfortunate, because EAPs are relatively inexpensive to operate, and they can be an important resource during a crisis. A trained staff is usually well equipped to deal with issues of stress, job insecurity, job loss, anger, and depression that accompany a crisis.

Ways to Influence Corporate Life

What, then, are the ways in which an EAP can expand its contribution to and influence on corporate life? Here are some of the areas in which mature programs have increased their involvement.

Management training. EAP staff conduct or contribute to seminars for management on a wide spectrum of issues related to the "people skills" of management. These seminars include such topics as understanding human behavior, motivation, managing change, giving constructive feedback, reducing stress, crisis management, confronting problem employees, and others of a similar nature.

"Wellness" promotion. Included under the heading of "wellness" promotion are primarily educational programs for employees as well as self-help or issue-oriented groups. The goals of these are education and prevention. For example, some programs conduct seminars for employees on timely issues such as stress management, drug awareness for parents, coping as a single parent, successful dual-career marriages, adjusting to retirement, principles of mental health, and others. In addition, some EAPs sponsor ongoing groups focusing on topics that range from weight control and smoking cessation to adjusting to re-entry (for returning expatriates), minority adjustment to business, professional women's issues, coping with divorce, and so on.

Consulting with senior management. EAP staff with access to senior management are in a position to offer important insights on the psychological impact of corporate policies, on stress-producing aspects of the corporate culture, on issues related to minority or female adjustment, and on helpful strategies for handling reductions in force, as well as offering insights into high-stress or high-conflict areas of the organization. Sometimes these consultations can lead to reduced tension or an improved work environment for whole groups of people.

Specialized counseling. Specialized counseling might include special guidance for individuals whose employment has been terminated. Another possibility is counseling for employees and their families being relocated to a different culture. One EAP program initiated group sessions for employees being laid off. There are any number of other emotionally tumultuous situations related to personal or organizational change for which an EAP can offer special help.

Benefit-cost containment. While involvement in benefit-cost containment does not directly impact on stress or corporate culture, it is nonetheless a potentially important contribution. One mechanism is for the EAP to act as a triage or screening unit for psychiatric benefit usage. Some programs, for example, have control over alcoholism treatment benefits. No employee may obtain insurance benefits for substance abuse without referral by the EAP. The program thus acts as gatekeeper for this treatment and utilizes the most cost-beneficial programs for each employee, choosing between alternatives ranging from residential care to AA alone.

Some companies are entertaining the notion of expanding the gate-keeping function of their EAP to include *all* psychiatric treatment. The staff would have to be well-trained mental health professionals to ensure that proper referrals are made. This level of control is not likely to occur in the near future, but it is being discussed as one possible way for companies to gain control over the psychiatric portion of their escalating medical costs.

Research. If an EAP is well utilized, it is probably accumulating a great deal of data on an organization's dynamics. Some of the data is anecdotal, but it may nevertheless be accurate. EAP aggregate data, in conjunction with other personal data (turnover, absenteeism, grievances, health-care utilization, in-house medical visits, and so on), can be used to identify high-stress areas of an organization. Other questions relevant to employee morale and welfare could be studied by EAP staff. Additionally, investigating the cost benefit of various health promotion and education programs sponsored by the company can be accomplished by the EAP working with other areas, such as accounting or personnel.

THE EAP OF CONTINENTAL ILLINOIS NATIONAL BANK

There are many employee assistance programs that have developed a broad organizational presence.* One example of a broadly integrated program is the EAP of Continental Illinois National Bank.

Continental Bank's EAP has developed over the past decade from a reactive counseling service handling individual employee problems to a proactive company-wide program with broad responsibilities. Used by as much as 12 percent of the 10,000 employees in the Chicago-based bank, the Employee Counseling Service (ECS), as it is known, is an exemplary program.

The success of Continental ECS does not mean it should be used as a model for other companies. Many factors contributing to its development are unique—historical circumstances, the bank's culture, the staff, and just plain luck. In fact, no EAP should try to duplicate the specific structure or procedures of another, because it is imperative that each program represent adaptation to a specific environment.

*This section is adapted from Nahrwold 1984, with permission of the publisher.

There are, however, lessons to be learned from more general factors, such as the underlying philosophy of the program and Continental's supportive environment, that are relevant to the success of any program in any setting.

The Importance of Management Support

Continental's program was developed at the request of the personnel director. Having top-level support from the beginning was very important for the program's subsequent development, because in a hierarchical organization, attitudes held by top management have a strong influence on management at lower levels. In fact, any program in a strong chain of command generally needs to be endorsed first by influential senior executives. This is particularly important for an EAP because of the need to rely not only on management referrals, but also on management cooperation in supporting individual rehabilitation programs.

Broad Spectrum of the Program

Continental's ECS is a broadly based program. It assists employees with a wide range of personal concerns. This includes issues such as alcoholism, drug abuse, emotional disorders, and job stress, as well as help for marital, family, legal, consumer, financial, vocational, and day-care problems. From the beginning, the program emphasized this broad concern for any problem that affected either an employee's job or personal well-being. One major assumption of the EAP movement is that the latter probably affects the former in some way. That assumption is more easily proved in cases of substance abuse and serious psychiatric disorders; it is less easily proved in less serious personal problems.

There were several reasons for this broad approach. As an institution handling people's money, and as the first bank EAP in Chicago, ECS had to avoid creating a negative image, and therefore could not be devoted specifically to alcoholism. Management also felt there would be less stigma on employees who made use of a broader program that did not involve an implied diagnosis. Furthermore, the bank's conservative and reserved culture did not support a crusade-style program aimed at eliminating a specific disease.

Employees come to the ECS office, which is staffed by a psychologist and a social worker, either on their own or because they are referred by the personnel department, medical department, or their supervisors. Most management referrals are acts of concern for any employee whose performance is adequate but who has confided to a supervisor that he or she has a personal problem. When job performance is affected, managers generally refer employees to ECS as a first step instead of taking disciplinary action. Employees are not required to follow through with this referral.

The Continental program is similar to most other EAPs in that it provides only evaluation, short-term counseling (two to six sessions), and referral to prescreened outside resources, most of which are eligible for health insurance coverage. It follows a policy of strict confidentiality, and no record of an employee's participation or problem is kept outside the program offices.

During the earlier years of the program, ECS was exclusively reactive, handling problems from individual employees seeking help and providing training to new supervisors on counseling policies and referral procedures.

Initially located in the employee relations division of the personnel department, ECS had an image as a personal problem and job adjustment counseling service. It subsequently became part of the health services division and took on more of a clinical image. Since 1982 the program has been a part of the training and development division, which has added a more proactive, organizational development approach to the traditional spectrum of EAP services. These changes have been the result of broad reorganizations within the personnel department as well as evolutionary developments in the program itself.

Taking a Proactive Stance

This new proactive thrust, while still developing, is often cited as the distinguishing characteristic of Continental's program and has earned it an excellent reputation. It is important to note that the broader mandate evolved gradually after ECS had established trust and credibility among both employees and management.

Much of the recent literature on employee assistance has discussed the development of proactive programs that, in addition to helping individuals with problems, intervene positively in the corporate culture by providing preventive programs, and even attempt to alleviate destructively stressful situations.

The proactive areas in which the ECS has become involved, both formally and informally, encompass a wide variety of activities, from seminars to management development to advisory services. For example, numerous seminars have been presented for employees, including: adolescents and drugs, parenting, stress reduction, handling difficult customers, self-defense for women, and adjusting to retirement. In addition, some seminars are directed specifically to management, on topics such as managing change, coping with conflict, reducing stress, new values in the workplace, interviewing skills, managing young people, and giving feedback. It is difficult to measure the outcome of these seminars in terms of efficiency and morale, but employees report anecdotally that they are useful. Additionally, this training opportunity provides a means for addressing group and organizational problems as they arise.

Closely associated with this, ECS staff have become involved in consultations with management about programs that address employee developmental needs as well as job testing and outplacement of employees, that is, assistance to employees whose jobs are terminated. ECS staff is also responsible for developing and sometimes teaching management development courses offered by the bank.

ECS gives periodic reports to senior personnel management on employee morale and issues of concern to employees. An example of this is ECS participation in personnel efforts to improve minority retention and satisfaction in the organization. ECS also coordinates the bank's personal feedback programs, which assist management and employees in assessing their interpersonal styles and needs. ECS acts as the psychological adjunct to the medical department and monitors all psychiatric disability claims, including authorizing the return to work following psychiatric leave. The staff also consults on corporate psychiatric benefits and on developing ways to promote quality mental health care as well as to reduce costs.

Another proactive part of the program involves coordinating the bank's relationship with outside psychological and management consultants, such as when executives receive self-development-oriented psychological assessments. The staff also evaluates requests for donations by social service organizations.

Important Considerations

In this process of expanding the influence of ECS in the bank's organizations, there have been both positive and negative developments. On the positive side are the increased variety and stimulation brought on by involvement in numerous projects. Broader responsibilities in the organization give program staff more opportunities to understand the business environment and its effect on personal problems. In addition, more responsibility generally means more chances for advancement. This addresses one of the problems many EAPs have—namely, keeping good staff. Most counseling staff positions tend to be set within a fixed job grade or level. After a few years, salaries may approach the top of the preestablished range, and future growth is limited. Additional responsibilities not only enrich a job, but allow the staff a career path beyond current job levels. Staff may stay longer and, for the functioning of the program, that is an extremely desirable outcome.

On the negative side, too many additional demands on staff can lead to burnout. It is important to learn how to prioritize requests and sometimes even to say no. But saying no should not apply to an employee seeking counseling unless he or she is abusing the service.

In addition, when a program is identified with a variety of tasks, role confusion can result, and the program's image and goals may become blurred. This is a tolerable risk as long as all program responsibilities are related to promoting employee welfare and quality of work life. Individual counseling, for example, must always come before other duties. Under no circumstances should the program or its staff become involved in hiring, firing, or promotion decisions. This is a conflict of interest that ultimately will undermine the program and discourage people from seeking help.

Another subtle potential problem occurs when a counselor thinks and sounds too much like management. This can be a natural development in an aspiring professional. However, EAP staff must maintain an empathetic objectivity similar to a psychotherapeutic situation. Therefore, the staff must never become strong advocates for either employees or management. As staff members take on more responsibilities within the organization, they may unwittingly overidentify with the company's culture, and thus be rendered less capable of helping its casualties.

Most successful EAP programs have demonstrated their value by developing a quality service, marketing it successfully, and generating a significant usage among employees at all levels. These are the basic ingredients for success and will contribute not only to a program's continued existence, but to its growth and influence.

REFERENCES

Ivancevich, J. M., M. T. Matteson, and E. P. Richards, III. 1985. "Who's Liable for Stress on the Job?" *Harvard Business Review* 3 (March-April): 60.

Nahrwold, S. C. 1980. "Ethics in Industrial Mental Health Programs." In *Mental Wellness Programs for Employees*, edited by R. H. Egdahl and D. C. Walsh (New York: Springer-Verlag).

_____. 1983. "Why Programs Fail." In *Occupational Clinical Psychology*, edited by J. S. J. Manuso (New York: Praeger), pp. 105-15.

_____. 1984. "Broad-Brush Employee Assistance Program Approach." *Business and Health* 2: 29-31.

Peters, T. J. and R. H. Waterman. 1983. *In Search of Excellence* (New York: Harper & Row).

Sherman, P. A. 1983. "The Alcoholic Executive." In *Occupational Clinical Psychology*, edited by J. S. J. Manuso (New York: Praeger), pp. 1-20.

Trice, H. M. and W. J. Sonnenstuhl. 1985. "A.A. and EAP: The Historical Link." *The Almacan* 15, no. 5: 10-12.

9

INNOVATIONS IN EMPLOYEE ASSISTANCE PROGRAMS: A CASE STUDY AT THE ASSOCIATION OF FLIGHT ATTENDANTS

BARBARA FEUER

Employee Assistance Programs (EAPs) are perhaps the fastest-growing human service field today. In less than two decades, the number of programs in this country has grown from some 200 to estimates of over 5,500, including 60 percent of the Fortune 500 companies (Roman 1981). This enormous growth has brought a dramatic expansion of the field's collective body of knowledge and a framework by which organizations can establish new EAPs or evaluate existing ones. Nonetheless, organizations that have implemented innovative nontraditional EAPs designed to meet the needs of their respective work organizations are often perceived as straying too far from the status quo. Best described as the "if it ain't broke, don't fix it" school of thought, this attitude is not only short-sighted, but it could potentially discourage the innovation and creativity necessary for continued future growth.

A BRIEF HISTORICAL PERSPECTIVE

To fully understand the implications of the above statement, it is imperative to review the events leading to the current status of the EAP field today. From the early 1940s through the late 1960s, early success from a cost-effectiveness and humanistic perspective contributed to increasing acceptance of occupational programs in the workplace. Decreases in absenteeism and lower use of health insurance coverage are cost benefits that have encouraged work organizations in the public and private sectors to implement occupational alcoholism programs.

During this period, a small but effective group of occupational alcoholism programs emerged in the medical and personnel departments of some major U.S. companies, such as DuPont, Eastman Kodak, and Western Electric. At the same time that occupational alcoholism programs were gaining a foothold in corporations throughout the United States, the AFL-CIO's Department of Community Services was also actively involved in training union counselors from affiliated locals to assist workers with alcohol-related and other personal problems. Independent unions, including the United Mine Workers and the International Brotherhood of Teamsters, provided services to members through their locals as well.

A look at recent statistics illustrates why alcoholism was, and still is, a primary focus of any effective occupational health program. The *Congressional Office of Technology Assessment* (1983) documented the economic costs of alcoholism and alcohol abuse (a major promotion of which is lost work productivity) to be a staggering $120 billion a year. The study also found that alcohol abuse alone may be responsible for up to 15 percent of the nation's health-care costs (Saxe et al. 1983).

These early programs relied on supervisors who suspected or identified alcohol abuse to refer a worker to a company EAP counselor. The absence of early identification and intervention was an inherent weakness of this popular approach, because workers were often not confronted until the later stages of their problem; chances for successful recovery were diminished. As the field grew and matured, job impairment, rather than the existence of alcoholism, became the key determinant in confronting an employee. Still, the majority of programs encouraged supervisors to approach a worker when they suspected alcohol abuse as the cause of job performance problems.

During the next stage of growth, program development moved from a purely occupational alcoholism focus to an expanded, multiservice employee assistance approach. Supervisors were accountable for monitoring work performance only. Assessment and diagnosis of problems causing impaired job performance were the domain of EAP counselors and treatment professionals. Programs still focused on alcohol-related problems, but dealt with other behavioral and medical problems as well. This enlarged scope of services was encouraged by the National Institute on Alcohol Abuse and Alcoholism (NIAAA), which played a key role in further legitimizing the field.

These new developments were welcomed enthusiastically by many, but with suspicion and mistrust by others in the field. Some of those unhappy with the new state of affairs felt that de-emphasizing the alcoholism focus of EAPs might prove the death knell for proven job-based mechanisms for reaching alcoholic workers. They believed that a broader scope of services would undermine the long-sought acknowledgment that alcoholism is a disease characterized by denial and is not prone to self-referral, as are most mental health problems. They also maintained that lessening the focus on employee alcohol problems would be detrimental to the field in the long run, since it is in this area that EAPs have established a clear-cut record of achievements (Roman 1981).

Nonetheless, the 1970s were a decade of great change for the employee assistance field. The proliferation of programs during these years clearly demonstrated their valuable contributions in the workplace. Programs flourished in all types of work organizations, and as an employee benefit they were simply considered a good idea. The view that all forms of chemical dependency (not only alcoholism), as well as all kinds of emotional and stress-related problems (personal, marital, family, legal, and so on), seriously affect productivity and profitability is a given in the world of work. Companies and unions also recognize that the historical method of dealing with such problems (namely termination) is simply not economical. Thus, the notion of giving rehabilitation a chance has taken center stage (Liebowitz 1982).

As the workplace evolved to accommodate more democratic and participatory forms of management, it became evident that the traditional job impairment model was not always the model of choice. It relies primarily on the supervisor to identify an employee with job performance problems, document the problems, confront the employee, and refer the individual to the EAP. In certain work settings, where employees have a high degree of autonomy and less direct supervision, this EAP model often doesn't fit well. Thus, modifications in program design and delivery were needed.

Identifying the potential users of EAP services in a given work setting is vital to program success. This is best determined by the nature of the organizational structure and the work itself. Wolfe (1982) classified case-finding methodologies into four categories: (1) the voluntary model; (2) the secondary referral model; (3) the confrontation model; and (4) the disciplinary/grievance board model. The voluntary model encourages employees to seek confidential help for problems on their own. The secondary referral model asks family, friends, and fellow workers to motivate an employee with problems to seek assistance from an EAP counselor. The constructive confrontation model is primarily employed in a pyramid structure (top-down) workplace where supervisors confront employees with documented work impairment. Finally, the disciplinary/grievance model is an alternative to punitive action for the employee with poor job performance.

Undoubtedly, the most widely utilized model today is the confrontation approach. As was mentioned earlier, this is not always most desirable, especially in union-based programs where it is incompatible with the philosophy of most labor unions. The cornerstone of this model, constructive confrontation, is a very effective tool in dealing with alcohol-related problems where psychological denial is an important factor. Used in situations where a clear-cut pattern of deteriorating job performance is present (absenteeism, lateness, unacceptable work output, and safety violations), the job-performance focus avoids the perception of "meddling" in an employee's personal life and violating her or his civil rights (McClellan 1982).

For a variety of reasons, constructive confrontation isn't always the most viable strategy for identifying troubled workers. It is a mistake to always assume that the supervisor is best qualified to deal with an employee, that she or he is the first to know about the problem or has the most information about impaired job performance.

With its reliance on the supervisor, the traditional EAP works best where superiors interact with subordinates on a day-to-day basis. In this type of hierarchical work setting, lines of authority are clear, and job descriptions have specific and measurable performance criteria (McClellan 1982). In many professional and technical work settings, however, the chain of command is less vertical, and work teams often replace more authoritarian supervisor-employee relationships. For example, when a flight attendant, teacher, or police officer does his or her job, the supervisor usually has little or no direct access to information regarding job performance. Since these jobs require a great degree of autonomy, supervisors often become involved only when major problems occur or new policies and procedures are implemented (McClellan 1982).

When choosing an appropriate program model, one must distinguish between organizational and occupational work settings. An occupation-specific EAP (like that of the Association of Flight Attendants) is implemented "where the program design is primarily concerned with matching policy and procedures to unique occupational conditions," Roman (1981). This model is appropriate "anywhere the program design is primarily concerned with the commonality of working demands and conditions among those sharing an occupation," Roman (1981).

Throughout the history of the employee assistance field, though the majority of programs focused on the impaired worker they paid little attention to the work setting as a whole. Ideally, EAPs should focus on the needs of all employees, as well as those in need of assistance (Molloy 1985). Unfortunately, the supervisory model is too often implemented in the workplace without regard to whether or not it really "fits."

Since the nature of the work environment is such an important factor, the Association of Flight Attendants (AFA) strongly supported a proposal to study the flight attendant work culture. In the fall of 1980 Joan Volpe, the program's "resident anthropologist," attended EAP trainings. As a participant-observer, she noticed that "flight attendant participants exhibited a cohesiveness and sameness that transcended individual members. Informal conversations among participants revealed 'we/them' distinctions which appeared to extend beyond the usual industrial group identity" (Volpe 1982). Tapping into this supportive "kinship-like" subculture, Volpe conducted an in-depth ethnographic study that enabled AFA to design an EAP that eventually fit "like a glove."

As Naisbett stated in *Megatrends* (1983), "We are moving away from hierarchies to a networking system in the workplace. Top-down management procedures need to be replaced by systems that offer equal participation for all employees. Under this type of system, *each spoke of the wheel is equally important . . .* " (p. 211; emphasis added).

If a supervisory-model EAP is not most appropriate in less-structured workplaces, what kind of progam would work best? The peer intervention model emerges as an attractive alternative, although for the most part, it remains relatively unresearched.

THE PEER REFERRAL MODEL COMES OF AGE

In the mid-1970s, the AFA actively addressed the issues of stress-related work-site problems and their affects on members. After receiving approval from the AFA's board of directors, flight attendants Lisa Eatinger and Jim Naccarato (the latter became the program's coordinator) prepared a grant proposal enabling the union to design and implement a peer referral member assistance program. In 1980 AFA was awarded a demonstration grant from the National Institute of Alcohol Abuse and Alcoholism, and the Association of Flight Attendants Employee Assistance Program was born.

The existence of such a program within a labor union continues to be somewhat unusual, but it is completely consistent with the purposes of unions in providing for the health, safety, and welfare of members and their families. The former director of the AFL-CIO's Department of Community Services, Leo Perlis, established the concept of a "human contract" that encouraged the development of occupational programs jointly administered by labor and management to address problems experienced by employees and their families that were not part of the negotiated contract. One advantage of providing such programs through the auspices of the union is that the union is generally able to be more responsive to the needs of members than community services are able to be. This helps to reduce the trade unionists' negative perception of counseling and related mental health care (Akabus 1977). The value of union participation has, however, received more lip service and publicity than commitment from management. Unions are frequently included only as a last detail in planning employee assistance services (Trice, Hunt, and Beyer 1977).

The need for a union-operated EAP was particularly great for flight attendants. The highly mobile and irregularly supervised employees required a program that was uniquely suited to their life styles and stressors. AFA believed that a program designed to rely on those who are available in the working environment would be most effective.

A flight attendant's work schedule varies from as many as 22 to as few as ten days a month, while the workday ranges from 3 to 17 hours within a 24-hour period. Trips last from one to five days, and rest periods are taken wherever and whenever the work assignment is completed. Flying partners usually change from month to month.

Daily job supervision in this high-stress, service-oriented profession is virtually nonexistent. It is not unusual for supervisory contact to occur only once during a three-month period, consisting solely of a 15-minute appearance evaluation. Under these circumstances, the probability of supervisory identification of personal or mental health problems is unlikely, at least in the early stages.

On the other hand, flight attendants not only work together in confined space, but room, eat, and socialize with other crew members during rest periods. These combined personal, professional, and social relationships give them the opportunity to observe potential problem behaviors in flying partners.

AFA capitalized on this unique set of circumstances by taking advantage of the social support dimensions of the flight attendant's work environment and developed a program model that acknowledges the importance of peer interveners as potential change agents. The leverage for getting help is peer pressure, a strong reinforcer of healthier behaviors (Whitfield 1973).

The peer model not only effectively identifies and refers workers in need of EAP services; it goes further than other models in its inherent ability to support recovery. We know it works for many adults, as evidenced by such proven successful peer support groups as Alcoholics Anonymous, Narcotics Anonymous, and Weight Watchers, to name a few.

In the *Journal of Drug Issues*, Trice, Hunt and Beyer (1977: 107) also suggest that the peer group may be the most knowledgeable about helping the alcoholic co-worker:

Perhaps it can be argued that current tendencies to emphasize only managerial detection of poor performance in work situations have gone too far, especially in situations where close, personal relationships occur on the job, often fostered by the nature of the work itself. Often union members and officials may readily see the poor performance and its causes more easily than professional and management personnel, and thus are willing to deal with it forthrightly.

The union's multiservice program offers a wide range of services to 23,000 members from 15 member airlines and their families nationwide. Services include referrals for: personal, marriage, and family issues; alcohol and other drug concerns; crisis situations, including rape and domestic violence; legal and financial referrals; and a 24-hour telephone hotline for members and their families.

AFA Committee Members: Catalysts for Change

EAP committee members are the foundation of the program. They have primary responsibility for recognizing signs of problem behavior and referring a troubled co-worker to the appropriate treatment professional or self-help group. Committees coordinate local program efforts with support from national headquarters. Committees are active in all of the 21 states and 26 cities where members are based.

Who are the committee members? They are full-time flight attendants chosen or elected to serve because they possess the qualities necessary to effectively assist their peers. Some of the 100-plus committee members have held previous union positions; others have backgrounds in the helping professions, while at least one-third are recovering alcoholics and/or Al-Anon members. They have been carefully selected because they are respected, trusted, and well-liked by their peers. Committee members understand and uphold the strict policy of confidentiality, which plays an essential role in the acceptance and utilization of the program by members.

TRAINING: AN ESSENTIAL INGREDIENT

EAP committee members receive approximately 96 hours of in-depth training developed by the national EAP staff. This rigorous training includes presentations by experienced EAP committee members, national office staff, and outside experts. Role-playing, films and videotapes, and experiential small-group exercises complement the lecture/discussion format.

Because individuals with alcohol and other drug problems are unlikely to self-refer themselves to the EAP, basic training focuses on chemical dependency. Committee members learn the essential skills needed to identify problem behavior and intervene when necessary. Presentations on the disease concept of alcoholism, treatment issues for women, and the importance of aftercare and follow-up are included. Intervention strategies are practiced, using simulated case studies, which give participants essential hands-on experience. Other topics covered are communication skills, developing community treatment resources, record-keeping, confidentiality, and burnout prevention (focusing on the committee members themselves). Understanding and accepting the concept of detachment, as well as responsibility *to*, but not *for*, troubled co-workers, is a major goal of each training area.

Advanced training concentrates on other problems that can affect union members on and off the job. Topics include crisis intervention, and suicide prevention, working with rape victims, domestic violence, eating disorders, continuing sobriety, adult children of alcoholics, and coping effectively with stress. These sessions also concentrate on program promotion, case management issues, working with other union committees, and advanced communication skills.

In July 1983, the EAP, in cooperation with the Air Safety and Health Department, organized the first EAP/Air Safety Training in the industry. Participants heard guest experts and AFA staff speak on accident investigation, the psychological aspects of aircraft emergencies, the proper response to hijackings, and stress management.

The goal of the training was to familiarize safety EAP committee members with each other's roles, responsibilities, and areas of expertise. The training fostered the idea of working together as a team to provide the most comprehensive services to members involved in any type of aircraft emergency. Following up on the training, the national office published for all EAP committee members a resource booklet entitled, "The Psychological Aspects of Aircraft Emergencies—Where to Turn When Flight Attendants Turn to You for Help."

Since the EAP is still the new kid on the block, integration into the existing organizational structure has a high priority. EAP committee members are encouraged to work with their Safety and Health Committee counterparts when flight attendants are involved in any type of unplanned aircraft emergency, be it a bomb threat, sudden loss of altitude, a hijacking, or a crash. They are trained to attend to the emotional needs of involved members, which allows their safety counterparts to focus on the technical aspects of the incident.

PROGRAM PRIORITIES: EDUCATION, PREVENTION AND PROGRAM PROMOTION

Effective EAP strategies focus on secondary prevention efforts, involving crisis intervention, early diagnosis and crisis monitoring as well as tertiary efforts focusing treatment and rehabilitation.

The prevention efforts of the AFA's EAP also emphasize early identification and intervention whenever possible. They make the assumption that educated members are more likely to recognize early warning signs of potential problems with co-workers or family members and take responsibility to try and do something about them. This encourages intervention *before* problems become more severe and/or discipline is involved. Interventions are usually informal, taking place between a committee member (or members) and the flight attendant in question, or with a committee member, concerned friends and a troubled member. More formal interventions might include a committee member who facilitates the meeting along with flying partners, friends, a supervisor, or family members.

Without compromising its secondary and tertiary prevention foci, primary prevention and education are also integral components of the EAP's scope of services. Educational brochures on how to get help from the EAP, coping with the stress of the holiday season, prescription drugs, PMS and hypoglycemia, stress management and anger have been mailed to all members' homes, including those who are laid off.

Promotional information (including the names and phone numbers of committee members on an 800 toll-free number) is displayed on crew lounge bulletin boards. Articles on smoking, loneliness and depression, money management tips, and stress appear regularly in local union newsletters. *Flightlog*, the Association's quarterly magazine, features articles on program services; EAP committees present at local union meetings; and national headquarter staff do the same at new officer leadership training. These are just some examples of the program's educational efforts. Committee members also organize local workshops on such subjects as weight and nutrition, stress, conflict resolution, and a host of other relevant topics. The key is to keep the EAP in front of the membership as much as possible.

DO THEY MEASURE UP?

Does the AFA EAP live up to its promise? From October 1980, when we began gathering data, through June 1985, more than 3,000 flight attendants and their family members sought assistance. The EAP is in its sixth year and a fourth utilization report has been completed by an independent research consultant.

From July 1, 1983 through June 30, 1985, utilization, based on a population of members and their families, was 3.6 percent. Given the paucity of reliable information on the ratio of penetration to utilization, this percentage compares with the very best. The Office of Personnel Management has estimated that a respectable utilization rate is 2 percent of the total work force.

The statistical analysis also shows that more than 31 percent of all cases were referred by peers, which includes flying partners, EAP committee members, and other union representatives. Fifty-one percent were self-referrals, with .1 percent from family members and 17 percent from supervisors or other management personnel. This last statistic is a good indication of the EAP's effectiveness; the adversarial barrier that usually exists between management and the union has crumbled in order to help members/employees.

During 1984-1985, the number of those seeking assistance increased by approximately 47.5 percent over the previous year, due to increasingly effective outreach efforts by local committees. Thus, when reviewing the standards of success set forth by the field, the AFA EAP does indeed measure up. But there is no room for complacency because there's much more to be accomplished.

New and exciting projects are in their development stages. As the corps of committee members grows, the EAP is exploring alternative training options. Training of trainers (using experienced EAP committee members to train new committee members) is being explored.

In the aftermath of the 1985 United Airlines strike, which affected 10,000 AFA members, the EAP is researching the psychological affects of a strike on members and their families, of which little or nothing has been written.

Stress in the workplace also looms as an issue that demands to be addressed. Stress seminars have been offered since the EAP first opened its doors, but the examination of the workplace as a stressor is a high priority.

When questioned about the reason for honoring the Association of Flight Attendants Employee Assistance Program with its 1985 EAP Humanitarian Award, Deborah Parker, executive director of the California Women's Commission on Alcoholism, stated, "Traditional EAPs operate from the top down, and rely on supervisors to refer troubled employees to the program. AFA's tremendous success is due to the peer referral approach."

Further evidence that the AFA EAP is on the right track comes from Don Godwin, associate director of Occupational Programs at the National Institute on Alcohol Abuse and Alcoholism and a man widely respected in the field. He wrote, "I consider AFA's program to be not only the most advanced in the flight attendant field, but also one of the most innovative programs in industry today."

REFERENCES

Akabus, S. 1977. "Labor: Social Policy and Human Services." *Encyclopedia of Social Work*: 737-44.

Liebowitz, B. 1982. "Employee Assistance Programs as an Employee Benefit and as Risk Management." *Employee Benefits Journal*; 14-16.

McClellan, K. 1982. "Changing EAP Services." *EAP Digest*: 25-29.

Molloy, D. 1985. "A Peer Training Initiative in an Industrial Social Work Program." Unpublished.

Naisbett, J. 1983. *Megatrends* (New York: Warner Books).

Presnall, L. F. 1981. *Occupational Counseling and Referral Systems* (Salt Lake City, UT: Utah Alcoholism Foundation).

Roman, P. 1981. *Barriers to Initiation of Employee Alcohol Programs*. Proceedings from a workshop on occupational alcoholism: A review of research issues (National Institute on Alcohol Abuse and Alcoholism).

Samuels, M. and D. Samuels. 1975. *The Complete Handbook of Peer Counseling* (Miami, FL: Fiesta Publishing).

Saxe, L., D. Doughtery, K. Esty, and M. Fine. 1983. "Health Technology Case Study 22: The Effectiveness and Costs of Alcoholism Treatment." *Office of Technology Assessment*: 3.

Trice, H., R. Hunt, and J. Beyer. 1977. "Alcoholism Programs in Unionized Work Settings: Problems and Prospects in Union-Management Cooperation." *Journal of Drug Issues* 7: 103-15.

Volpe, J. 1982. "The Flight Attendant Subculture." *Association of Flight Attendants.* Unpublished.

Wolfe, K. 1982. "Casefinding Models to Identify and Refer the Impaired Professional." *EAP Digest*: 37.

Whitfield, P. T. 1983. *Peer Group Training: A Positive Force in Influencing the Status-oriented Behaviors: Smoking, Alcohol, and Drug Abuse.* Symposium presented at the meeting of the Intrenational Congress on Drug Education. Montreux, Switzerland.

10

UTILITY ANALYSIS: A PRIMER AND APPLICATION TO ORGANIZATIONAL STRESS INTERVENTIONS

PHILIP BOBKO

The purpose of this chapter is to indicate how the *utility* of organizational stress interventions can be quantified—in dollar metrics, or otherwise. The assumption will be made that such stress interventions are geared to particular organizational dysfunctions and individual symptomology. The *type* of intervention (including method, length, and so on) will not be considered, as these issues have been dealt with in other chapters in this book. Rather, concern will be with the question, "Given that management is considering implementation of an organizational stress-related intervention, how can the financial gain to the host organization be determined?"

In the stress management literature, answers to these questions have often focused on *costs* and *losses* due to stress—both to the individual (such as physical and mental disease) and the organization (for example, health-care costs, absenteeism, and so on). These approaches are briefly reviewed below in the first section on cost accounting.

However, it is argued that the above approach casts the answer in a *negative* frame (by focusing on losses/costs) rather than a *positive* frame. As such, the cost accounting of stress has tended to focus on workers who are absent from the job, and often fails to consider the positive gains associated with workers who stay on the job and "overcome" the effects of stressors. The second section discusses a procedure that can be used to directly estimate *overall* organizational utility. The technique is adapted from well-known theory on the utility of selection devices (that is, the usefulness of particular tests for selecting individual workers). This technique is described in detail and then applied to results from a recent meta-analysis of organizational interventions that are potentially related to individual stress reduction.

The third section of this chapter provides a brief overview of yet another technique, conjoint analysis. This technique is useful when the source of stress (overload, ambiguity, and so on) can be reliably dimensionalized. The result of conjoint analysis is a set of utility weights that can help guide the organization to direct its efforts toward those dimensions that are deemed most important. The application of one of these techniques, whether cost accounting, conjoint analysis, or selection utility analyses, is imperative if organizations are to provide energy and resources for stress interventions.

Finally, several related issues are considered. For example, are there metrics other than dollars (for example, "life years gained") that might be more useful, more readily accepted by users, et cetera? Do the stress interventions considered for utility analysis really ameliorate stress-related problems, or do they provide only "band-aid" solutions while ignoring the causal agents of stress? And, given the past 30 years of industrial/organizational theory, should we expect stress interventions to enhance organizational *productivity* (in contrast to intervention effects on individual health and worker satisfaction)? These questions will generally have only partial answers, indicating a greater need for a union of clinical/stress research and industrial/organizational research.

COST ACCOUNTING

As Schwartz (1980) has noted, there is "a growing body of literature [which] specifically documents the effects of occupational stress in the etiology and development of physical and mental disease" (p. 99). He also notes, however, that research on the direct effects of stress *interventions* are scarce. Usually the cost effectiveness analysis of such interventions has focused on outcome variables that are quantitatively defined and relatively easy to operationalize. These variables often include absenteeism from work, cost of medical care and insurance, turnover, self-reports of stress and dissatisfaction, blood pressure, and physical correlates of anxiety. This list of variables is not surprising given the empirical interrelatedness of stress factors and physical/mental disease.

In the cost accounting method, a list of measurable outcome variables (for example, absenteeism) is generated. Then, estimates of dollar costs are attached to each of these outcomes. The costs are then summed across outcomes. In addition, the cost of the intervention (for example, consultant costs) is estimated. The savings on the outcome variables are then compared to the cost of the intervention program, either by direct subtraction or by the computation of a cost/benefit ratio.

A Short Example

Cascio (1982) provides an excellent cost accounting for the effects of smoking at the workplace. The present example draws heavily from Cascio's framework.

Suppose we are interested in the cost-effectiveness of a stress intervention program. First, the analysis should generate a list of outcome variables that are salient to the individuals and the organization. For example, high levels of stress may directly impact on

Absenteeism

Medical care

Morbidity and early retirement

Turnover

Insurance

On-the-job time loss and

Effects on other co-workers

Second, there needs to be an analysis of the *differential* rates (or costs) at which the above factors occur for populations that are extremely stressed and populations that are not. For example, Kristein (1982) reports differential mortality rates between hypertensive and control groups. The earlier mortality for the hypertensive group can then be translated into an expected number of person-years lost due to this factor. Assuming that estimates of the cost of training workers are available, dollar values can be attached to each person who is expected to manifest early mortality.

Kristein (1982) has also reported that hypertensives spend between $170 and $300 per year in extra medical care. He further provides estimates of the number of hypertensives in the work force. Again, these data can be combined and translated into "costs per person" and summed with the previous analysis on costs of early mortality.

As a further example, suppose data exist for differential absenteeism rates for highly stressed and control groups. These rates can be translated into an expected number of days lost for the stressed individuals. Then, the analysis typically computes dollar losses from the use of daily salary figures. [As an aside, it is interesting to note that Cascio (1982) has reported a substantial differential absenteeism rate for smokers. In contrast, Schwartz (1980) reports that, in a study by Manuso, there was *no* difference between the absenteeism of High Anxiety and Headache subjects and an overall corporate average.]

This mode of analysis is continued for each of the outcome factors listed above. In order to sum the results, data are placed in a common metric (usually dollars). The sum represents the potential gain/benefit of an effective stress intervention program.

The *cost* of the intervention must then be evaluated. Again, a list of factors must be generated and costs attached. For example, if a treatment program were to be conducted at the employees' health center, factors would include the cost of:

a. identifying particular individuals for treatment,
b. maintenance of the health center and training of medical staff for the intervention program,
c. employee time away from the job to visit the health facility, and
d. gaining acceptance from the individual's supervisor.

As was done for the list of benefits, the costs of implementing the intervention are estimated and summed across factors. Cost/benefit differences and ratios for the entire program can then be determined.

It should be noted that these gains are initially expressed at the *individual* level of analysis. For example, Cascio (1982) estimates that the total cost to an organization of *one smoker in one year* is $4,737. This type of figure is greatly magnified if one shifts levels of analysis to the entire organization and to a span of years. For example, suppose this figure is applied to a small organization of 400 employees, of whom 30 percent are smokers. Assume that there is a stable level of effectiveness, across time, for the stress intervention. Then, over a 5-year period, smokers will cost the organization a total of $5 \times .30 \times 400 \times \$4,737 = \$2,842,200$ in current dollars! Similarly, Kristein (1982) has estimated that the number of hypertensives in the work force is at least 30 million. Then assume that the excess medical care of hypertensives (the figure of $170 to $300 per year given above) is absorbed totally by the employers. Then, each year, hypertensives are costing U.S. organizations over $30 \text{ million} \times \$170 \approx \$5$ billion in excess health care! It should also be noted this $5 billion figure is conservative, in that it is simply for excess health care and does not incorporate other outcome factors of hypertension.

A TRANSITION: FOCUSING ON PRODUCTIVITY

The cost accounting procedure above does a thorough job of delineating specific factors and translating outcomes into dollars. The current feeling, however, is that the analysis misses several crucial factors because it is cast in a *negative* frame. Outcomes are almost exclusively cast in losses to the organization and the use of *interventions to avoid losses,* that is, avoiding turnover, absenteeism, and high health care costs, and so on. In contrast, the next section is cast in a more positive frame because it focuses on an individual's overall contribution to an organization. This includes the avoidance of negative outcomes, but also allows for the possibility that stress interventions can lead to *increases* in productivity, *increases* in a willingness to help co-workers, and other positive outcomes.

The use of productivity as an outcome variable is relatively rare in previous stress intervention literatures. For example, Kristein (1982: 35) notes that productivity is not included in his dollar analyses, implying that inclusion of this outcome would enhance the resultant intervention utility. Probably the most widely known stress management study in the industrial psychology literature, by Ganster et al. (1982), does *not* include a measure of productivity gain. Following the line of thought that stress is a *health* psychology issue (cf. Kaplan 1984), Ganster et al. assessed criteria such as individual anxiety, depression, and urinary catecholamines.

There are some serious concerns, however, about the lack of productivity as an outcome variable. First, Schwartz (1980) speaks for many researchers when he talks about the need for stress management programs and then states, "Whether the challenge will be met depends on the cooperation and collaboration of industry, labor, government, and the behavioral and bio-medical sciences. . ." (p. 108). It is believed that the greatest appeal to management is through industry's frequent bottom line—an individual's overall contribution (usually in *dollars* to the organization). This, by necessity, includes productivity. Second, in a marketplace shaped by unemployment, dual-career families, and increasing housing costs, it is simply not feasible for many employees to consider changing jobs. Thus, the frequently cited organizational measure of turnover may not really be a strong contributor to cost. Similarly, absenteeism can often be controlled by stronger organizational policy. However, this does not deny the possibility of *psychological* absenteeism, which would again be reflected in productivity gains and losses.

As an aside, it should be noted that a review of the literature found three studies on stress interventions that used productivity measures—by Manuso (reported in Schwartz 1980); Peters, Benson, and Porter (1977); and Riley, Frederiksen, and Winett (1984). Unfortunately, the study by Riley et al. had difficulties in comparing productivity measures across subjects working in different organizational units (Riley, personal communication). Also, Peters et al. used *self-report* measures of productivity, which, as a self-report, could be equally well interpreted as (or, confounded with) measures of worker satisfaction. Finally, it is not clear what the Manuso measures consisted of. In any case, the need for studies that directly assess the effect of stress interventions on organizational productivity is clear. Such studies would enhance theory *and* provide more direct evidence for a focusing of organizational resources on stress interventions.

The following section presents a methodology for assessing organizational utility that implicitly includes both costs and productivity as factors. Whereas the cost-accounting methods operate on the divide-and-conquer philosophy (list the factors, cost the factors, then add), the utility analysis is wholistic. Thus, an estimate of *overall* utility will be gained (at the expense of knowing the contributions of an individual factor, although even this shortcoming can be modified in utility analyses). In addition, as will become clearer, proponents of utility analysis are quick to note that the wholistic analysis is substantially easier to do and is less time-consuming (and cost-consuming!) than traditional cost-accounting analysis.

UTILITY ANALYSIS

Several decades ago, Brogden (1949) and Cronbach and Gleser (1965) derived sets of decision-theoretic equations that can be used to determine the utility of selection devices (for example, tests) in organizational settings. "Utility" is defined in any linear metric, although it is usually conceived in dollar values. There are restrictions to these formulations, as well as flexibility. For example, if the criterion for worker success is dichotomous (for example, either you keep up with an assembly line or you do not), then the equations are inappropriate and should be replaced by those of Taylor and Russell (1939). However, if output is assumed to be continuous, then the choice of metric is extremely flexible, from dollars, to worker hours gained, to expected number of life years, and so on (see discussion below).

In essence, Cronbach and Gleser demonstrated that the utility of a test is a direct multiplicative function of the correlational validity of that test (r), the selection ratio, the standard deviation of worker output (SD_y) in the metric of choice, and the costs associated with implementing the testing procedure (C). That is, the gain in utility, per person, by using the test in question, is evaluated by the formula

$$\Delta U = r \times SD_y \times Q - C \qquad 10.1$$

where Q is some mathematical function that depends on the selection ratio (the percentage of applicants chosen for the job).

Equation 10.1 is useful for estimating the utility of selection devices and has received substantial use in the last several years, due to advances in the ability to estimate its parameters. However, the form of Equation 10.1 is inadequate for the present purpose of assessing the impact of stress intervention that might be made available to *everyone* (or *anyone*) in the workplace, thus making the concept of "selection" moot. Fortunately, Equation 10.1 can be readily modified to accommodate that change.

The essential features of this modification include two issues. First, as noted above, stress interventions are usually applied to on-the-job workers. As such, selection ratios (and hence the factor Q) make little sense. Second, there is usually a desire for a direct comparison between the possible results of a stress intervention *and* the status quo. In validity terms, this implies a shift in interest from r to a difference in r's (say $r_1 - r_2$). Using these notions, two sets of researchers (Landy, Farr, and Jacobs 1982; Schmidt, Hunter, and Pearlman 1982) have independently derived utility equations that assess the impact of organizational interventions on work-force productivity. The result is

$$\Delta\,U \text{ per individual} = d_t \times SD_y - C \qquad\qquad 10.2$$

where SD_y is the standard deviation of performance, in the metric of choice, for the status quo group of workers; d_t is the expected difference, in standard deviation units, in job performance between an employee who has undergone the intervention and one who has not; and C is the cost, per person, of the intervention. Finally, assuming that N employees are subjected to the intervention, and that the effect of the intervention remains relatively stable for T years, the overall gain in utility to the organization is

$$\Delta U \text{ for organization} = T \times N \times d_t \times SD_y - N \times C \qquad\qquad 10.3$$

Parameter Estimates

Equation 10.3 provides a mechanism for estimating organizational gain (for example, in dollars) of a stress intervention. The parameters T and N are defined in a rather straightforward manner. The definition of C is also straightforward but, as in cost accounting methods, may be time-consuming to operationalize. This parameter is often overestimated, such that the overall utility equation provides a conservative estimate.

The parameter d_t (the expected difference in productivity between a "treated" and "nontreated" employee) can be estimated from a well-designed study that reflects the effect on productivity of the intervention of interest. Unfortunately, as noted earlier, these studies are extremely rare. This leaves two alternative approaches to estimating d_t. First, the value of d_t may be estimated from effect sizes of meta-analytic studies that use similar interventions. This is the approach taken in this chapter, and will be described in the next section. Second, the value of d_t may be, by definition, directly translated into a point-biserial correlation. Then, either empirical or rational estimates of this correlation may be obtained. The latter approach, rational estimation, is often accomplished by asking several judges (for example, supervisors, managers) to estimate the degree of relationship between interventions and worker performance. These estimates are then averaged. Such procedures have been used successfully in the past and provide the fundamental basis for a related area in industrial/ organizational psychology—validity generalization (cf. Burke 1984).

Estimation of the parameter SD_y (the standard deviation of worker performance) has received substantial attention in recent years. In fact, the lack of good estimates for SD_y is usually cited as the reason why the Cronbach and Gleser models received so little application in the 1960s and 1970s. Recently, however, Schmidt et al. (1979) proposed an estimation technique for SD_y that is extremely straightforward to implement. Assuming that productivity is approximately normally distributed across all potential workers in a particular job, they note that one standard deviation is approximately equal to the difference between a 50th percentile and an 85th percentile worker. Thus, supervisors are asked to estimate the overall worth (for example, in dollars) to the organization of an average worker and an 85th percentile worker. The difference between these two percentile estimates provides an estimate of SD_y. These estimates are then averaged across supervisors, and the resultant average is substituted in Equations 10.1, 10.2, or 10.3.

Given that utility is a direct function of SD_y, it is crucial that estimates of SD_y are relatively accurate. In a recent study, Bobko, Karren, and Parkington (1983) compared supervisory estimates of one component of performance (yearly dollar sales of insurance counselors) to actual, archival records. In this case, the average supervisory estimates of SD_y (for sales) was extremely accurate. In addition, this particular index of performance was essentially normally distributed across workers. Although these results bode well, it is crucial to remember that this study focused on one component of performance, and not on *overall* performance. Bobko et al. also suggested that the estimation process could be psychometrically enhanced by providing feedback to supervisors about the average of their 50th percentile estimates *before* they estimated 85th percentiles. This has recently been confirmed in a study by Burke and Frederick (1984). It appears, therefore, that progress is being made in estimating the parameters of Equation 10.3.

Further Refinements

Although not considered in the example below, several researchers have provided further refinements to the basic utility equations. For example, in order to compute estimates of SD_y, supervisors are asked for their estimates of *overall* performance. Several researchers (Cascio 1982; Janz 1982) have indicated methods that analyze performance into component parts. Supervisors then provide estimates about these *components* of performance, and the resulting estimates are *statistically* combined. These methods seem to provide greater acceptance on the part of the supervisors who are making the estimates, although results are equivocal regarding any increases in the quality of SD_y estimates.

Extensions to the utility equations have also been accomplished by embedding results within econometric models. For example, Boudreau (1983) has added to the basic model the impact of tax rates, variable costs associated with changes in productivity, the effect of employee flows, and the effect of discounting for future benefits. The last factor has also been cited as a major factor in health intervention estimates (Kaplan 1984). Finally,

Alexander and Cronshaw (1984) have extended these capital budgeting modifications by systematically assessing the effect of uncertainty on utility estimates.

AN APPLICATION

In order to provide for current applications of Equation 10.3, it will be necessary to enhance the scope of what is meant by an organizational stress intervention. The opinion of this author is that this enhancement is useful, not only for application, but points to a potential flaw in current stress intervention approaches.

Often stress interventions are focused at the *individual level of change*— for example, time management programs, self-monitoring programs (Riley, Frederikson and Winett 1984), cognitive restructuring programs (Ganster et al. 1982; Meichenbaum 1975), or muscle relaxation programs (Ganster et al. 1982; Jacobson 1938). However, suppose the *source* of the individual's stress is due to poor supervisory structuring in a matrix management setting, with conflicting (and perhaps variable) time demands being placed on the individual from a variety of supervisory sources. It can then be argued that time management programs that are focused on any particular individual have missed the root source of the problem, that is, a need to restructure the work demands. As Neale et al. in Chapter 7, suggest, "If the problems of stress involve an interconnected whole, . . . then selective attention to one aspect is not only doing less than a complete job, but threatens to be useless in the long run." Perhaps Ganster et al. (1982: 541) summarize the issue best:

The present program is one that attempts to alter the reactions of employees to presumed noxious and stressful organizational, task, and role characteristics. In this sense it represents an innoculation approach, and does not, in fact, remove objective stressors from the employee's organizational environment. Training employees to better tolerate poorly designed organizations would seem to be a less desirable strategy than one that attempts to make the organization inherently less stressful.

Thus, as argued earlier, the need for increasing organizational involvement is even more imperative, because a large part of the solution to ameliorating stress may lie within the organizational, not individual, purview.

Thus, for the current example, suppose that dysfunctional time demands on workers are seen as the root cause of individual stress. As such, it is believed that a work rescheduling intervention may help reduce stress and, in turn, increase individual productivity. The empirical effects of such rescheduling interventions have been recently documented in a meta-analysis of psychologically based work interventions by Guzzo, Katzell, and Jetty (1985). They review 27 studies of work rescheduling that give empirical estimates of impact on worker *productivity*. The analysis indicates that the average effect size, $d_{interventions}$, is .21. Substituting into Equation 10.3 yields

$$\Delta U \text{ for organization } = T \times N \times (.21) \times SD_y - N \times C$$

Guzzo et al. do not give any data useful for estimating SD_y, the standard deviation of performance in dollars. However, Schmidt and Hunter (1981) have recommended that a *conservative* estimate of SD_y is 40 percent of the mean salary of employees. A recent review of over 18 studies (Schmidt and Hunter 1983) found support for their contention. Thus, for our purposes, assume that the average salary of the workers in our "stressed" organization is $15,000. A conservative estimate of SD_y would then be (.4) $\times$ $15,000 = $6,000.

There are at least two ways to approach the use of Equation 10.3. First, assume the remaining parameters are specified. For example, let the number of identified employees be $N = 100$ and suppose the effects of the intervention will remain stable for $T = 4$ years. Also, assume that the cost to the organization of rescheduling work activities is $50,000. This yields a cost per employee of $500. Then Equation 10.3 yields a gain to the organization of

$$\Delta U \text{ for organization } = 4(100)(.21)(6000) - 50,000$$
$$= \$454,000 \text{ in productivity.}$$

A second approach would be to start with Equation 10.3 and work in reverse, in order to estimate what a break-even figure would be for the "cost of the program." For example, assume organizational interest is only in a one-year effort ($T = 1$), or that the cost of implementing the program does not decline from year to year. Then, Equation 10.3 yields

$$\Delta U \text{ for organization } = 1(100)(.21)(6000) - \text{(total cost)}$$
$$= \$126,000 - \text{(total cost).}$$

Then any intervention that had a total cost of less than $126,000 would provide positive productivity utility to the organization.

Of course, the values that were used in estimating the parameters of Equation 10.3 are only that—estimates. It is often useful to try a *range* of values for each parameter and then document the sensitivity of the analysis to variations in parameter estimates. In general, these analyses will indicate that organizational utility gains are substantial across a wide variety of values.

A TRANSITION: OTHER METRICS OF UTILITY

The previous discussions have generally presumed a utility metric of *dollar* gains. This metric was clearly connected to the need to appeal to and motivate organizations to invest resources in stress interventions. There are organizational cultures, however, in which financial metrics may be inappropriate—for definitional reasons, acceptability (by management) reasons, and so on. For example, Kaplan (1984) notes that a dollar metric has "not been popular among social and health care scientists because it tends to favor programs that benefit the rich" (p. 761). Instead, Kaplan argues that benefits of health programs may best be expressed in the number of life-years they produce.

The use of other metrics, such as life-years, has intuitive appeal. These metrics may be more socially/politically acceptable to decision-makers and more useful in conveying cost/benefit information. For example, the Army Research Institute is currently conducting a seven-year study of selection and classification procedures. One major focus is the assessment of the utility of new selection devices. Initially, these evaluations were conceived in dollar metrics. However, it quickly became clear that dollar values of "winning a war," "maintaining peace," and so on were extremely difficult, if not impossible to define. The fear of political, public, and policy-maker reactions to such dollar evaluations was also quite real. Subsequent discussions with Army experts led to a new metric derived from the question: "I can provide either the intervention *or X* average infantrymen to make an identical gain in Army effectiveness. What is the value of *X*?" The metric is therefore in terms of "equivalent numbers of infantry." This metric is readily accepted by Army experts, and policy-makers may feel more comfortable when assessing the impact of alternative interventions.

CONJOINT ANALYSIS

Given that the metric of evaluation is flexible, a variety of other policy-capturing techniques may become useful for evaluating stress interventions. In particular, it may be that organizations need to *choose* between interventions that focus on *different sources* of stress. If "cutthroat competition" and "role ambiguity" are two operative sources of organizational stress, then where should an organization focus its finite energy and/or resources?

One technique that can help resource expenditure allocations is known as *conjoint analysis* (cf. Green and Srinivasan 1978, for a review of this technique). Essentially, conjoint analysis begins with a set of "case histories" or scenarios that depict theoretical individuals who systematically vary across dimensions of interest. These dimensions might be sources of organizational stress, such as work overload, work ambiguity, role conflict, cutthroat competition, contact with stress carriers, or constant change (see Schwartz 1980, or Neale et al. 1987, for extended lists of organizational stressors). Then experts are asked to rate these scenarios on some criterion. The criterion might be "likelihood of inducing a decrement in performance"; likelihood of causing dysfunctional stress"; "estimated percentage reduction in performance"; "estimated percentage increase in early retirement and/or turnover"; and so on. Clearly, the criterion is flexible and can reflect any concern that might motivate organizational involvement. The experts might be managers or incumbent workers. The former experts (managers) are usually assumed to be more knowledgeable about overall criteria; the latter group (incumbent workers) are more knowledgeable about the direct effects of the stressors.

These types of ratings are conducted on a variety of scenarios that systematically vary the stress inducing dimensions. Application of conjoint analysis will then yield a set of "utilities" for each dimension considered. These utilities can be directly compared across dimensions; that is, the analysis will allow statements such as, "Given that interest is in increasing performance (the criterion), a 20 percent decrease in role conflict is equivalent to a 50 percent decrease in work overload." Then, within the organization's resources, decisions can be made whether to focus on role conflict interventions or work overload interventions.

The utility of conjoint analysis is therefore in the capacity to choose between potential interventions (based on expert judgment). In addition, the technique makes no assumptions about linearity (an assumption inherent in Equations 10.1 through 10.3). Thus, conjoint analysis is useful for demonstrating the *shape* of the utility function as well. For example, it may be that a 10 percent (or 15 percent) decrease in role conflict is equivalent to a 10 percent (or 15 percent) decrease in work overload, yet a 20 percent decrease in role conflict is equivalent to a 50 percent decrease in work overload.

Finally, as is often done with conjoint analyses, studies could be conducted across several populations of interest. That is, separate analyses could be done for varying expert levels (supervisor versus incumbent), varying demographics (male versus female; blue collar versus white collar), or varying organizational characteristics (public versus private sector, product versus service orientation). The results of these comparisons could further help our understanding of how organizational and individual variables impact on the emergence and effects of stress.

EMBEDDING STRESS IN I/O THEORY

Performance versus Satisfaction

As stated earlier, it would seem that knowledge of *productivity-based* utility would be useful for increasing an organization's focus on stress interventions. As noted, however, there are precious few studies that directly relate stress interventions to productivity. The most common organizationally relevant measure of individual behavior is withdrawal, evidenced by either absenteeism or turnover. Most of the other measures include physiologically based indices or self-reports of affective states (including satisfaction).

The question will arise, then, as to whether or not we should *expect* stress interventions to be associated with productivity measures. For example, for many decades, researchers in I/O psychology were concerned with the relationship between satisfaction and performance. A prevailing view, based on accumulation of research findings, is that no such relationship exists (cf. Blum and Naylor 1968; Jackofsky 1984). Satisfaction *is* related to absenteeism and turnover (Vroom 1964), but this is seen as an affective-affective relationship. Thus, the utility of stress interventions for decreasing dissatisfaction may be documented, but this implies no suggestion that such interventions will impact on performance.

A decade of studies by Peters and O'Connor on the effects of organizational constraints may have implications for the above statement. A recent review by Peters, O'Connor, and Eulberg (1985) indicates that in the *laboratory*, situational constraints (improper tools and equipment, extreme noise, inefficient communication patterns, and so on) have an effect on performance. However, in field experiments, this relationship vanishes. They suggest that "constraints may not be the significant real world variable we had expected." Given that actual constraints may not be as severe as initially thought, "they may be no more than a nuisance factor one encounters while doing the job." Assuming that organizational constraints are precursors of stress, the "nuisance" effect could explain the stress-affect relationship. However, there is little reason to expect that stress interventions will impact on performance levels. Or, given the low performance satisfaction relationship, some aspects of stress interventions might impact on stress, other aspects on performance.

Intervention Scope

As noted earlier, the developers of stress interventions are encouraged to increase the scope of their activities; while the outcomes of stress may be observed at the individual level, the source of the problem may be at the organizational (or larger system) level. The typology set forth by Neale et al. (1984) provides an excellent source of multiple levels of stressors, including sociocultural, organizational, psychological, and so on.

Also, as noted earlier, the derivation of the Cronbach and Gleser utility equations (for example, Equation 10.1) was developed in a *selection* context. Perhaps, then, in support of the above paragraph, stress interventions can include actions taken by the organization *before* the individual enters it. The importance of early intervention has been noted by Kaplan (1984), who states that "most of the highly cost-efficient programs have been in the area of primary prevention and screening" (p. 762). Similarly,

Cascio and McEvoy (1984) have found that implementation of realistic job previews results in reduced turnover and increased organizational profit ($40,000 for every 100 new hirees), presumably through a maximization of employee/employer fit and a reduction of role ambiguity (Wanous 1980).

Thus, we have come full circle. Concerns about the value of organizational involvement in stress interventions led to utility (and conjoint) analyses. These analyses led to considerations of the utility of extended definitions of organizational interventions and to the unknown magnitude of organizational stress-performance relationships. In turn, these unknowns lead back to the need for basic involvement in stress research. Future researchers are encouraged to consider all facets of the circle.

SUMMARY

Three possible strategies for estimating the utility of organizational stress interventions were considered: cost accounting, conjoint analysis, and utility analysis based on the work of Cronbach and Gleser. All of the techniques provide a quantitative evaluation of stress intervention programs. The resultant metric can then be used to compare and select among *types* of intervention (such as physiologically based versus cognitively based). In addition, such quantitative measures can aid in the choice of *level* of intervention (individual, group, organization, community, and so on).

We encourage practitioners to avail themselves of the above techniques. The choice of which of these techniques should be used depends on the availability of parameter estimates and on organizational needs. For example, if cost-accounting data are available and the organizational focus is on minimizing loss, then traditional cost-accounting techniques are appropriate. If, however, the organizational focus is on potential overall productivity gains, *and* if the subject matter experts are available to make valid overall-worth estimates, then Cronbach/Gleser-based utility analysis is more appropriate. Furthermore, if the interest is on determinants of stress *and* if sources of stress can be dimensionalized, then conjoint analysis becomes a strong third alternative. In all cases, these "bottom-line" outcomes should be useful in motivating and directing organizational energy toward work-site stress intervention programs.

REFERENCES

Alexander, R. and S. Cronshaw. 1984. "The Utility of Selection Programs: A Finance-Based Contingency Perspective." Paper presented at the meeting of the American Psychological Association, Toronto (August).

Blum, M. and J. Naylor. 1968. *Industrial Psychology*, rev. ed. (New York: Harper & Row).

Bobko, P., R. Karren, and J. Parkington. 1983. "The Estimation of Standard Deviations in Utility Analyses: An Empirical Test." *Journal of Applied Psychology* 68: 170-76.

Boudreau, J. 1983. "Effects of Employee Flows on Utility Analysis of Human Resource Productivity Improvement Programs." *Journal of Applied Psychology* 68: 396-406.

Brogden, H. 1949. "When Testing Pays Off." *Personnel Psychology* 2: 171-83.

Burke, M. 1984. "Validity Generalization: A Review and Critique of the Correlation Model." *Personnel Psychology* 37: 93-113.

Burke, M. and J. Frederick. 1984. "Two Modified Procedures for Estimating Standard Deviations in Utility Analyses." *Journal of Applied Psychology* 69: 482-89.

Cascio, W. 1982. *Costing Human Resources: The Financial Impact of Behavior in Organizations* (Boston, MA: Kent Publishing).

Cascio, W. and G. McEvoy. "Extension of Utility Analysis Research to Turnover Reduction Strategies." Paper presented at the meeting of the American Psychological Association, Toronto (August).

Cronbach, L. and G. Gleser. 1965. *Psychological Tests and Personnel Decisions* (Urbana, IL: University of Illinois Press).

Ganster, D., B. Mayes, W. Sime, and G. Tharp. 1982. "Managing Organizational Stress: A Field Experiment." *Journal of Applied Psychology* 67: 533-42.

Green, P. and V. Srinivasan. 1978. "Conjoint Analysis in Consumer Research: Issues and Outlook." *Journal of Consumer Research* 5: 103-23.

Guzzo, R., R. Katzell, and R. Jetty. 1985. "The Effects of Psychologically Based Intervention Programs on Worker Productivity: A Meta-Analysis." *Personnel Psychology* 38: 275-92.

Jacobson, E. 1938. *Progressive Relaxation* (Chicago, IL: University of Chicago Press).

Jacofsky, E. 1984. "Turnover and Job Performance: An Integrated Process Model." *Academy of Management Review* 9: 74-83.

Janz, T. 1982. "Preliminary Comparisons of Direct vs. Behavioral Estimates of the Standard Deviations of Performance in Dollars." Paper presented at the meeting of the Academy of Management, New York (August).

Kaplan, R. 1984. "The Connection between Clinical Health Promotion and Health Status." *American Psychologist* 39: 755-65.

Kristein, M. 1982. "The Economics of Health Promotion at the Work Site." *Health Education Quarterly* 9: 27-36.

Landy, F., J. Farr, and R. Jacobs. 1982. "Utility Concepts in Performance Measurement." *Organizational Behavior and Human Performance* 30: 15-40.

Meichenbaum, D. 1975. "A Self-Instructional Approach to Stress Management: A Proposal for Stress Innoculation Training." In *Stress and Anxiety*, vol. 1, edited by C. Spielberger and J. Sarason (New York: Halsted Press).

Neale, M., J. Singer, and G. Schwartz. 1987. "A Systems Assessment of Occupational Stress: Evaluating a Hotel During Contract Negotiations." Chapter 7 this volume.

Peters, L., E. O'Connor, J. Eulberg. 1985. "Situational Constraints: Sources, Consequences, and Future Considerations." In *Research in Personnel and Human Resources Management*, vol. 3, edited by K. Roland & G. Ferris (Greenwich, CT: JAI Press).

Peters, R., H. Benson, and D. Porter. 1977. "Daily Relaxation Response Breaks in a Working Population. I. Effects on Self-Reported Measures of Health, Performance, and Well-Being." *American Journal of Public Health* 67: 946-53.

Riley, A., L. Frederiksen and R. Winett. 1984. "Stress Management in the Workplace: A Time for Caution in Organizational Health Promotion." Report submitted to NIOSH under contract no. 84-1320.

Schmidt, F. and J. Hunter. 1981. "Employment Testing: Old Theories and New Research Findings." *American Psychologist* 36: 1128-37.

————. 1983. "Individual Differences in Productivity: An Empirical Test of Estimates Derived from Studies of Selection Procedure Utility." *Journal of Applied Psychology* 68: 407-14.

Schmidt, F., J. Hunter, R. McKenzie, and T. Muldrow. 1979. "Impact of Valid Selection Procedures on Work Force Productivity." *Journal of Applied Psychology* 64: 609-26.

Schmidt, F., J. Hunter, and K. Pearlman. 1982. "Assessing the Economic Impact of Personnel Programs on Work Force Productivity." *Personnel Psychology* 35: 333-47.

Schwartz, G. 1980. "Stress Management in Occupational Settings." *Public Health Reports* 95: 99-108.

Taylor, H. and J. Russell. 1939. "The Relationship of Validity Coefficients to the Practical Effectiveness of Tests in Selection: Discussion and Tables." *Journal of Applied Psychology* 23: 565-78.

Vroom, V. 1964. *Work and Motivation* (New York: John Wiley).

Wanous, J. 1980. *Organizational Entry: Recruitment, Selection, and Socialization of Newcomers* (Reading, MA: Addison-Wesley).

11

OCCUPATIONAL MENTAL HEALTH: A CONTINUUM OF CARE

ROBERT H. ROSEN
and FREDERICK C. LEE

Emotional problems, stress-related illness, and substance abuse present the most difficult challenges to work-site health maintenance. It is estimated that each year 15 percent of the U.S. population requires some form of treatment for mental disorders (Sharfstein, Muszynski, and Arnett 1984). One-fourth suffers at any given time from mild to moderate depression, anxiety, and other emotional symptoms that affect work performance (President's Commisson on Mental Health 1978). Approximately 3 to 7 percent of the population is afflicted with alcoholism, while 10 to 20 percent drink excessively (Shain 1982). In addition, both prescribed and illegal drug use among workers has been recently described as a "crisis epidemic" in U.S. industry ("How Drugs Sap the Nation's Strength" 1983).

Related research implicates stress and other psychological factors in the etiology of various physical disorders. When families and co-workers are considered, the consequences multiply geometrically. Substance abuse and emotional problems disrupt not only personal and family lives, but also have costly human resource consequences for organizations and society in general.

THE COSTS TO ORGANIZATIONS

On the macro level:

- Ten to twenty percent of the labor force is considered "troubled," suffering various mental health and substance abuse symptoms.

- Employees with "burnout syndrome" may be as high as 35-40 percent.
- Nineteen billion dollars in lost work days was due to excessive drinking in 1979 (Cunningham 1982).
- Workers who inhale, inject, snort, or swallow both legal and illegal substances cost industry $25 billion annually ("How Drugs Sap the Nation's Strength" 1983).
- Approximately 20 percent of all employee medical claims are for emotional illness and substance abuse, and the percentage is growing each year (Lee and Schwartz 1984).

On the micro level, controlled studies have demonstrated that compared to nonalcoholics and their families, alcoholic or "problem-drinking" employees:

- Use eight times the in-patient and out-patient medical care (Holder and Hallans 1981; Rosenbloom and Gertman 1984)
- Are absent 2.5 times more
- Use triple the dollar amount of sickness insurance payments
- Have 3.6 times the number of accidents on and off the job
- Are ill or injured 2.5 times more, resulting in eight or more lost workdays (Observer and Maxwell 1959)

Compared to the average employee, a recreational alcohol or drug user:

- Is late three times as often
- Uses triple the normal sick-leave benefits
- Is five times as likely to file workman's compensation claims (U.S. Dept. of Health 1983)

In addition, covert medical costs include insurance claims for "surrogate illnesses" or complications of chemical dependency and mental disorders (Chapman-Walsh 1985). Much of this research has focused on the costs of substance abuse at the workplace; few studies have examined the parallel human resource costs associated with stress and other mental health disorders (Manuso 1983; Elliott and Einsdorfer 1982).

Increasingly, legal suits have been brought successfully by workers against their employers for job-related mental distress, cumulative trauma, and progressive occupational stress diseases under workman's compensation and tort liability systems. Table 11.1 outlines the direct and indirect costs to industry of emotional distress (Chapman-Walsh 1985).

In response to this vast array of human, corporate, and social costs associated with substance abuse and stress disorders, corporate mental health policy has moved in two seemingly opposite directions. On the positive side, the following program developments have occurred: evolution and expansion of mental health insurance coverage, state-mandated mental health

Table 11.1 Costs to Industry of Emotional Distress

	Overt	Covert
	(1)	*(2)*
Direct (medical)	Insurance claims that elevate experience-rated premiums for covered care for chemical dependency and mental illness (employees and dependents)	Insurance claims for care of "surrogates" or for complications of chemical dependency and mental distress (employees/dependents)
	Visits to medical department	
	(3)	*(4)*
	Grievances and disciplinary actions	Potential legal liability for "job-related" mental distress under workers' compensation and tort-liability system
	Absenteeism, lost productivity, turnover, industrial spoilage, accidents on the job	Damage to labor and public relations, morale

Source: Chapman-Walsh, D. 1985. p. 3.

Cell 1: Costs to treat the disorders directly.

Cells 2-4: Costs of failing to treat them successfully.

benefits, growth of mental health services in HMOs and alternative delivery systems, rapid proliferation of EAPs, and the inception of work-site health-promotion activities. Four employee populations have been directly affected by these changes: (1) asymptomatic employees with interest in stress management; (2) employees "at risk," such as those with poor stress management skills; (3) those already suffering symptoms, such as "troubled workers" and substance-abusing employees; and (4) those with existing psychiatric disabilities. The federal government has responded by funding risk factor and intervention research examining such topics as: occupational stress (Kahn 1981; Kasl 1984), type A personalities (Friedman and Rosenman 1974), hardiness (Kobasa 1979), person-environment fit (Caplan et al., 1980), the buffering role of social support (House 1981), burnout (Cherniss 1980; Golembiewski 1985), stress management (Murphy 1984), and EAP evaluation research (Chapman-Walsh 1985; Kurtz, Googins, and Howard 1984; Roman 1981; Trice and Beyer 1984).

On the negative side, despite these developments, most corporate health policies discriminate against mental health compared to physical health and, more specifically, preventive coping skills and stress management activities. The traditional stigma against open recognition of mental health problems combines with the fear of excess utilization to make employers cautious about adding additional coverage. Considerable in-fighting over reimbursement by mental health professionals has given executives the impression that the field cannot monitor itself effectively. In addition, some employees are not convinced that treatment is cost-effective or even has demonstrated benefits. In many companies, these benefit deficiencies have fostered an attitude among employers that workers neither need treatment nor wish to pay for it. Compounding the problem, workers fear possible consequences at work for reporting the use of psychological services or for discussing the stress of work conditions. Certainly one factor contributing to these conditions is that executives consistently underestimate the prevalence of alcohol, mental health, and stress-related problems in their respective companies when compared to mental health specialists (Roman 1981).

A similar discrepancy exists between the actual use of existing employee counseling programs and the number of employees in need of services. For example, despite the National Institute on Alcoholism and Alcohol Abuse (U.S. Dept. of Health 1981), Conference Board (Weiss 1980), and WBGH (Kiefhaber and Goldbeck 1979; Rosen 1984) surveys documenting the thousandfold increase in EAPs, and rapid growth of stress management activities (Hewitt Associates 1984; Towers et al. 1983), the penetrance rates for work-site alcohol, drug, and mental health (ADM) programs are far below what epidemiologic projections would suggest to be necessary. For example, although 3 to 7 percent of the population are alcoholic, and 10 to 20 percent are considered problem drinkers, the average penetrance rate of EAPs with regard to alcohol cases is 0.63 percent of the work force per annum (Shain 1984). Penetrance rate is defined as the actual number of substance abuse cases treated in an organization. Similarly, in contrast to the estimated 10 to 20 percent of the work force who suffer emotional and stress-related symptoms, EAPs treat, on an average, only 2 to 4 percent of the work force (composed primarily of lower-level employees and their families; Washington Business Group on Health 1984). Those at moderate levels of risk are often not referred until problems are sufficiently well advanced to interfere with work performance. Going beyond the numbers, current corporate mental "wellness" programs are conceptualized as tertiary or secondary prevention activities; primary prevention efforts at the workplace, aimed at reducing stressful organizational policies and programs, have been minimal.

The typical focus of EAPs and work-site stress management activities on improved coping skills and employee responsibility for health further reflects this conceptualization of stress disorders and limits the efficacy of corporate mental health programs. In contrast, unions consistently cite stressors in the work site as etiologic of ADM disorders and, therefore, propose structural interventions that change organizational policy, programs, and procedures (Singer et al. 1985). There is a range of reasons why companies have been reluctant to acknowledge not only the full significance of mental health and substance abuse problems, but also their own role in making employees unhealthy (Groepper 1985).

The future of occupational mental health rests on our ability to design comprehensive work-site mental wellness strategies that provide primary, secondary, and tertiary services. In this framework, mental health strategic planning includes not only in-house counseling programs and stress management activities, but also therapeutically efficient/cost-effective benefit designs, innovative mental health delivery systems, prevention and other wellness programs, and other related human resource activities, such as selection and matching of employees, management training, and health-promoting manpower development. Otherwise, add-on alcohol, drug, and mental health programs will be viewed merely as ancillary services, never fully integrated into the corporate culture, and therefore vulnerable to cost-cutting measures.

CORPORATE BARRIERS TO MENTAL HEALTH PLANNING

Increasingly, mental health experts are concluding that stress plays a prominent role in the development of many physical and emotional disorders. Various physical, psychological, and environmental conditions are capable of producing stress. Outcomes of prolonged stress may be physiological, behavioral, organizational, or financial in nature. People with emotional problems use more medical services than their healthier counterparts, whereas providing short-term mental health treatment decreases the need for these physical health services. This so-called offset effect has been fairly well documented (Jones and Vischi 1979). Some specialists contend that as much as 75 percent of all physician visits can be attributed to emotional rather than physical causes. In addition, there are those in the health-care industry that estimate that 20-25 percent of total health costs in a company stem from mental health and chemical dependency. This evidence suggests that stress reduction/mental wellness services could be a cost-effective corporate health management strategy. Unfortunately, few companies to date have designed mental health services and benefits that fully capitalize on this research.

There are several reasons why companies have had difficulty acknowledging the importance of stress and mental health and the link between organizational factors and mental health/substance abuse outcomes. Management and health professionals often speak different languages and have different attitudes toward employees. This has made it difficult for both parties to fully appreciate the relationship between business settings and the health of workers. For example, physical health specialists, such as corporate medical directors and occupational health nurses, study the impact of organizational stress and emotional symptoms by measuring somatic symptoms and physiological disturbances within the body. Often these symptoms are visible through physical health insurance utilization and visits to in-house medical departments. Only recently have these departments been viewed as "cost centers." In contrast, mental health experts, employee assistance counselors, psychologists, and psychiatrists observe the psychological impact of stress. Nervousness, boredom, depression, indecisiveness, diminished concentration, substance abuse, perceptual deficits, progressive lack of initiative, and loss of interest in work are internal symptoms that are easy to hide and difficult to measure. Irritability, tense work relations, work withdrawal, accident proneness, and lack of commitment to product quality and organizational goals are external symptoms more visible to others in the workplace. Often these symptoms are expressed first in the offices of health professionals or in work-site clinics. Yet both types of symptoms affect organizational measures of performance. In fact, low morale and productivity decrements are likely to be expressed first as subtle physical and mental health problems.

Industrial specialists and human resource analysts are concerned with the impact of corporate settings on organizational factors such as work behavior, group and departmental functioning, and measures of productivity. Poorly designed and inadequately managed work environments affect work behavior in many ways—for example, in the form of job dissatisfaction, poor quality of work life, decreased motivation, lack of cooperation, and poor morale. Other effects include lateness to work, early departures, extended lunch periods, increased error rates, time spent redoing work, missed deadlines, and a slowdown in the work pace. Organizational stress can affect departmental functioning by increasing group conflict and antagonism among employees, by sabotaging teamwork, and by disrupting healthy relationships between supervisors and subordinates. Stress, mental health, and substance abuse problems can also lead to increases in transfer, demotion, temporary replacement costs, increases in supervisory time spent on conflict resolution, and employee counseling. Productivity and labor costs include increased absenteeism and turnover, time lost due to medical visits, in-house medical care for stress-related illness and injury, strikes, grievances, and the costs associated with disciplinary proceedings.

Financial analysts are interested solely in the bottom line. Cost factors at this level, such as increased premiums for health-care expenses, disability payments, work compensation claims, accidents on and off the job, training costs, and early pension payments are often gross measures and frequently overlook many of the subtle effects of organizational stress.

Each department views the employee mental health problem from its unique perspective and measures the effects by its own evaluation tools. The presence of language barriers and the absence of integrated data systems have made it difficult to account for the full impact of mental health and stress at the workplace. Inadequate health claims information and limited employee tracking systems have made it difficult to document the importance of stress to the bottom line. For example, in analyzing annual health claims, benefit managers often are asked to report the top ten payments, and more often than not express shock when noting several in-patient psychiatric care episodes for spouses or dependents on this high-cost list. Although these expressions of concern or surprise may not be called for (in that the company's total mental health costs could be moderate despite two or three large claims), they generate attention and sometimes stimulate cuts in benefits or coverage. Outlays for mental health benefits are like other health benefits in that a relatively small proportion of the pool consumes a vast amount of the entire payments.

In recent years, however, companies have grown more concerned about mental health benefits and costs because they are now better apprised of their outlays by improved data collection and reporting. Although the assessment of corporate mental health use and costs is still rudimentary compared to the more state-of-the-art health-care data collection, the very process of receiving reports and analyzing trends will draw attention to areas that previously have not been scrutinized, like psychiatric benefits and stress management. As employers enhance their data sets, improve their understanding of overall use of benefits, and understand better the connection between physical and mental health, they will want to upgrade their mental health data and programs as well.

Another barrier to effective mental health planning is that work and workplaces have been designed almost exclusively with reference to criteria of efficiency, costs, and short-term profits. As a result, technological advances and capital investment have taken precedence over the development of human capital. Consequently, managers often have ignored the presence of stress-related problems and conditions, denied the connection between corporate stress and health, and disguised many of these problems by using more acceptable organizational actions such as transfers, demotions, terminations, outplacement counseling, and technically oriented training. Many, in fact, still believe that excessive stress is a mark of excellence. Furthermore, stress conditions at the workplace do not produce entirely predictable reactions, but rather they have a dispersion effect. In the same workplace, workers experiencing the same stresses may develop a variety of different reactions. This dispersion encourages managers to interpret stress reactions as strictly personal problems rather than as reactions at least in part, to stressful work conditions; hence, the relationship between corporate settings and health is underestimated.

Confidentiality issues have also led employers to underestimate the health needs within organizations, and to minimize their responsibility as producers of stress. The stigma attached to certain physical and mental health treatment inhibits insurance utilization, particularly mental health coverage, and inhibits involvement in company counseling programs.

Unwillingness by many corporate executives to speak out about mental wellness has produced a "hands off" philosophy among the middle management ranks. Many corporate executives see mental health problems and stress-related ailments as illnesses resulting from a temporary loss of control. Lapses in functioning like these are viewed as threatening and indicative of inadequate business performance. Understanding the workplace as a major source of stress mandates an examination of management values, communication patterns, and hierarchical decision and control structures within organizations. This is complicated and involved. Additionally, changes in these areas may be perceived as threatening to existing organizational life, and as likely to disrupt power and control dynamics within organizations. Consequently, these changes may be met with resistance by all levels of management. Moderating these obstacles is the most significant challenge to efforts in worksite health management.

CORPORATE MENTAL HEALTH: A CONTINUUM

Corporate mental health policy can be viewed on a continuum, ranging from mental health benefit design on one hand to corporate culture interventions on the other. There are four major program areas in a comprehensive mental health plan: benefit design, employee counseling services, health promotion/wellness activities, and corporate culture/human resource interventions. Each plays a necessary and critical role in solving the mental health problems of employees and their families.

As Figure 11.1 indicates benefit design includes both in-patient and out-patient care, typically offered through third-party insurance benefits. Programs are frequently financed with large initial deductibles and significant co-payments paid by the employee. Increasingly, alternative health-care delivery systems, such as health maintenance organizations and preferred provider plans, are creating new mental health packages for employees. Most services offered under traditional third-party insurance coverage are tertiary interventions for symptomatic individuals or for those with existing psychiatric disabilities.

Employee counseling services are a second type of work-site mental health program. Psychological services are offered either at the work site or in conjunction with work-site-initiated community services. Employee counseling programs can be of two types: substance abuse and broad-brush. Health promotion and prevention programs are a third type of programming. Stress management seminars have received the most attention by workers and their companies. Yet other work-site wellness activities, such as weight management, smoking cessation, and fitness, can also be effective in

Figure 11.1 Organizational Mental Health

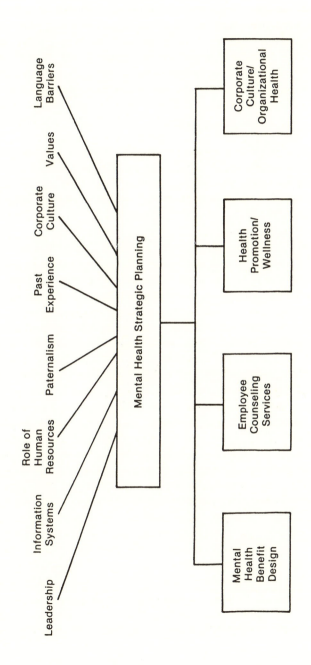

reducing stress. Organizational health and corporate culture interventions represent the largest part of the continuum, and are based on a growing body of research implicating organizational life as a major etiological factor in the development of stress-related illness (Rosen 1985).

These four components of a mental health strategic plan are influenced by numerous factors, including the availability of current management information systems; corporate culture, paternalism, and organizational values concerning mistakes, risk-taking, and growth; language barriers across departments; past mental health claims experiences; leadership; and emphasis on human resource development in the company.

Mental Health Benefits

The design of health benefits is the most critical component of a corporate mental health policy. It is through the availability of these benefits that workers and their families gain access to mental health services in the community. Recently employers have become more involved in managing their health-care dollar, thus struggling more directly with the search for effective mental health strategies in their benefit packages.

In light of the rapid changes occurring in the health-care marketplace, the following discussion on mental health benefits will be presented as a survey of benefits in large companies. This 1984 mental health survey by the Washington Business Group on Health is based on a sample of 76 companies that currently provide health-care benefits to approximately 21 million people (Lee and Schwartz 1984). The survey concentrates on the trends in services provided, benefits offered, changes implemented, costs accrued, and overall approaches to mental health coverage. The companies are mostly Fortune 500, and in the authors' opinion, represent trend-setters in the field. The years ahead will likely see thousands of large and small, public- and private-sector organizations following the lead of these surveyed corporations. The survey collected employee per capita health-care data for both 1982 and 1983. In 1982 the responding companies spent an average (mean) of $1,348 per capita; $1,543 per capita was spent in 1983. The average per capita increase between 1982 and 1983 was 13 percent.

Treatment population and overall costs. In 1982 total health insurance benefits allocated to mental health by employers in this sample ranged from less than 1 percent to 26.6 percent. From 1 percent to 5.6 percent of all employees used mental health benefits. In 1983 the number of employees using mental health services at one company grew to 6.4 percent. In 1982 some companies spent less than 1 percent of their total hospital costs on mental health, whereas other companies spent as much as 15 percent. By 1983 that range had been reduced to a fraction of a percent to 10.5 percent. Costs of providing stress management services and employee counseling programs are seldom included in these determinations. Furthermore, in attempting to quantify the mental health services component of an employer's total health costs, none of the data provided accurately measures the digestive and circulatory disorders that are stress related. Experts have estimated that as much as 25 percent of total medical claims can be linked to emotional illness, including these types of somatic manifestations (Lee and Schwartz 1984).

Two kinds of employers emerge from an examination of this data. Many companies, when witnessing a growth in mental health expenditures, act without questioning the underlying reasons for the increases. These kinds of companies have elected to cut in-patient days covered, annual dollar maximums, percentage of company co-payment, or number of covered mental health out-patient visits in order to reduce economic exposure. Nor do they respond proactively by trying to prevent stress-related illness through employee counseling and stress management services. They seem oblivious to long-term strategic planning and evidence a lack of investment in human capital.

On the other hand, there are as many companies who, in response to growing mental health claims, have either expanded benefits or introduced management tools like case management, preadmission certification, utilization review, or mental health programs. The prevailing attitude of these companies is to accept increased costs as long as the outlays are associated with appropriate treatment. Furthermore, they are intensifying their efforts to obviate inappropriate treatment. It is in the field of monitoring mental health treatment where change is rapidly occurring. In fact, by employing effective utilization review programs, companies have the greatest opportunity for effecting changes in the escalating costs and growth of mental health-related claims.

In-patient coverage. Coverage for in-patient psychiatric care is the mental health benefit most generously offered by employers. The in-patient bias is well rooted in tradition. Most companies have stop/loss coverage built into their plans, exempting patients from financial liability over a certain dollar amount. More than two-thirds of businesses have a stop/loss provision with a specific in-patient psychiatric clause. The average in-patient psychiatric stop/loss is around $1,500. Restrictions in out-of-pocket costs are usually set at $1,000. The company typically pays the additional costs. Employers also rely on co-insurance (a financial strategy where employees and employers share the cost) as a cost management strategy for their in-patient psychiatric benefits; only one-fourth still have first-dollar coverage.

The inpatient/outpatient debate is particularly controversial for psychiatric care. According to the survey, 25 percent of all in-patient days are attributable to mental disorders, and more importantly, 70 percent of every mental health dollar goes to inpatient treatment (Mosher 1982). Although many employers are implementing incentives to encourage their employees to use out-patient instead of in-patient services, few have extended those policies to the psychiatric sector. The relatively uncontrolled out-patient setting could be as costly if lower unit prices are multiplied by a high volume of services, no matter what the medical service provided. On account of this well-known principle, few employers are adopting reduced co-payment policies for use of out-patient mental health settings. This phenomenon underscores the employer's trepidation that out-patient psychiatric care will be used excessively; whereas employers are confident that out-patient surgery will be cost-effective, predictably finite, and controllable.

Many companies have begun to restructure benefit plans to incorporate alternatives to in-patient psychiatric coverage. Although this trend is becoming apparent, there is little available data to substantiate the associated cost savings. Reimbursing for day treatment centers and night hospitals, which allow patients to work during regular employment hours, is no longer isolated or rare. Extended-care facilities have also been added to the benefit plans of a few companies. It is likely that this trend of covering alternatives to in-patient psychiatric care will become more widespread in corporate mental health packages and programs.

Out-patient coverage. Out-patient coverage remains an area of concern for employers. Most have implemented some conventional limitations to protect against induced demand. Despite philosophical leanings toward reviewing employee health-care claims, few companies have identified utilization review as an effective check on psychiatric use. Consequently, companies use benefit design as a way to check unnecessary out-patient use. The three most commonly employed strategies are: maximums on the employer's annual payment per employee for out-patient services, limits on the number of reimbursable outpatient visits per year, and dollar limits on reimbursement per visit. Few of the surveyed businesses limit the number of annual out-patient visits, but those that do usually constrain use to either 25 or 50 visits per year. Stress management seminars and work-site counseling programs are similarly constrained by limits on the number of sessions and visits offered. Some counseling programs are paid through the insurance system; stress management programs typically are not.

Utilization review. Although many companies have adopted utilization review programs, the provision of separate mental health review is less common. This deficit seems primarily related to a lack of proven review entities in the mental health area with a track record of successful utilization management. Nevertheless, the field is changing dynamically, with many vendors scurrying to implement mental health review capabilities.

The best way to save on in-patient utilization is to keep patients out of the hospital entirely. Companies have adopted pre-admission certification programs for surgery, but are now finding the same strategy works for mental health treatment. More importantly, aggressive concurrent review (in which psychiatrists are queried about treatment plans), psychopharmacology, and discharge plans have yielded significant reductions in lengths of stay.

One example of an effective utilization review program is the St. Louis Area Business Health Coalition, which has joined forces with the Eastern Missouri Psychiatric Society (EMPS) to create a concurrent in-patient review program. Specifically, objective criteria have been outlined by a Chicago firm, InterQual, for determination of appropriateness of care for different mental diagnoses. InterQual convened a group of psychiatrists to develop these criteria, on which determination of hospitalization can be based. Through delegated review, patient records are monitored on the first working day after admission and every week thereafter. Physician advisors from EMPS intervene after the twenty-first day of stay, working with the providers until discharge.

An analysis of the aggregate review data is conducted periodically. The program is being funded at $2.50 per admission which covers review costs. The St. Louis Area Business Health Coalition conservatively estimates a reduction of 5.38 days per stay, which would result in a $1,614 savings per psychiatric admission. The ambitious goals of business, in conjunction with the determination of the providers to demonstrate that needed mental health care can be made available without leading to unnecessary or inappropriate use of resources, holds promise for communities across the country seeking relief from the escalating costs of psychiatric services.

Preferred provider arrangements. Corporations are becoming more aware of their ability to successfully negotiate with providers for lower hospital rates and a more cost-effective benefit design. The local health-care coalition movement has helped corporations to combine their purchasing power. Many providers have also realized that they can be competitive by negotiating with employers who are looking for a more cost-effective method to provide services. Currently, 141 preferred provider organizations (PPOs) have formed nationwide to meet this demand. Over time other mental health consultation services, such as employee counseling and stress management services, are likely to be incorporated within these packages.

Mental health-oriented PPOs will be slower to catch on than other more general PPOs. Psychiatrists, psychologists, and social workers are eager to form PPOs because they are aware of the competition among themselves. Offering a good utilization review (UR) program is critical to the marketing success of a PPO that provides mental health services. In fact, companies that already have good utilization review programs in mental health may be among the first to initiate mental health PPO negotiations. However, most companies will be reluctant to embrace mental health PPOs, because they appear to be a risky, novel concept. In addition, as a rule, most corporations avoid product development of untested services.

Providers and facilities. Purchasers of health care, whether public or private, are exploring the use of alternative health-care practitioners and individuals, like psychiatric nurses and social workers, who may be more cost-effective in the provision of care. This is especially true in mental health because of the availability of alternative providers. Corporations are diversifying by directly reimbursing a variety of mental health professionals. The majority of employers have always reimbursed psychiatrists and psychologists. Fewer than 5 percent of employers do not reimburse clinical psychologists. In addition, almost half of the major corporations reimburse social workers. Furthermore, employers have almost doubled the use of psychiatric nurses in the last three years; psychiatric nurses are currently covered by one-third of employer group insurance plans.

Business has moved to control the admission of patients through gatekeeper functions (to triage employees into the appropriate mental health modality). Increasingly, companies have designated individuals responsible for identifying persons in need of mental health treatment, referring patients to other providers, monitoring ongoing treatment, or overseeing long-term psychiatric disability cases. In most cases, these tasks are performed by one individual who may be an RN, medical or counseling department staff member, physician, psychiatrist, EAP coordinator, plant personnel manager, benefit manager, administrator, or psychologist.

The changes that have occurred in the companies surveyed in this sample presage potential changes that could be adopted in the years to come. Many companies have initiated data collection efforts and acknowledge that, depending on the information collected, they may make changes. The most common alteration will be focused on out-patient care. Companies intend to enhance the incentives for out-patient use by decreasing the employee's level of co-insurance, usually from 50 to 20 percent. Effective case-management is also being proposed. Such an approach is combined with concurrent utilization review. A waiver policy that permits case managers to waive benefit coverage restrictions, when a more cost-effective model can be activated, may also become more pervasive. Companies could leave out-patient restrictions intact, while permitting cost-effective exceptions on a case-by-case basis. Case management in general seems particularly well suited to the mental health sector, where 10-15 percent of the work force consumes 90 percent of a company's psychiatric expenditures.

Employee Counseling Programs

Employee counseling programs, offered at the work site or through work-site-initiated community-based programs, are a second approach to organizational mental health planning. This approach is more proactive than solely providing mental health benefits, because it attempts to identify employees earlier in the illness process, and requires that the organization plan for the identification and treatment of the problem.

Most existing employee counseling programs are founded on three basic assumptions: (1) an employee's psychological pain and personal troubles can be brought under control, (2) employees who experience emotional or stress-related problems should be helped by organizational services, and

(3) a distressed employee is not a corporate asset. Based on these principles, helping employees is considered good business. If organizations can reduce the stress and emotional symptoms of employees and help them deal with personal troubles early on, then it is hoped that this will improve their work performance. At the simplest level, employee assistance programs are a set of company policies and procedures for identifying (or responding to self-identified) employees experiencing personal or emotional problems that may interfere, directly or indirectly, with acceptable job performance.

Recently the United States has witnessed a rapid proliferation of employee counseling services. Estimates from the National Institute on Alcohol and Alcohol Abuse Fourth Special Report to Congress, published in 1981, showed exponential growth in EAPs from the four to six programs available in 1940-1945 to the 4,400 existing in 1980. This is a thousandfold increase in just 40 years (U.S. Dept. of Health 1981). More current surveys estimate that there are now 5,000-6,000 such programs (Chapman-Walsh 1985). Many of these contemporary programs are broad-brush in nature (in contrast to the more traditional EAP services, which focus solely on alcoholism problems) and treat employee problems ranging from substance abuse to child care.

The proliferation of work-site counseling services reflects a wide range of managerial motivations, ranging from a concern about a company's public image to a desire to fulfill an internal paternalistic commitment to manage in humanitarian ways. Yet health-care cost containment has been the primary reason most companies have instituted EAPs. Typically, programs are initiated to reduce absenteeism, turnover, disability, work compensation, and health-care costs associated with substance abuse, emotional illness, and stress-related ailments.

It is difficult to describe the "prototype" EAP program, as companies design their EAP to satisfy a unique set of objectives and a corporate culture. EAPs can be offered as in-house programs with counseling sessions provided on the premises, or as contracted services offered by existing community settings. If offered at the work site, the program can be free-standing inside the company or a division of the medical, personnel, or benefits department, or it can be responsible directly to top management. Care can be offered during release time from work, or before or after work hours. Some programs are free, others have a minimal charge. Still others are experimenting by using increasing employee co-payments to control the overutilization of services.

Most EAP programs are offered to all employees, yet few middle and top managers use the services. Programs are expanding more and more to include dependents and retirees, but not as quickly as appears necessary. This is disturbing both on business and clinical grounds. On the economic side, 65 percent of benefit costs are for dependents and retirees. By excluding these two important populations, programs clearly limit their potential cost-effectiveness. From a clinical perspective, the connection between work and family life rarely goes unnoticed in clinical practice. Without addressing both of these social spheres, therapeutic effectiveness is questionable.

Finally, programs can cover single issues or the full range of personal and group problems, and can be staffed by various professional groups (such as clinical/industrial psychologists, recovering alcoholics, psychiatrists, social workers, or human resource specialists). The availability of programs offered and the training of the staff determine the distribution of diagnoses seen (for example, substance abuse, family, emotional, financial, child care), and the kinds of problems to which they are prepared to respond. The most successful programs are confidential, easily accessible, open to all employees and their families, and provide focused, manageable care (cf. Nahrwold, Chapter 8, and Feuer, Chapter 9).

Work-site Stress Management

Stress management activities comprise the third area of occupational mental health programming. The aim of stress education at the work site is to help individuals manage their own health, ultimately reducing their health risk and minimizing the need for services within the traditional, fee-for-service health-care system.

Approaches to work-site stress education and management can be directed at changing the individual and/or changing the organization. Individual change programs are by far the most popular, and include instruction in stress management techniques such as physical, cognitive, and emotional strategies for managing physiological and psychological stress reactions. Existing stress reduction programs are of two types: (1) Preventive programs teach skills that help educate employees about the negative effects of stress, and review techniques that can help to prevent more serious physical and psychological breakdowns. (2) Intervention programs focus on people with particular stress-related symptoms, teaching them self-management of stress as a way to overcome or reduce existing pain and reduce the risk of further problems.

Most stress programs focus on the following five individual goals:

1. To facilitate greater awareness of the role of stress in one's life and its effect on physical and emotional health of workers
2. To explore one's current coping styles and their effectiveness
3. To learn practical techniques for modifying one's response to stress and to identify alternative responses
4. To learn to utilize stress in a positive way in one's family, interpersonal, and work lives
5. To learn how to apply stress knowledge and stress management techniques to situations outside of the seminar

Companies deliver stress programs in three formats:

1. Workshops
2. Self-learning (for example, workbooks, audio and videotapes, self-study material, computer-assisted instruction)
3. Personal counseling

Typically, some combination of awareness building, skill building, stress assessment, and counseling are offered through one or more of these media. Most company programs are of the workshop format, often utilizing self-study material as an adjunct. Increasingly, companies are turning to self-help methods and emerging computer software technologies.

Most stress management programs focus on three basic skills: (1) Relaxation skills include meditation, progressive muscle relaxation, self-hypnosis, guided imagery, and autogenic training, and help the body release built-up chronic stress. (2) Coping skills include all the ways that people respond to stressful situations. These include type A behavior modification, inflexible thinking, time management, altering the perception of stress, and managing the emotional aspects of stress such as in anger and feelings of inadequacy. (3) Interpersonal skills training focuses on relations with other people as a source of stress. Social support, assertiveness training, communication skills, active listening, conflict resolution, and team building are included in this category.

Research on the effectiveness of work-site stress management programs indicates that a variety of techniques can be effective in helping workers reduce physiological arousal levels and psychological manifestations of stress (McLean 1979). Although too few studies have been conducted to determine the relative merits of certain techniques and cost-benefit ratios, such programs appear to have potential for improving worker well-being and partially offsetting the costs of occupational stress arising from productivity losses and stress-related disorders (Jaffe and Scott 1985).

Organizational Interventions

Management is just beginning to recognize the tremendous costs associated with organizational stressors and the associated employee burnout that often escape traditional cost controls. The impact of work conditions and corporate culture on health is also gaining attention. It is imperative that management recognize these hidden costs, and realize the significance of work environments as part of the problem and ultimately part of the solution in the management of employee health and health-care costs.

The connection between job factors and health is finally being recognized, and the relationship between work stress, health breakdowns, and productivity is better understood. Ten years of government-sponsored research documents the direct impact of organizational policies and procedures on stress and unhealthy breakdowns of workers (Rosen 1985b).

There are six factors inside organizations that place workers at risk for health breakdowns. These include:

- Stressful work conditions
- Career progression
- Lack of control/participation
- Change and emerging technologies
- Work relations
- Job role

Each area is grounded in scientific evidence linking these organizational factors to the health risk of employees.

Stressful work conditions. Traditionally, work-related dangers have been limited to the blue-collar environment. While this concern is warranted, it has diverted attention from the stressful nature of jobs themselves, and the growing dangers associated with the psychosocial work environment and white-collar work. Examples of stressful work conditions include:

- Crowding or social isolation
- Psychological effects of a negative physical environment
- Inadequate regulation of temperature, noise, and lighting
- Inadequate safety regulations
- Too much work with inadequate resources
- Time pressure
- Repetitious, monotonous work

Corporate programs designed to protect workers against these stressful effects of work include: accident prevention programs, redesign of the physical setting, and job rotation opportunities.

Career progression. In today's workplace, employees are looking to their organizations for career development and personal growth opportunities that once were provided outside the workplace and during leisure hours. Companies focusing on mental wellness view their organization as a "cultivator of human potential," and emphasize training and career development as critical to the long-term planning of human resources.

Unhealthy companies, in contrast, pay little attention to developing workers; their focus is short-term, and the concept of "human capital" is ignored. Examples of stressful career progression include lack of adequate skills preparation, inadequate career development, and unhealthy matches between workers and jobs. Solutions might include career and dual tracking programs, lateral transfers, assessment centers, and improved job placement.

Lack of control/participation. Workers need to feel some sense of control over their own destinies. Without this control many become alienated and angry or develop a variety of physical and emotional symptoms. Examples of sources of stress associated with lack of control include inadequate control over rewards and promotions or lack of input in decison-making. Numerous studies show that lack of control and limited participation in decision-making place workers at health risk. Examples of corporate programs designed to protect workers against the stressful effects of lack of control at the workplace include upward communication programs, control over work pace, participative management opportunities, and organization-wide reward/compensation programs.

Change and emerging technologies. Constant change and unpredictable movement inside organizations can be a disruptive form of organizational stress and a potential health hazard for employees. Examples of sources of stress associated with the change process include fear of automation and mass technology, absence of retooling and training, fear of layoffs and unexpected market shifts, and organizational restructuring.

Corporate programs designed to protect workers against their stressful changes might include cross-training and job rotation opportunities, retooling programs, job security contracts, and educational strategies preparing workers for upcoming change.

Work relations. Work relations are one of the greatest determinants of employee health. Companies concerned with mental wellness and productivity are open, trusting, stimulating, and supportive. In contrast, unhealthy companies are viewed as distrustful and manipulative, and characterized by selfish one-up-manship, with closed, formal communications. Examples of sources of stress associated with work relations include unhealthy management values and policies, poor supervision, presence of stress-carriers, and lack of management/peer support.

Solutions to this type of stress might include healthy management philosophies, positive organizational health norms, mentor programs, team building, job-sharing programs, and group incentives.

Job role. Organizations are networks of interconnected roles. When these roles are clearly defined and the rules of the game clearly stated, employees are able to perform their jobs without much difficulty. In many organizations, however, these expectations are unclear, leading to various health and performance consequences. Examples of stress associated with these role conflicts include work and family conflicts, unclear job descriptions, unclear expectations and goals, and conflicting performance demands.

Solutions to job role stress include improved job descriptions, goal-setting programs, performance appraisal training, and flexibility in defining work. Work and family strategies include variable work schedules, child-care programs, and retirement transition programs.

All of the stressors listed above have been linked in some way to the development of physical and emotional disorders (Kahn 1981; Jaffe and Scott 1985). The challenge to organizations will now be to incorporate this research into a wholistic approach to management, where relationships between health, morale, and productivity are fully appreciated. For example, policies such as flex-time, job sharing, and part-time employment underscore a company's concern for a healthy workplace. Physical amenities such as quiet rooms for relaxation, noise control, day-care facilities, and attractive work environments all promote good health. Healthy management practices such as open communication channels, quality circles, health-enhancing performance appraisals, and career development opportunities are additional examples of how corporate culture can reduce stress and promote healthy lifestyles. Increased attention to quality of work life issues, identification of pockets of organizational stress, and placement of mental health professionals on occupational health and management teams will help to identify and solve stress-related problems.

FUTURE TRENDS

Today's organizational leaders are struggling with the question of how to manage the escalating costs of mental and physical health care and the deleterious effects of organizational stress on the bottom line. Many employers now realize that they are paying high costs for mental health and occupational stress, yet they have little understanding of what they are purchasing, and how it gets translated into human resource costs. The recent movement toward collecting and analyzing health data and toward a more enlightened approach to managing people has brought employers closer to a solution. Organizations are recognizing that mental health services can be provided through a wide range of alternatives, ranging from traditional health benefits to in-house management training programs. This enlightened view offers top management unlimited opportunities to manage occupational mental health in the same way they manage any other product or business venture. Below are some trends for the future:

- Corporations are becoming more concerned about high health-care costs, absenteeism, disability costs, and lost productivity associated with mental health and organization stress.

- Organizations will continue to balance the cost of benefits with quality of care. With increasing competition among provider groups, companies will have a better understanding of what works, with whom, in what settings, and with which providers.

- Benefits managers will grapple with how to redesign reimbursement for mental health coverage to reflect new options in service delivery and alternative providers (for example, Health Maintenance Organizations, PPOs, day and night hospital treatment), with a greater appreciation for case management and a continuum of care from acute to nonacute facilities.

- There will be changing attitudes about mental health; an increasing link between physical and psychological health; reduced stigma; and a better articulated definition of mental wellness.

- There will be an increasing sophistication in monitoring company health data (health claims, medical screening, health risk appraisals, human resource factors). Medical care cost management information and health risk assessment will be used to target mental wellness programs.

- There will be increases in legal precedents, tort liabilities, psychiatric disabilities, and work compensation claims for organizational stress and mental health reasons.

- There will be a move toward a "healthy corporation" concept, with human resource departments working around a central theme of organizational health. The impact of corporate culture variables on health and productivity will be fully appreciated.

- Employers will continue to increase the number of employee counseling programs, broadening their scope to include more areas (counseling disabled employees, child care issues, preretirement). A move toward more in-house stress programs offered by a variety of departments through a variety of mediums will be evident.

- Greater reliance on emerging technologies, such as computer-assisted education programs, mental health computer and diagnostic systems, and video-assisted instruction.

- Increases in corporate self-help activities and the self-care movement will predominate.

- Greater union cooperation.

- Improved services and communication systems for families, dependents, and retirees will be both cost-effective and therapeutically effective.

In closing, the era of passive purchasing of health care is rapidly being eclipsed by knowledgeable, aggressive employers seeking ways to prevent disease and optimize the mental health of their employees. Occupational mental health planning is critical to this long-term solution.

REFERENCES

American Association of Preferred Provider Organizations. 1985. Unpublished communication (Washington, D.C.).

Caplan, R. D., S. Cobb, J. R. P. French, R. V. Harrison, and S. R. Pinneau. 1980. *Job Demands and Worker Health*, (Washington, D.C.: HEW Publications no. (NIOSH) U.S. Department of Health, Education, and Welfare), pp. 75-160.

Chapman-Walsh, D. 1985. "Employee Assistance Programs and Untested Assumptions." *Corporate Commentary* 1, no. 3: 1-10.

Cherniss, C. 1980. *Staff Burnout: Job Stress in the Human Services* (Beverly Hills, CA: Sage Publications).

Cunningham, R., Jr. 1982. *Wellness at Work: An Inquiry Book* (Chicago, IL: Blue Cross and Blue Shield Association).

Elliott, G. R. and E. Einsdorfer, 1982. *Stress and Human Health: Analysis and Implications of Research* (New York: Springer Publishing).

Friedman, M. and R. H. Rosenman. 1974. *Type A: Your Behavior and Your Heart* (New York: Knopf).

Golembiewski, R. 1985. "Worksite Burnout: Realities and Emerging Challenges." *Corporate Commentary* 1, no. 5. pp. 7-15.

Groepper, R. C. 1985. "Role of Treatment in EAP." Paper presented at the Employee Assistance Program Research Conference, Elkridge, Maryland.

Hewitt Associates. 1984. *Company Practices in Health Care Mansagement* (Lincolnshire, IL).

Holder, H. and J. Hallans. 1981. *National Institute on Alcoholism and Alcohol Abuse.* Report submitted to NIAAA. (Washington, D.C.).

House, J. S. 1981. *Work, Stress, and Social Support* (Reading, MA: Addison-Wesley).

"How Drugs Sap the Nation's Strength." 1983. *U.S. News and World Report*, May, p. 55.

Jaffe, D. and C. Scott. 1985. "Worksite Stress Management Programs." In *DHHS/WBGH Cooperative Agreement on Worksite Wellness and the Media* (Washington, D.C.: Washington Business Group on Health), pp. 1-30.

Jones, K. R. and T. R. Vischi. 1979. "Impact of Alcohol, Drug Abuse and Mental Health Treatment Medical Care Utilization: A Review of the Literature." *Medical Care* 17 (Supplement): 1-82.

Kahn, R. L. 1981. *Work and Health* (New York: John Wiley and Sons).

Kasl, S. V. 1984. "Stress and Health" *Annual Review of Public Health* 5.

Kiefhaber, A. and W. B. Goldbeck. 1979. "Industry Response: A Survey of Employee Assistance Programs." In *Mental Wellness Programs for Employees*, edited by Egdahl, Walsh, and Goldbeck (New York: Springer-Verlag), pp. 19-26.

Kobasa, C. K. 1979. "Stressful Life Events, Personality, and Health: An Inquiry into Hardiness." *Journal of Personality and Social Psychology* 37: 1-11.

Kurtz, N. A., B. Googins, and W. C. Howard. 1984. "Measuring the Success of Occupational Alcoholism Programs." *Journal of Studies on Alcoholism* 45, no. 1.

Lee, F. C. and G. Schwartz. 1984. "Paying for Mental Health Care in the Private Sector." *Business and Health* 1, no. 10: 12-16.

Manuso, J. S., ed. 1983. *Occupational Clinical Psychology* (New York: Praeger).

McLean, A. A. 1979. *Work Stress* (Reading, MA: Addison-Wesley).

Mosher, L. R. 1982. "Alternatives to Psychiatric Hospitalization: Why Has Research Failed to be Translated into Practice?" *New England Journal of Medicine* 309, no. 25: 1579-80.

Murphy, L. R. 1984. "Occupational Stress Management: A Review and Appraisal." *Journal of Occupational Psychology* 57: 1-15.

Observer, B. and A. Maxwell. 1959. "A Study of Absenteeism, Accidents, and Sickness Payments in Problem Drinkers in One Industry." *Quarterly Journal of Studies on Alcoholism* 20: 302-12.

Report to the President from The President's Commission on Mental Health. 1978. Stock no. 040-000-00390-8 (Washington, D.C.: U.S. Government Printing Office).

Roman, P. M. 1981. "From Employee Alcoholism to Employee Assistance." *Journal of Studies on Alcohol* 42: 244-72.

Rosen, R. 1984. "Worksite Health Promotion: Fact or Fantasy?" *Corporate Commentary* 1, no. 1: 1-8.

Rosen, R. H. 1985a. "What Really Ails Employees?" *Training and Development Journal.* December, pp. 54-56.

_____. 1985b. "Healthy Companies." In *DHHS/WBGH Cooperative Agreement in Worksite Wellness and the Media* (Washington, D.C.: Washington Business Group on Health), pp. 1-55.

Rosenbloom, D. L. and P. M. Gertman. 1984. "An Intervention Strategy for Controling Costly Care." *Business and Health* 1, no. 8: 17-21.

Shain, M. 1984. "An Exploration of the Ability of Broad-Based EAPs to Generate Alcohol-Related Referrals." In *The Human Resources Management Handbook: Principles and Practices of EAPs*, edited by J. L. Francek, J. H. Klarreich, and C. E. Moore (New York: Praeger).

_____. 1982. "Alcohol, Drug and Safety: An Update Perspective on Problems and Their Management in the Workplace." *Accident Analysis and Prevention* 14, no. 3: 239-46.

Sharfstein, S., S. Muszynski, and G. M. Arnett. 1984. "Dispelling Myths about Mental Health Benefits." *Business and Health* 1, no. 10: 7-11.

Singer, J. A., M. S. Neale, G. E. Schwartz, and J. Schwartz. 1985. "Conflicting Perspectives on Stress Reduction in Occupational Settings: A Systems Approach to Their Resolution." In *Behavioral Medicine in Industry*, edited by T. Coates and M. Cataldo (New York: John Wiley and Sons).

Trice, H. and J. Beyer. 1984. "Employee Assistance Programs: Lending Performance-Oriented and Humanitarian Ideologies to Assist Emotionally Disturbed Employees." *Research in Community and Mental Health* 4: 245-97.

Towers, Perrin, Forster, and Crosby. 1983. *Corporate Health Promotion Survey* (Boston: Towers, Perrin, Forster, and Crosby).

U.S. Department of Health and Human Services. 1983. *Conference on Worksite Health Promotion and Human Resources: A Hard Look at the Data* (Washington,D.C.).

U.S. Department of Health and Human Services, Public Health Services National Institute on Alcohol Abuse and Alcoholism. 1981. *Fourth Special Report to the U.S. Congress on Alcohol and Health*, DHHS Pub. no. (ADM)81-1080 (Washington, D.C.: U.S. Government Printing Office), pp. 124-27.

Washington Business Group on Health. 1984. Unpublished manuscript (Washington, D.C.).

Weiss, R. 1980. *Dealing with Alcoholism in the Workplace* (New York: The Conference Board).

BIBLIOGRAPHY

Anderson, C. R. 1976. "Coping Behaviors as Intervening Mechanisms in the Inverted-U Stress-Performance Relationship." *Journal of Applied Psychology*
61: 30-34.

Antonovsky, A. 1979. *Stress, Health and Coping: New Perspectives on Mental and
Physical Well-Being* (San Francisco, CA: Jossey-Bass).

Arsenault, A. and S. Dolan. 1983. "The Role of Personality, Occupation and
Organization in Understanding the Relationship between Job Stress, Performance, and Absenteeism." *Journal of Occupational Psychology* 56: 227-40.

Beehr, T. A. and R. S. Bhagat. 1985. *Human Stress and Cognition in Organizations:
An Integrated Perspective* (New York: Wiley).

Beehr, T. A. and J. E. Newman. 1978. "Job Stress, Employee Health, and Organizational Effectiveness." *Personnel Psychology* 31: 665-98.

Billings, A. G. and R. H. Moos. 1982. "Work Stress and the Stress Buffering Roles
of Work and Family Resources." *Journal of Occupational Behaviour* 3:
215-32.

Cannon, W. B. 1914. "The Interrelations of Emotions as Suggested by Recent
Physiological Researches." *American Journal of Psychology* 25: 256-82.

_____. 1929. *Bodily Changes in Pain, Hunger, Fear, and Rage* (Boston, MA:
C. T. Branford).

Cascio, W. 1982. *Costing Human Resources: The Financial Impact of Behavior in
Organizations* (Boston, MA: Kent Publishing).

Cherniss, C. 1980. *Staff Burnout: Job Stress in the Human Services* (Beverly Hills,
CA: Sage Publications).

Coelho, G. V., D. A. Hamburg, and J. E. Adams, eds. 1974. "Adjustment as

Person-Environment Fit." In *Coping and Adaptation* (New York: Basic Books).

Cohen, S. 1980. "After-Effects of Stress on Human Performance and Social Behavior: A Review of Research and Theory." *Psychological Bulletin* 88: 82-108.

Cooper, C. L. and J. Marshall. 1978. *Understanding Executive Stress* (London: Macmillan).

Cooper, C. L. and R. Payne, eds. 1978. *Stress at Work* (London: Wiley).

_____. 1985. *Current Concerns in Occupational Stress* (London: Wiley).

Cooper, C. L. and M. J. Smith. 1985. *Job Stress and Blue Collar Work* (London: Wiley).

Foote, A. and J. C. Erfurt. 1981. "Effectiveness of Comprehensive Employee Assistance Programs at Reaching Alcoholics." *Journal of Drug Issues* 2: 217-32.

French, J. R. P., Jr., and R. D. Caplan. 1973. "Organizational Stress and Individual Strain." In *The Failure of Success*, edited by A. J. Marrow (New York: AMACOM).

French, J. R. P., Jr., R. D. Caplan, and R. V. Harrison. 1984. *Mechanisms of Job Stress and Strain* (New York: Wiley).

Friedman, M. and R. H. Rosenman. 1974. *Type A: Your Behavior and Your Heart.* (New York: Knopf).

Ganster, D. C., B. T. Mayes, W. E. Sime, and G. D. Tharp. 1982. "Managing Organizational Stress: A Field Experiment." *Journal of Applied Psychology* 67: 533-42.

Goldberger, L. and S. Breznitz, eds. 1982. *Handbook of Stress: Theoretical and Clinical Aspects* (New York: The Free Press).

Guzzo, R., R. Katzell, and R. Jetty. 1985. "The Effects of Psychologically Based Intervention Programs on Worker Productivity: A Meta-Analysis." *Personnel Psychology* 38: 275-92.

Hackman, J. R. and G. R. Oldham. 1980. *Work Redesign* (Reading, MA: Addison-Wesley).

Hoiberg, A. 1982. "Occupational Stress and Disease Incidence." *Journal of Occupational Medicine* 24: 445-51.

Holmes, T. H. and R. H. Rahe. 1967. "The Social Readjustment Rating Scale." *Journal of Psychosomatic Research* 11: 213-218.

House, J. S. 1981. *Work, Stress, and Social Support* (Reading, MA: Addison-Wesley).

House, J. S. and J. R. Rizzo. 1972. "Role Conflict and Ambiguity as Critical Variables in a Model of Organizational Behavior." *Organizational Behavior and Human Performance* 7: 467-505.

House, J. S., J. A. Wells, L. R. Landerman, A. J. McMichael, and B. H. Kaplan. 1979. "Occupational Stress and Health among Factory Workers." *Journal of Health and Social Behavior* 20: 139-60.

Ivancevich, J. M. and M. T. Matteson. 1980. *Stress and Work: A Managerial Perspective* (Glenview, IL: Scott, Foresman, & Co.).

Ivancevich, J. M., M. T. Matteson, and E. P. Richards, III. 1985. "Who's Liable for Stress on the Job?" *Harvard Business Review* 63: 60.

Kahn, R. L., D. M. Wolfe, R. P. Quinn, J. D. Snoek, and R. A. Rosenthal. 1964.

Organizational Stress: Studies in Role Conflict and Ambiguity (New York: Wiley).

Karasek, R. A. 1979. "Job Demands, Decision Latitude, and Mental Strain: Implications for Job Redesign." *Administrative Science Quarterly* 24: 285-307.

Kasl, S. V. 1984. "Stress and Health." *Annual Review of Public Health* 5: 319-41.

Katz, D. and R. L. Kahn. 1978. *The Social Psychology of Organizations* (New York: Wiley).

Kobasa, S. C. 1979. "Stressful Life Events, Personality, and Health: An Inquiry into Hardiness." *Journal of Personality and Social Psychology* 37: 1-11.

Kristein, M. 1982. "The Economics of Health Promotion at the Worksite." *Health Education Quarterly* 9: 27-36.

LaRocco, J. M., J. S. House, and J. R. P. French, Jr. 1980. "Social Support, Occupational Stress, and Health." *Journal of Health and Social Behavior* 21: 202-18.

Lazarus, R. S. 1966. *Psychological Stress and the Coping Process* (New York: McGraw-Hill).

Lazarus, R. S. and S. Folkman. 1984. *Stress, Appraisal and Coping* (New York: Springer).

Liebowitz, B. 1982. "Employee Assistance Programs as an Employee Benefit and as Risk Management." *Employment Benefits Journal*: 14-16.

Manuso, J. S. J., ed. 1983. *Occupational Clinical Psychology* (New York: Praeger).

Margolis, B., W. H. Kroes, and R. P. Quinn. 1974. "Job Stress: An Unlisted Occupational Hazard." *Journal of Occupational Medicine* 16: 659-61.

Maslach, C. and S. E. Jackson. 1984. "Burnout in Organizational Settings." *Applied Social Psychology Annual* 5: 133-53.

McGrath, J. E. 1976. "Stress and Behavior in Organizations." In *Handbook of Industrial and Organizational Psychology*, edited by M. D. Dunnette (Chicago, IL: Rand McNally), pp. 1351-95.

McLean, A. 1974. *Occupational Stress* (Springfield, IL: Charles C. Thomas).

Meichenbaum, D. 1985. *Stress Innoculation Training: A Clinical Guidebook* (New York: Pergamon).

Murphy, L. R. 1984. "Occupational Stress Management: A Review and Appraisal." *Journal of Occupational Psychology* 57: 1-15.

Newman, J. E. and T. Beehr. 1979. "Personal and Organizational Strategies for Handling Job Stress: A Review of Research and Opinion." *Personnel Psychology* 32: 1-42.

Parasuraman, S. and J. A. Alutto. 1984. "Sources and Outcomes of Stress in Organizational Settings: Toward the Development of a Structural Model." *Academy of Management Journal* 27: 330-50.

Quick, J. C. and J. D. Quick. 1984. *Organizational Stress and Preventive Management* (New York: McGraw-Hill).

Sarason, I. G. and D. C. Spielberger, eds. 1979. *Stress and Anxiety*, vols. 1-6 (Washington, D.C.: Hemisphere).

Schuler, R. S. 1980. "Definition and Conceptualization of Stress in Organizations." *Organizational Behavior and Human Performance* 25: 184-215.

Schuler, R. S. and S. E. Jackson. 1986. "Managing Stress through PHRM Practices: An Uncertainty Interpretation." In *Research in Personnel and Human Resource Management*, vol. 4, edited by K. M. Rowland and G. R. Ferris

(Greenwich, CT: JAI Press).

Schwartz, G. 1980. "Stress Management in Occupational Settings." *Public Health Reports* 95: 99-108.

Seyle, H. 1956. *The Stress of Life* (New York: McGraw-Hill; 2d ed., 1976).

———. 1976. *Stress in Health and Disease* (London: Butterworth).

Sharit, J. and G. Salvendy. 1982. "Occupational Stress: Review and Reappraisal." *Human Factors* 24: 129-62.

Trice, H., R. Hunt, and J. Beyer. 1977. "Alcoholism Programs in Unionized Work Settings: Problems and Prospects in Union-Management Cooperation." *Journal of Drug Issues* 7: 103-15.

ABOUT THE CONTRIBUTORS

TERRY A. BEEHR is currently Professor of Psychology and Director of Doctoral Training in Industrial/Organizational Psychology at Central Michigan University. Well known for his numerous publications in the areas of leadership, job design, women in the workplace, and job stress, his two-article review and analysis of job stress, co-authored with John Newman, made a significant early contribution to our understanding of stress in the workplace. He is author of *Human Stress and Cognition in Organizations: An Integrated Perspective*, with co-author Rabi S. Bhagat.

PHILIP BOBKO is currently in the Department of Management at the University of Kentucky, Lexington, Kentucky. During the period this work was completed he was Associate Professor of Psychology and Director of the Applied Behavioral Science program at Virginia Polytechnic Institute and State University. He has conducted research and published in many areas, including the philosophy of science, research methods, industrial/organizational psychology, the application of psychometric theory, and utility or cost-benefit analysis.

ROBERT D. CAPLAN is Senior Study Director in the Social Environment and Health Program at the University of Michigan's Institute for Social Research. He is author of *Job Demands and Worker Health* and *The Mechanisms of Job Stress and Strain*, co-authored with John R. P. French,

Jr. and colleagues. Dr. Caplan's research in work stress has covered a large number of occupational groups and work settings, ranging from the assembly line to the air traffic control tower, from the engineer's lab to the executive's office. He has a special interest in social support and coping as moderators of the effects of stressors on well-being.

CARY L. COOPER is Professor of Organizational Psychology at the University of Manchester Institute of Science and Technology, Manchester, England. He is editor of the *Journal of Occupational Behavior*, a fellow of the British Psychological Society, and the author of over 30 books in the fields of organizational psychology and stress. He has been an advisor to the World Health Organisation on occupational stress and health, and is on the board of trustees of the American Institute of Stress.

BARBARA FEUER is Director of the Association of Flight Attendants' Employee Assistance Program, AFL-CIO, which provides human resource services to more than 23,000 members and their families on 15 airlines nationwide. The AFAEAP received the first Humanitarian Award given by the California Women's Commission on Alcoholism in June 1985 in recognition of providing outstanding services to women in the workplace. An instructor at the University of Maryland, she teaches a course on the fundamentals of employee assistance programming. She has lectured extensively and written on such diverse topics as women and alcoholism, communication skills, domestic violence, and stress/burnout issues. Ms. Feuer is a member of ALMACA (Association of Labor-Management Administrators and Consultants on Alcoholism) and served as vice-president and president of the Washington, D.C. chapter. She is also a member of the Coalition of Labor Union Women and the American Society for Training and Development.

JOSEPH J. HURRELL is Research Psychologist in the Applied Psychology and Ergonomics Branch, Division of Biomedical and Behavioral Science, National Institute for Occupational Safety and Health (NIOSH), and is Adjunct Assistant Professor at Xavier University, Cincinnati, Ohio. He has authored numerous scientific articles in the area of job stress, with a focus on machine pacing, police officers, coal miners, and postal workers. His current research centers on ascertaining health risks in information-processing work and the development of physiological and self-report indicators of cognitive task demands.

SUSAN E. JACKSON is on the faculty of the Graduate School of Business Administration at the University of Michigan, Ann Arbor. During the period this work was completed, she was on the faculty of the Department of Management and Organizational Behavior in the Graduate School of Business at New York University. She is an active researcher, with publications in the areas of job stress, burnout among human service professionals, shift work, and the causes and consequences of role ambiguity and conflict in the workplace. She has developed a model of the effects of uncertainty with Randall S. Schuler that provides an integrative framework for understanding how organizational events are translated into the experience of organizational stress.

FREDERICK C. LEE is director of Public Policy for the Washington Business Group on Health (WBGH), in which he tracks all federal health legislative developments for the 200 large corporations that comprise the WBGH membership. In addition, he is a featured columnist in *Business and Health*, the WBGH's topical monthly health publication. He acts as task force staffer for key WBGH committees and serves on several local health committees. A hospital administrator by training, Mr. Lee has also held health policy positions in the office of former Congressman David Stockman and at the National Health Policy Forum.

LAWRENCE R. MURPHY is Research Psychologist in the Applied Psychology and Ergonomics Branch, Division of Biomedical and Behavioral Science, National Institute for Occupational Safety and Health (NIOSH) and Adjunct Assistant Professor at Xavier University, Cincinnati, Ohio. He was formerly Research Fellow at the Psychosomatic and Psychiatric Institute, Michael Reese Medical Center, Chicago, Illinois, during which time he studied memory and information processes of psychiatric inpatients. He is co-editor of *Mass Psychogenic Illness* and author of research articles and a review paper on stress management in work settings. His current research involves the development of a stress management training manual and examination of health risk across occupational categories.

STEVEN C. NAHRWOLD is Second Vice-President and Manager of the Employee Counseling Services at Continental Bank of Chicago. He was instrumental in establishing the program as a respected and important function of management within the bank, and is currently active in the development of programs and policies to enhance the ability of all levels of staff to address the problems of work and personal stressors more effectively. He is a contributing author to several books relating to health in industry, including *Mental Wellness Programs for Industry*, and *Occupational Clinical Psychology* (Praeger, 1983).

MICHAEL S. NEALE is currently at the West Haven Veterans Administration Medical Center, West Haven, Connecticut. He completed early investigation into the effects of flexible work schedules on family life and methods for decreasing residential energy consumption, in coordination with Richard A. Winett of Virginia Tech. His clinical and research activities at Yale University, in conjunction with his doctoral studies, centered around applications of systems theory and behavioral medicine approaches to occupational stress and disability.

ANNE W. RILEY is currently on the faculty of the Kennedy Institute, Johns Hopkins University School of Medicine. During the time this work was undertaken, she was in the Department of Psychology, Virginia Polytechnic Institute and State University. Her research publications are in the areas of Organizational Behavior Management, stress at work, health promotion, diffusion of health care technology, and medical care utilization.

ROBERT H. ROSEN is Assistant Clinical Professor of Psychology at the George Washington University School of Medicine, where he participates on the National Collaborative Depression Treatment Research Project. As a Clinical Psychologist he is active nationally in the areas of worksite health enhancement and organizational health policy. As Consultant to the Washington Business Group on Health (WBGH), the only national organization devoted exclusively to the health policy and cost management needs of major employers, Dr. Rosen directs the Institute on Organizational Health and coordinates the Worksite Health Evaluation Forum, a group of corporate health managers interested in the evaluation of work-site health programs. At the WBGH, he is also the Editor of *Corporate Commentary*, a national quarterly report on the evaluation of work-site health strategies. He has served as consultant to numerous organizations and government-sponsored projects on health promotion and disease prevention, representing the employer's perspective.

RANDALL S. SCHULER is Associate Professor at the Graduate School of Business, New York University and Editorial Board Member for *Human Resource Management*, *Journal of Management*, and *Group and Organizational Studies*. He has formerly served on the review boards of four academic journals, including the *Academy of Management Journal* for six years. He has worked as an associate editor and as an ad hoc reviewer for over a dozen other journals. He has authored over 70 articles, and is author or editor of several books, including *Personnel and Human Resource Management 2e.*, *Case Problems in Management 3e.*, *Effective Personnel Management 2e.*, *Resource Management in the 1980s*, and *Managing Job Stress*.

GARY E. SCHWARTZ is Professor of Psychology and Psychiatry at Yale University, and serves as Director of the Yale Psychophysiology Center and Co-Director of the Yale Behavioral Medicine Clinic. He is formerly President of the Health Psychology division of the American Psychological

Association and Associate Editor of *Health Psychology*. Author of numerous articles, Dr. Schwartz has also edited nine books. He is internationally known for his research and clinical work in emotion, cardiovascular disease, and stress management as an aid to promoting health.

JEFFERSON A. SINGER is currently at the Langley-Porter Institute of the University of California, San Francisco. As a research psychologist pursuing the study of occupational stress he has worked with Marianne Frankenhauser in Sweden investigating the psychophysiological responses to work stress, and more recently with Gary Schwartz at Yale. His recent research involves approaches to the management of stress in the workplace, focusing in particular on the differing perspectives held by unions and management.

DONALD J. VREDENBURGH is Professor of Management and Assistant Provost at Baruch College, City University of New York. He is author of many articles on leadership and organizational politics, and has contributed to such journals as the *Academy of Management Journal, Journal of Applied Psychology, Human Relations,* and *Journal of Vocational Behavior.*

STEPHEN J. ZACCARO is Assistant Professor in the Department of Psychology at Virginia Polytechnic Institute and State University. He formerly taught at the College of the Holy Cross. His research interests have taken him into the areas of such organizational issues as absenteeism, work motivation, group processes, and stress in the workplace. He has published research in the *Journal of Applied Psychology* and *Group and Organizational Studies.*

INDEX

ability, 10
absenteeism, 7, 20, 217
accidents, workplace, 42
air safety training, 224
Alcoholics Anonymous (AA), 207
alcoholism, 207, 218; constructive
  confrontation, 219; cost of, 246;
  health care cost, 218; and job performance, 218; psychological denial,
  220
ambiguity: positive effects, 157; and
  uncertainty, 147
ambiguity tolerance, 156
anxiety, 5
Association of Flight Attendants
  (AFA): committee members, 223;
  employee assistance programs,
  217-226; occupational stress
  problems, 221
autonomy, job, 220

bank employee, job stress, 150
Beehr-Newman mode of job stress,
  85-88
burnout syndrome, 246

career progression, 262
challenge, 141
cognition, 103
cognitive complexity, 156
competition, 7
conflict management, 213
constructive confrontation, 219
contract negotiations: employees'
  sensitivity to, 199; stress assessment,
  sociocultural factors, 179; stress
  reduction intervention, 177
control, in organization, 103
coping: management of, 12-16; PE
  fit, 131
coronary heart disease (CHD), 60;
  job characteristics for, 36-37
cost accounting, of stress intervention,
  230; example, 213
cost-benefit ratio, 230
cost effectiveness, calculations, 231
cross-cultural interactions, 84
cumulative trauma, 64

decision making process, 115;
  employee participation, 153

decision theory, 154
depression, 7, 245
deregulation of industry, 150
disability payments, 250
dissatisfaction, in employment, 104
dogmatism, 156
drug abuse, 206, 245; cost to employer, 246
dual career stress, 59

emotional disturbances, 38
emotional problems, physical health, 249
emotional support, 65
employee(s): benefit costs, 208; compensation suits, 205; fair treatment, 197; management demands, 176; satisfaction with management, 195; wellness programs, 206
employee assistance programs (EAPs), 205-215; acceptance in workplace, 217; access to senior management, 209; Alcoholics Anonymous, 207; Association of Flight Attendants, case study, 220-226; benefit-cost containment, 211; broad spectrum, 212; confrontation model, 219; Continental Illinois National Bank case study, 211; cost-effectiveness, 217; counseling office, 207; crisis intervention, 224; decrease in absenteeism, 217; design modifications, 219; disciplinary model, 219; drug abuse help, 206; educational programs, 210; effective strategies, 224; employee benefit costs, 208; employee developmental needs, 214; employee population, 209; environment specificity, 211; expenses, 210; facility location, 209; group counseling, 208; and health insurance use, 217; health programs, 218; history, 207, 217; influence on corporate life, 210; innovations, 217; job adjustment service, 213; job impairment model, 219; for laid-off employees, 208; limitations, 215;

management cooperation, 212; management referral, 207; management support systems, 212; management training, 210; minority affairs, 210; models, 207; multiservice programs, 218; negative effect, 214; occupation specificity, 220; in the organization, 206; and organizational stress, 208; for personal problems, 212; positive effects, 214; prerequisite criteria, 208; proactive programs, 213; problems, 215; psychiatric benefit usage, 211; psychiatric help, 206; psychosocial support, 207; psychotherapy, 207; reactive counseling service, 211; referral model, 219; rehabilitation programs, 212, 219; research, 211; responsibility, 211; senior management consultation, 210; skill training, 208; specialized counseling, 210; staff influence, 209; staff knowledge about, 209; staff quality, 209; success, 209; supervisory model, 220; supportive environment, 209; types, 206; usage rate, 209; voluntary model, 219; wellness promotion, 210
employee counseling programs, 258; cost-effectiveness, 260
employee-supervisor relationship, 220
engineering psychology, 72
environmental uncertainty, in organizations, 160
expectancy theory, 88
expectation, 120
extra-organizational stress, 35

factor analysis, 186
fatigue, 7
fear and death, 30
field dependence, 156
fight-or-flight response, 2, 4, 30
flight attendants: job environment, 222; occupational stress, 221; peer referral assistance program, 221; social relationships, 222; stress coping training, 224; supervision,

222; work schedule, 222
flight attendants, employee assistance programs: air safety training, 224; committee members, 223; promotional information, 225; success, 225; training, 223; utilization, 225

general adaptation syndrome (GAS), 29
group counseling, 208
group motivation, 11
group performance, 10

hardiness, 141, 156
health maintenance organizations, 252
health promotion programs, 46
health screenings, 168
heart diseases, and job characteristics, 36
high-strain jobs, 36
hotel employees, 176; cooperation in stress survey, 185; front desk employees, 185; management as stressor, 198; racial discrimination, 179; stressors, level of, 178
hotel employees, stress assessment studies, 176; data collection, 183; departments, 181; factor analysis of survey, 186; feedback from employees, 179; labor-management relations, 181; questionnaire, 182; research process, 179; stressor specificity, 183; stress survey, 182-183; survey distribution, 183; survey results, 186
humane employee relations, 208
human information processing, 143
human resource management, 151, 159
hypertension, medical cost, 231

illnesses, stress-related, 205
industrial psychology, 208; stress management study, 233
information distribution, 155
information processing, 41
information theory, 153
inter-group conflict, 156

irritability, 7
insomnia, 7

job(s): complexity level, 114; demands, 114; expectation, 54; enrichment strategies, 44; insecurity, 32; performance, 1; strains, 11
job adjustment, 213
job characteristics, 31; and stress, 170
job design, 41
job impairment model, 219
job performance, 1; and alcoholism, 218; and depression, 245; and mental health, 245; and person-environment fit, 105
job satisfaction, 1
job-seeking behavior, 55
job title and job demands, 114

labor and psychology, 177
leadership skills, 10

maladaptive behavior, 31
management-labor relations, 173
management policy, 195
management practice, 195
management training, 210; coping with conflict, 213
meditation, 42
mental health: and accidents on job, 250; burnout syndrome, 246; and disability payments, 250; and early pension, 250; and job behavior, 250; and loss of control, 252; treatment cost, 248, 254; "wellness" program, 248; and work compensation claims, 250; and work environment, 250
mental health benefits, 254; in-patient coverage, 255; out-patient coverage, 256; utilization review, 256
mental health care, cost to organizations, 245
mental health disorders, 37
mental health planning: benefit design, 252; corporate barriers, 249; cost, 251; employee counseling programs,

252, 258; health promotion, 252;
psychological services, 252; wellness
activities, 252; worksite stress
management, 260
mental health survey, 254
mental illness, job-related, 246
mortality rate, 231
motivation, 5, 10; and strains, 11
(*see also* group motivation)
motivational occupational fit, 124

National Health Interview Survey
(NHIS), 41
National Institute on Alcohol Abuse
and Alcoholism (NIAAA), 218
National Institute for Occupational
Safety and Health (NIOSH), 30
negative emotions, 191; and management policy, 197; and work, 195
neurophysiological rhythms, 56
neurosis, 90
nonmanagerial employees, stress
management program, 167

occupational alcoholism programs, 218
occupational categories, and job
strains, 41
occupational health, 30
occupational health programs, 218
occupational mental health, 245-267
occupational stress: assessment,
system principles application, 171;
bank employees, 150; Beehr-
Newman model, 85; cardiovascular
response, 76; as a cognitive state, 91;
complexity, 205; concept, 29; and
co-worker's behavior, 150; different
perspectives, 167; dynamics of, 170;
economic aspects, 75; employee
assistance programs, 208; employee-
environment exchange, 5; environmental requirements, 85; and
environmental resources, 85; estimation methods, 74; evaluation grid,
172; extra-organizational stress, 35;
family responsibilities, 172; flight
attendants, 221; front desk
employees, 185; health consequences,

30; and individual characteristics, 31;
individual responsibility, 200; intervention utilization, 229; job characteristics, 31, 36; job demands, 33;
and job insecurity, 32; low level, and
job performance, 106; management,
group approach, 20; and management attitude, 176; model, 5; negative coping behavior, 34; optimal
level, 1; an organizational problem,
3; and participative management, 21;
person-environment fit theory, 84;
and personality, 87, 205; person's
needs, 85; and person's skill, 85; and
productivity loss, 75; psychosocial
stress, 4; research method, for
systems assessment, 172; and role
ambiguity, 81; role conflict, 80;
scope of, 74; socioeconomic factor,
172; and supervisor's behavior, 150;
symptóms, 206; systems assessment,
167-203; and systems theory, 3; and
task anxiety, 5; underutilization of
skills, 93; and work environment,
31; workload, 31; and workplace
accidents, 42; and work productivity,
35; and work setting, 150
occupational stress measurement: data
collection, 31; limitations, 32;
techniques, 30
occupational stress research, 29, 76;
ergonomic studies, 39; expectancy
theory, 91; field studies, 40; goals,
88; hotel employees, 176; laboratory
studies, 40; longitudinal studies, 36;
methodological needs, 40; moderator
variables, 33; natural experiments,
39; obstacles, 94; record studies, 36;
role theory, 80; theory-guided work,
90
occupational stress sources, 56, 172;
career development, 58; dual career
strees, 59; home-work interface, 59;
organizational structure and climate,
59; and physical danger, 57; and
poor working conditions, 56; relationships at work, 58; role in
organizations, 57; shift work, 56;

and work overload, 57; and work underload, 57

open systems theory, 7

opportunity, 141

organizational effectiveness: goals, 10; strain and, 7-8; in stress management, 1, 7

organizational interventions, in stress management, 261

organizational performance, 106; ability, 10; determinants, 9; external constraints, 10; motivation, 10

organizational psychology, 82

organizational stress, coping framework, 16

organizations: and behavior, 105; business strategy, 152; component systems, 5; counseling office, 207; decentralization, 155; employee relations departments, 206; and employee satisfaction, 195; environmental uncertainty, 160; group power, 156; human resource management, 151, 159; interdepartmental communication, 152; management policy, 195; mental health care costs, 245, 255; mental health policy, 246; mental health survey, 254; participatory decision making, 152; personnel selection, 123; power distribution, 103; profit sharing, 105; research on, 153; reward system, 105; role conflict, 152; stress intervention cost, 229; uncertainty and stress, 151; and work setting, 190

organizations, mental health benefits, 254; preferred provider arrangements, 257; utilization review, 256

participative management, 21

patient evaluation grid, 172

pension payments, 250

personality: differences, 153; research, 157, 158; and stress experience, 205

personal strain, and person-environment (PE) fit, 168

person-environment (PE) fit, 103; application in workplace, 106; change in, 105, 129; cognitive fit, 125; commensurate dimensions, 110; conceptual distinctions, 107; constructive value, 133; coping, 131; and denial process, 109; dimensions, 119; dynamic theory, 104; improvement, 104, 116; individual adjustments, 117; and job security, 109; motivational fit, 125; needs and ability, 107; needs-supplies fit, 128; objective fit, 107; and occupations, 113; and performance, 105; person's control, 129; realities and expectations, 170; research, 113; responsibility, 126; social support, 131; subjective fit, 107; time frame, 119

person-environment interactions, 113, 169

physiological strain, 78

positive emotion, at work, 191

problem solving, 15

process theories, 144

productivity increase, and stress intervention, 232

profit sharing, 105

psychogenic illness, 65

psychological fatigue, 9

psychological stress, and health, 31

psychological theories: guiding-idea theory, 143; process theories, 144; systems theory, 143; taxonomic theories, 144

psychosocial stress, 4

psychosomatic dysfunction, 42

psychotherapy, 207

racial discrimination, 179

regression analysis, 187

relaxation, 19; and work performance, 43

retirement adjustment, 210

role conflict, 83, 152

role expectations, 87

role overload, 93

role theory, 80

self-esteem, 7

self-hypnosis, 261

self-respect, 54
shift work, 56
sleep disturbance, 198
smoking cessation, 252
smoking cost, 232
social psychological stress, 71
social support: and health conditions,
    34; and psychological resources, 34;
    and stress, 33
strain, 4, 7; and job performance, 11;
    and motivation, 11
stress: adaptive coping responses, 34;
    beneficial effects, 9; and challenge,
    141; and competition, 7; coping
    responses, 7, 34; coping strategies, 4,
    13-14; definition, 72; duration, 7;
    and environmental stimuli, 72;
    formal responses, 172; at group
    level, 10, 12; group motivation, 11;
    impact of different stressors, 11;
    informal response to, 172; informa-
    tion theory view, 153; intensity, 11;
    and job performance, 8; and job
    satisfaction, 1; labor perspectives,
    176; in life, 71; management per-
    spectives, 176; managing and coping,
    12; and medical costs, 206; and
    mortality rate, 231; and motivation,
    5; in nonaversive situations, 141; and
    organizational performance, 2; or-
    ganizational withdrawal, 3; physical
    response to, 29; physiological
    response, 4; as political concept,
    170; psychological impact, 250;
    research vs. managerial perspectives,
    2-3; and social support, 33; somatic
    response to, 29; and strain, 7; and
    task anxiety, 5; and uncertainty, 90,
    142; and unemployment, 55; unsuc-
    cessful coping, 7; and work perfor-
    mance, 1 (*see also* occupational
    stress)
stress assessment, 168; data collection,
    183; demographic data, 184; during
    contract negotiations, 169; ecological
    perspective, 169; employees involve-
    ment, 200; of hotel employees, 176;
    management involvement, 177; from
        management point, 176; physical
    symptoms, 198; research process,
    180; sociocultural factors, 179; stress
    as dynamic concept, 178; stressors
    assessment, 177; stress survey, 182;
    survey results, 186
stress experience, 53
stress intervention: activity scope,
    241; cognitive restructuring pro-
    grams, 237; conjoint analysis, 239;
    cost effectiveness, 230; direct effects,
    230; economic aspects, 229;
    employee identification cost, 232;
    evaluation techniques, 239; muscle
    relaxation programs, 237; organiza-
    tional gain, 235; organizational in-
    volvement, 237; and productivity
    increase, 232; self-monitoring pro-
    grams, 237; time management
    programs, 237; utility analysis, 234,
    235; utilization, 229; work inter-
    vention, 237
stress intervention cost accounting,
    229; absenteeism cost, 231; example,
    231; health center maintenance cost,
    232; insurance cost, 231; medical
    care cost, 231; morbidity and retire-
    ment, 231; on-the-job time loss, 231;
    potential gain/benefit, 231
stress management: daily relaxation,
    18; employee assistance programs,
    205-215; health promotion efforts,
    168; health screenings, 168; inter-
    vention strategies, 16, 18; and labor
    management, 167; and labor unions,
    168; and medical benefit plans, 206;
    for nonmanagerial employees, 167;
    personal counseling, 168; public
    education about, 206; safety and
    health committees, 168; strain pre-
    vention, 12; in turbulent times,
    141-166; work rescheduling interven-
    tion, 237; at work site, 19, 260
stress management training (SMT):
    effectiveness, 42; at work site, 43,
    260
stress measurement, in organizations,
    29-51

stress model, 4
stressors, 3; different impacts, 11; identification, 73
stress process, 2; stress experience, 3
stress reduction: individual oriented technique, 42; by meditation, 42; organization centered approach, 44, 45; by relaxation, 42
stress response, 2
stress survey, 182; factor analysis, 186; individual psychology, 189; work setting, 188
substance abuse (*see* drug abuse)
supervisor-employee relationship, 220
survey feedback research, 173
systems theory, 143; application to occupational stress, 169; embedding systems, 149; and occupational stress, 3; and organization, 4
systems theory principles: emergence, 198; redundancy, 198

tension, 81
time management program, 237
trauma, 141

ulcers, 7
uncertainty, 90, 94; and ambiguity, 147; and behavioral stress, 142; definitions, 146; and groups, 155; individual reactions to, 157; and information availability, 154; and information distribution, 155; and inter-group conflict, 156; organizational responses, 160; and organizations, 146, 151; reduction, 156; and systems theory 143; taxonomic component, 144; and unpredictability, 154
unemployment, 53; and mental health, 55; and self-respect, 54; and stress, 55
unionized employees, 176; stressors assessment, 177

union-management collaboration, 173

video display terminal, 46

weight management, 252
women, non-work roles, 83
work: career development, 58; and emotions, 191; employee participation, 61; environment and stress, 31; flexible hours, 39; health protection issues, 46; high-demand-low control, 183; informal social support, 66; and negative emotions, 195; objective characteristics, 39; organization support, 61; person-environment interactions, 171; physical danger, 57; poor conditions, 56; positive emotions, 191; psychological environment, 208; relationships at, 58; and responsibility, 104; social psychological characteristics, 71; social support at, 60, 131; support systems, 63; understaffing, 185
work environment, 31
worker compensation, 64
working conditions, poor, 56
workmen's compensation laws, 206
work overload, 57
work performance, and relaxation training, 43
work process characteristics, 39
work productivity, 35
work setting: control, 189; correlations with organization, 190; co-worker relations, 188; external control, 189; interpersonal, 188; job characteristics, 188; physical environment, 189; supervisory relations, 188

workplace accidents, 41
work-site alcohol program, 248
work-station design, 39
work stress (*see* occupational stress)
work underload, 57